John Calvin
Genius of Geneva

John Calvin
Genius of Geneva

A Popular Account of the
Life and Times of John Calvin

by

Lawrence Penning

INHERITANCE PUBLICATIONS
NEERLANDIA, ALBERTA, CANADA
PELLA, IOWA, U.S.A.

Library and Archives Canada Cataloguing in Publication

Penning, L. (Louwrens), 1854-1927.
  John Calvin : genius of Geneva : a popular account of the life and
times of John Calvin / by Lawrence Penning.

Translation of: Het leven van Johannes Calvijn.
ISBN 1-894666-77-1

1. Calvin, Jean, 1509-1564. 2. Reformation—Switzerland—Geneva—
Biography. I. Title.
BX9418.P4313 2006a 284'.2'092 C2006-900422-6

Library of Congress Cataloging-in-Publication Data

Penning, L. (Louwrens), 1854-1927.
  [Leven van Johannes Calvijn. English] John Calvin : genius of
Geneva : a popular account of the life and times of John Calvin / by
Lawrence Penning.
    p. cm.
  ISBN 1-894666-77-1 (pbk.)
  1. Calvin, Jean, 1509-1564. 2. Reformation—Switzerland—Geneva
—Biography. I. Title.
BX9418.P4313 2006
284'.2092—dc22
[B]

                                                            2005037049

Originally published in Dutch as *Het leven van Johannes Calvijn*
(1909) by J.M. Bredee, Rotterdam, The Netherlands

Translated by B.S. Berrington
Cover Design: Roelof A. Janssen

Contents

Publisher's Introduction

(for the 101ˢᵗ book of Inheritance Publications)

The publishing of this book is a direct fruit of the reading and publishing of *Under Calvin's Spell* by Deborah Alcock. Shortly after Gary den Hollander and his wife lent me their copy of the Alcock book in 1990 with the advice to republish it, I read the book and agreed that it would be worth republishing. It was the first book by Alcock that I read. Later I read *The Spanish Brothers* and enjoyed it very much as well (and was encouraged by Joanne Barendregt to publish that). However, it was not until I read *Crushed Yet Conquering* that I realized that Alcock was likely the greatest author of Christian historical fiction that ever lived. In this regard there are some interesting parallels with her contemporary Lawrence Penning, possibly the most famous Dutch author of historical fiction (Piet Prins, the author of the Scout books, read all the books of Penning when he was still a child and prayed to God that he would become such an author as well). Several of Alcock's books were translated into Dutch (and into many other languages) while Penning's book on Calvin was soon translated into English. Its present edition is at least the third English edition.

However, when the time was ripe to re-publish *Under Calvin's Spell*, which I intended to be the one hundredth book published by Inheritance Publications, I found that, although this great novel gave a very good description of life in and around Geneva — with one of the best plots of a (fictional but very realistic) love story (possibly second only to the true love story of William III and Mary II, told in Marjorie Bowen's *Defender of the Faith*) — it told very little about Calvin himself. As a result I read Penning's book and was quickly convinced that both books should be published as companion editions, Alcock's book being the introduction and Penning's book the "full" story. Also today the world needs to know it's most important historical facts and since upon the mouth of two witnesses the truth of a matter is to be established we send out in these two books the true story of John Calvin.

Calvin is perhaps the most important person who lived after Biblical times (seconded by Martin Luther, William of Orange, Michael de Ruyter, and William III of Orange). To know and understand how the Lord has used these people in the history of His Church and world will stir in any reader the desire to follow them in their footsteps.

May the Lord use these books for the glory of His Name and the well being of His Church which especially today needs to be united in Him in order to present a clear message to the world.

— Roelof A. Janssen, September 28, 2005

Chapter I

THE DARK NIGHT

FORTUNATELY we have left behind us the damp houses and tortuous streets of Paris. And over there — outside the gates — between the trees, rises stately and impressive, the abbey Saint-Germain des Prés, where the kind abbot, William Briconnet, sways his sceptre.

Like a fortress the abbey is surrounded by deep moats to prevent surprise from any sudden and unexpected attack; and a sweet resting-place it affords to the man, who worn out by the moil and toil of the great city, wishes here to end his days in tranquillity and peace.

There in the great hall with its costly library, sits a solitary man. The friendship of Briconnet brought him to the place. And on the parchment, that is lying before him on the massive writing-table, he writes: "Anno 1509."

For it is the year 1509.

His hand trembles with age as he writes.

Yes, that solitary man is old; along that face run deep furrows; his hair is blanched by the seventy-four winters which have passed over it.

He stands up, stiff from sitting, goes to the window and stares through the cross-leaded panes into the Herbary, where grow the simples, used by the monks skilled in medicine, for sick and suffering humanity.

Now you see that the man is short of stature; he does not even reach to the shoulder of his king, who is called Louis XII.

Nevertheless, he is a king — O deny him not that title!

As a king he rules in the domain of minds, as Louis rules in the domain of the French kingdom.

That face of his attracts us; at the first sight of it we feel sympathy for the man; those eyes express intelligence, reconciliation, love.

Speak, noble old man! Of what are you thinking?

He does not answer; more and more thoughtful grows his face; all the remembrances of a long life, perhaps, are passing before his mind's eye.

He was eighteen years of age when European Christendom turned pale with terror at the tidings that Constantinople had fallen under the furious attacks of the Turk's crooked sword; he was not forty-four, when the Sultan snatched Moldavia away from the Polish kingdom.

The pitiful end of Charles the Bold, who, stripped naked, was found at Nancy, sticking frozen in the ice, was not unknown to him. Laurence Koster and John Gutenberg, the inventors of printing, were his contemporaries, and his life's sun was already declining in the western horizon, when Columbus discovered America.

A new world — son of Rome! Cover your face!

For the army of Franciscan and Dominican monks, that went to America to convert the heathens, murdered those heathens by thousands and made the survivors ten times worse than they ever were before.

Hark! There is another cry going up to heaven: the cry of a hero and martyr, who is fast bound to the strangling-post. It is Savonarola, who preferred the gallows to a Cardinal's hat, offered by the hand of a pope, and whose only crime was, that he preached a poor sinner and a rich Christ.

Savonarola

THE POPES!

Is it unknown to you, O son of Rome, that Europe once saw the unheard-of spectacle of two, three popes, who at the same time laid claim to the chair of St. Peter, and hurled at each other the thunders of the Vatican? That Innocent VIII made himself notorious by introducing into Germany trials for witchcraft, and by being the father of sixteen illegitimate children?

And Alexander VI, who died six years before — did he do anything else than neglect, to his own advantage, the interests of the Church, which are dear to your heart? Was his son not a Cain, a fratricide? And did not the people consider him guilty of incest with his own daughter?

Degenerate, corrupt, sick to her very life's core has the Church become; the immorality of the monks and the shameless ambition of the priests cry to God; the traffic in indulgences and image-worship has assumed revolting proportions.

True it is that the incursion of the Turks and the fall of Constantinople caused Greek literature to seek refuge in Italy and Western Europe; in those regions it became a rich source of civilization and brought with it treasures of knowledge.

A revival of knowledge is discernible; new universities are founded; the names of Reuchlin and Erasmus will be spoken of with honour even after centuries to come.

In another department, too, Art shows what she can do, when her efforts are approved by God.

It is fifty-nine years since, in the city of Rome, the foundations were laid of St. Peter's Church, and they will have to go on building for more than a century before that imposing production of human art and of Michael Angelo's genius will be completed. This old man has seen the unfinished church, and, dumb with astonishment and admiration, he claps his hands together in ecstasy at the sight of the splendour before him.

Yet appearances are deceptive; this St. Peter's Church, built in honour of the Almighty and true confession of faith, is a lie; and the hundred and forty-four million guilders, which the building of the church will cost, will, for the greatest part, have to be covered by the sale of indulgences.

The atmosphere is sultry, oppressive; the air is infected; centuries before, the necessity had been felt for a reformation

The noblest minds have pleaded for that reformation; every nation of the Christian West has had its martyrs, whose conscience-cry has re-echoed through the dark night like a wail for help.

John Huss

But the reformation has not come; councils, convened for that object, broke up without result; and the synod of Constance could do no more than erect a stake, on which to burn God's holy witness, John Huss.

The piety of the old man, spoken of in the beginning of this chapter, is renowned. The Roman Catholic Church, that burns heretics, lets scoffers live; yet in the seat of scoffers this old man, this Le Fèvre (or Fabri) has never sat. He is a faithful son of his church; never has any one sung the Mass with more reverence than he; kneeling before the images he reads his prayers.

But in his soul, which none can see save God, it seethes and foams — it is the storm, by God awakened; the storm that is beginning to blow over Western Europe, and, breaking the dry branches, foretells the spring.

Le Fèvre is not unacquainted with the history of the Middle Ages. Better than any one else does he know how Dante, who with angels and devils alike held communication, met on his terrible journey to hell more than one pope in the abodes of the damned —

and that more than one mouth uttered the awful words: "The Pope is Antichrist!" — O, this is not unknown to him! The old man sits down again.

Once more we are struck by the shortness of his stature, the delicacy of his appearance, his insignificance. And yet Erasmus, the great scholar of Rotterdam, who even in the saddle pursues his studies, once said of this man: "That Le Fèvre — that pious, good, and learned man, who has rendered such great services to science and to all learned men, deserves to remain always young!"

This same Le Fèvre shall, with the strength of a Samson, attack the Sorbonne and fell it to the ground. There he sits and muses. Then suddenly the eyes under those gray brows light up, and over that furrowed face runs a thrill of silent, pent-up enthusiasm.

Of what is he thinking? Is his patriotic heart aglow at the thought that his king Louis XII has just destroyed the power of the proud Republic of Venice?

Is it the brilliant light of national glory, which makes his old heart beat faster?

He is thinking, indeed, of a brilliant light, and taking up the pen to write the preface to his fivefold version of the Psalms, he speaks thereof.

But yet it is another, a higher, a more blessed light, the splendour of which makes his old eyes rejoice; it is the discovery of a new world, compared to which the discovery of Columbus, of seventeen years before, sinks into insignificance.

And he writes: "For a long time I have devoted myself to classical studies, and scarcely touched upon theology, for it is of an exalted nature and must not be taken in hand without serious reflection.

"But in the distance such a brilliant light has already shone upon my eyes, that in comparison with what theology offered, the humanities seemed to me darkness, and the study of theology to diffuse such a sweet fragrance, that on earth there is nothing that can be compared to it."

It is remarkable, that in the year 1509 the regeneration of the noble Le Fèvre took place, and, in the same year, the last and greatest of the Reformers of the sixteenth century was born.

Chapter II

THE SON OF FISHERS AND SAILORS

LE FÈVRE had spoken of a brilliant light — no, Gérard Calvin, the father of the Reformer, perceived little of that heavenly light. The man had something else to do. With him it was working hard all day; he wanted to get on in the world; to be independent, a substantial citizen of the town of Noyon — that was his ambition.

Gérard Calvin was born in the little fishing village of Pont l'Evêque, not far from Noyon. Following the old road, in half an hour you reach the town, the towers of which rise up pleasantly above the high trees. And in the background the eye is agreeably struck by an undulating line of little hills.

Calvin was in heart and soul a son of his country, a real Picardian: of that race, from which sprang the celebrated hermit, Peter of Amiens, who, by his flaming words, had once set all Christian Europe on fire.

The Picardians have a warm temperament. They are warlike; the spirit of contradiction rests on them; they are the Frisians of the French nation: resolute, hardy, obstinate, and with strong democratic tendencies. In them the Reformation and the Revolution found their staunchest defenders; this province was the cradle of the French Protestantism, which attacked the Roman Catholic Church in her very vitals, and of the Ligue, that with blood and steel strove to root out Protestantism. Gérard Calvin had seaman's blood in his veins. Although his father was a cooper, the family of the Calvins were a seafaring people, with a love for adventure. And that seaman's blood was of service to his son, the Reformer, for none of his forefathers ever went through such a storm as he did before his little barque reached the haven in safety.

Gérard Calvin knew what he was about when he turned his back upon the little fishing village. In his father's workshop he had learned something more than how to knock the staves around the barrels. He was a writer; clever moreover, quick and discerning. And his heart yearned for the town.

He was suited for Noyon. And Noyon was the cradle of his fortunes. He became successively apostolical notary, procurator fiscal, clerk of the Ecclesiastical Court of Justice, secretary of the Diocese, and *promoteur* of the Chapter.

"He has so many irons in the fire," wrote one of his opponents, at a later period, "that all his life long he never knew which way to turn." He took everything he could get — that is true, but it required a good deal to perplex him.

As actuary he had a great name; he was held in high repute by the nobility, and was respected as a citizen of Noyon.

Pont l'Evêque

There he married, and his neighbours said that this cooper's son of Pont l'Evêque had made good use of his eyes when he knocked at the door of Mr. Johannes le Franc.

Le Franc had been a hotel-keeper at Cambrai, had sold or let the business and become an inhabitant of Noyon. People said, that this Cambrai hotel-keeper had feathered his nest well, and they were right. The man's ship had come home, he became one of the leading men of the town, member of the corporation, and paid four pounds a year income tax, while his future son-in-law never paid more than fourteen pence.

Johanna, his daughter, was a desirable match. She was lovable, winsome, and of a beauty calculated to make the hearts of the young unmarried men of Noyon beat faster.

Gérard Calvin was the fortunate man who led her to the altar, and from there to his own dwelling, close to the Cornmarket, in the neighbourhood of her parents' house.

In character and way of thinking, they were different. The mother of the Reformer was a quiet woman, deeply attached to the Church, while one has a strong impression that Gérard Calvin's eyes were firmly set on earthly things.

His ideals were not exalted. He loved his wife and his children, but his desire to get on in the world overruled everything else. And although the heavenly lights were burning, we have not a single proof that his eye saw those lights.

It was not an unhappy marriage, but there is reason to conjecture that the severe social struggle maintained to the end by the father with such indomitable and admirable perseverance was but too frequently like a thick mist, that intercepted the joyous light of the Sun. One of the biographers of Calvin has said, that his father's system of education consisted in concealing his love from his children, whom he really loved. This is perhaps an exaggeration. But yet it is to be feared that the children had to suffer through the endless cares of their father, and experienced but little of that affection which to a young heart is like dew and summer rain.

We are sorry and grieved to say that it was so. We are grieved more especially about that little Johannes.

For he was a very impressionable child, with a sensitive soul. In his little body beat a heart. And on account of his father's many occupations it was impossible for that heart to receive what it was entitled to.

So we see the stamp of suffering already imprinted on Calvin's childhood. Suffering indeed followed him like a shadow all through his life, with scorn and revilings. And have not that scorn and those revilings — side by side with passionate love and veneration — been his lot to the present day?

Of the three sons Charles was the eldest, Johannes the second, and Antony the third.

Amazed and startled at the elasticity afterward displayed by Johannes Calvin, his enemies have examined his genealogical tree, taken notice of the swarm of gnats which flew up at his birth, and even consulted the stars, in order to explain his wonderful and extraordinary influence. And to these astrologers we are indebted for the hour of his birth being settled with horoscopical exactitude as having taken place on the 10th of July, 1509, at twenty-seven minutes past one in the afternoon.

Johannes was brought up by his mother, who probably died early, in all the solemnities and ceremonies of the Roman Catholic Church. He took part in the processions; he pressed his lips with reverential awe on the relics of the saints; it did not trouble him much, that from time immemorial the

Courtyard of Calvin's birthplace at Noyon

town of Noyon had been divided, with regard to the relics of St. Eloy, into two hostile camps, who were always at war with each other.

Who really possessed the true genuine remains of St. Eloy? The chapter of the Cathedral or the abbey of St. Eloy, for both laid claim to them? The people wanted to know this; they would know it, for it was a matter that affected their eternal interests, and, furious with rage, they asked who were the falsifiers and deceivers: the clergy or the monks?

For two generations a lawsuit went on about it; the Parliament had acted as judge between the two; a decision had been given and new decisions followed. But the uncertainty was not removed.

The violent disputes did the Church no good. The respect for the clergy decreased alarmingly. A spirit of doubt and mockery was awakened. The sharp-sighted Gérard Calvin must have had difficulty in suppressing a scornful laugh, and, more than thirty years later, the son who had sprung from his loins lashed image-worship with whips and scorpions.

In that remarkable writing, Johannes Calvin enumerates the principal relics in order then to make the following observations:

The wooden cross: if you were to collect all that has been found of it, you would have a good shipload.

The three nails of the cross: there are fourteen of them.

The point of the spear: you must assume that the crucible of the alchemist has quadrupled them.

The crown of thorns: you must take for granted that they have been planted again in order to produce new ones — or else how could they have increased so?

"Everything is so contradictory and confused," says Calvin, "that you cannot worship the bones of a martyr without running the risk of reverencing the bones of some thief or robber, or of a donkey, a dog, or a horse. And one cannot worship a ring, a comb, or girdle of the Blessed Virgin Mary, without being in danger of bowing the knee to the ornaments of some shameless woman."

Gérard Calvin saw clearly the advisability of giving his children a sound education. His idea was that the money spent on the education of one's children is well invested, and it was a load off his mind when he was in a position to send his boys to a good boarding and day-school just outside the gates of the town.

Especially for the second son, who was one day to attract the attention of Europe, he began to entertain great expectations.

He was a child of quiet and retiring disposition, weak, delicate, and pale; nervous, timorous, and irritable. Yet the penetrating eye of the father saw through all those externals; and he was surprised at the judgment, the intelligence, and the quick, cheerful spirit which animated this child.

He was a peculiar child; into those pale cheeks of his came colour and glow when he sat poring over his books; and the powerful aristocratic family of Montmor was so struck by the wonderful talent of this extraordinary boy, that he was educated with their children.

Here Johannes came into a new and strange world; his heart yearning for love, was refreshed by the charming kindness of this excellent household, and all his life long he thought of them with deep-felt gratitude.

In this circle he quickly learnt the first principles of science; there, too, he acquired those refined forms and distinguished manners, which afterward enabled him to associate with the highest aristocracy, even with princes and kings.

By Gérard Calvin, who was busy night and day in order to help his children on in the world, it was soon settled that Johannes should be educated for the Church.

The seriousness of the boy and his talent, fitted him for this; the worldly side of the matter would not be lost sight of by the father. By his connections he succeeded indeed in getting his son appointed chaplain when only twelve years of age; he received the tonsure, and enjoyed a yearly income of three bushels of corn and the produce of twenty grain fields.

Does it sound strange, that a boy of this age could be chaplain? In the eyes of the world, such as it was then, there was nothing strange in it; people did not know better; the state of things was so bad that they would have been astonished at the man who had dared to make remarks about it.

In the century before, there had been popes of eighteen years of age; Benedictus IX was a boy of twelve when the triple papal crown was placed upon his head; John of Lotharingia, who in 1502 was appointed Bishop of Metz, was a child of ten; and Leo X had no scruples about appointing a cardinal — another child of eight.

There was almost as great a traffic then in Church appointments as there is now in Russian and American Consols at our Exchanges. The house of God was made a house of merchandise; the Pope and money ruled there, but for Christ there was no place. And while, abusing what is sacred, a man became purchaser of an ecclesiastical office, that sacredness had to be profaned a second time in order to obtain money for a substitute.

Later on, Calvin was loaded with reproaches for not having fulfilled the duties connected with his office.

But the reproaches were silly. He could not do so. He had not the right to say Mass and administer the sacraments. For that he had to be a priest, and he could not be a priest till he was twenty-five years of age.

Time did not stand still. Johannes was now fourteen years old, and the father's eye began to rest with pride and pleasure on his child. He saw himself reflected in that boy: the same resoluteness of will; the same perseverance; the same unflagging energy. There was something in that boy; he gave promise of becoming a great man; he would be his father's glory, his father's crown. Gérard Calvin, no doubt, consulted wise men of his surroundings, as to where he should then send the boy. And the advice to send Johannes to the University of Paris coincided with his own views.

This University, founded in the beginning of the thirteenth century, owed its greatness to the struggle which it maintained against the despotism of the Church, and in the short period of half a century had become the glory of France and of Western Europe. The Sorbonne and the Pope were in that century considered indispensable; they formed the two pillars of the Church; the Sorbonne looked after the unity of doctrine, the Pope after the unity of authority.

The Sorbonne was the beaming sun in the scientific world; it was the Mecca of studious young men; it would have sounded like a strange contradiction if any one had become a learned man without having attended the lectures of the professors in Paris.

Yet this University, whose morning had foretold such a gladsome and bright summer day, fell into the same despotism that it had suppressed with so much glory. It became reactionary, as stubborn as a self-willed pony, the violent opposer of all real progress.

The age of sophism reigned in the seats of the audience-halls: the question whether it was an apple or a pear that Adam had eaten was eagerly discussed; the authority that was to be given to the testament of Lazarus after his resurrection, called forth the most passionate disputes. And in the sixteenth century the University had gone down so far, that Erasmus could not resist the temptation of shooting at it his sharpest arrows dipped in mockery and contempt.

"At this worm-eaten gate then," says Doumergue,[1] "Calvin knocked in 1523, when the plague and heresy were threatening Noyon and Picardy."

---

[1] E. Doumergue, *Calvin's Youth.*

Chapter III

THE GREAT DAY OF THE REFORMATION

MUCH had happened in Europe during the last six years; the dark thunder-clouds had begun to gather rapidly, and over Wittenberg the first storm had burst, when, on October 31, 1517, a former Augustine monk, in the strength of his God, nailed to the principal door of the Wittenberg Schlosskirche, his ninety-five theses against the traffic in indulgences.

On the market-place of Jüterbock, Tetzel threw Luther's theses into the fire; Luther answered by burning the papal bull outside the

gate of Elster. And at the diet of Worms, before an assembly of princes and prelates more brilliant than Europe had scarcely ever seen before, he sealed his conviction with the immortal words: "Here I stand; I cannot do otherwise; God help me. Amen!"

The day of the Reformation had come; over Europe passed a breath of God; the hearts of men were moved as the sea in a storm.

19

It was a stream, that could not be turned aside; it was another Nile stream, which flowing far over its banks, fertilised the arid and sunburnt lands.

This stream was irresistible; it knew no bounds; the writings of Luther and his brave helpmates were disseminated like strong germinating seed, over the field of the world, and in the spring of 1519 Luther wrote triumphantly that his letters were read in Paris and gave satisfaction to many.

But if he for one moment imagined that among those well-wishing readers the professors of the Theological Faculty were included, he was greatly mistaken.

The Sorbonne was terribly incensed. Luther was in its eyes worse than Mohammed; against such a cursed heretic nothing could avail but sword and fire. And mad with rage, the Sorbonne issued an edict, that whoever possessed a book of Luther's and did not bring it within a week, should be imprisoned and fined a hundred livres.

Is Luther, then, the father of French Protestantism? Not so!

In 1512, when the Augustine monk on his bare knees, bewailing with tears of blood his sins and misery, had climbed Pilate's staircase at Rome, without a kindly star to illumine his darkness, and Zwingli, like another crusader, had crossed the Alps to risk his life and all that he had for the Pope, Le Fèvre with increasing enthusiasm had followed the shining and everlasting light, that had appeared to him three years before.

He was the pioneer of Protestantism; and the Exposition of the Psalms, which was printed in 1512, was the first Protestant book that appeared in France and in Europe.

He did not, indeed, possess Luther's heroic courage. It never entered his head to burn a papal bull, while the resolute consistency of John Calvin was nothing for this gray-headed old man, inclined to silent speculations. He was a Protestant in the monk's cowl, and while Luther fought with heroic courage against priests and devils, the soul of Le Fèvre longed for rest and reconciliation.

Yet the fire that burned there on the altar of his heart had been lit by God; he had gazed upon the unveiled face of Christ; and his spirit had accepted the sacred secret of reconciliation through Christ's blood.

Le Fèvre did more; by his instruction he won his first pupil: a man who, for burning zeal, untiring energy, and matchless intrepidity, was excelled by none of the Reformers. That man was William Farel.

"My son!" said the gray-headed old man of nearly eighty, in the year 1512, while his aged eyes were illumined with prophetic glow, "God is going to renew the world, and you will live to see it!" With all the strength of his young, passionate heart, Farel had clung to the Roman Catholic Church, but she had not been able to satisfy the yearnings of his soul. Then he had turned to Aristotle, but the Greek philosophy brought him no light. And the Bible had left him just as perplexed, since it was impossible for Farel to place the authority of God's Word higher than the authority of the Church.

Then on his life's path he met Le Fèvre, and, as if by inspiration, he understood that this man possessed the herbs wherewith to cure his sick soul.

The two so totally different characters attracted each other with strong magnetic power; in the gentle and lovable old man, whose one foot rested on the earth, while the other stood on the golden strand of eternity, there was a charm which William Farel could not resist.

Did Le Fèvre lead the child of Rome, thirsting for righteousness, immediately to the fountains of life?

Alas! Le Fèvre himself was still tossed to and fro like a reed in the storm. He took the young man by the hand and together they knelt before the mother of Jesus, the Virgin Mary.

There in earnest worship they lay absorbed, and then with flowers they would adorn the object of their veneration.

Yet Le Fèvre could not remain standing where he was; truth drove him on with irresistible force, and he took his pupil with him on the way.

"My son!" he once said, "it is all grace!"

They were four simple words, and they struck Farel with the strength of a flash of lightning. The scales fell from his eyes; his soul drank in the words as the parched traveller in the desert drinks the cool water. He was saved, redeemed, blessed; in the twinkling of an eye it had been done. And from that time forth Farel would declare to the four corners of the earth, that all our merits are like

William Farel

a garment, that is only fit to be cast aside. He took the pilgrim's staff in his hand and preached the word of life; he came to the great city of Paris and there founded a community — in the same year that Calvin had entered the city and taken up his abode with his uncle Jacob Calvin, the locksmith, in order to attend the lectures in the College Cordier.

Chapter IV

TWO METHODS OF PEDAGOGY

"WHAT do you know?" asked Cordier.

And overcoming his bashfulness, Calvin replied: "Nothing that I do not think to learn better from you!"

Never could Calvin have been more fortunate; Cordier was the ideal of a teacher: learned, acute, full of patience, the originator of a new pedagogy.

He had his own way of looking at things, and said that more could be done by gentleness and love, than by the whip and harsh words. A strange and singular assertion at a period when the scholars, if they did not learn, were thrashed like dogs.

He tried to implant in their youthful hearts the love of God; they should be imbued with the spirit of Christ; he longed to write the sacred name of the Saviour in their hearts with ineffaceable letters, and went on the hypothesis, *that the fear of the LORD is the beginning of wisdom.*

From this excellent master, Calvin learned the elegant Latin that awakened the admiration of his enemies, and that vigorous, temperate, and lucid French with which he exercised such powerful influence over the French nation.

From Cordier College, Calvin went to Montague College. It was a leap over a precipice. Cordier represented progress, spring, gentleness; Montague, winter, the old method, the strictest conservatism and the whip. The whip was the commonest means in resort to make young men learn; more than once the rectors of the University impressed seriously upon the minds of the teachers the necessity of thrashing their pupils well; Margaret of Valois, sister of Francis I, received in her youth many bloody stripes from this terrible whip.

Erasmus paid particular attention to the life scholars had in the notorious Montague College, and thus described it: "Thirty years ago I was at a college in Paris, where you swallowed so much theology that the walls were impregnated with it; but I took nothing else of it away with me than a cold disposition and a number of vermin. The beds were so hard, the food so wretched, the sitting up and studying at night so difficult, that in the first year of their stay in that college many young men of great promise became bandy-legged, blind, or leprous, if they did not die. Some bedrooms, near which were the privies, were so dirty and infected that nobody who had slept in them came out alive or without the germ of some terrible sickness. The punishments consisted in flagellations, which were dealt with a severity that can only be expected from a hangman.

"The Principal wanted to make monks of us all, and so to teach us fasting, he gave us no meat at all! O, how many bad eggs did I eat there!" When Calvin went to this college, the gloomy, fanatical Noel Béda was at the head of the institution. And this Béda was the successor of the celebrated Dutchman Standonck, of whom it is said that when young he had reached Paris in the greatest poverty, and at night climbed into the tower to study by the moonlight, as he had no money for candles.

It was a hard school this, that Calvin had to go through, but he went through it with heroic courage. His mind was polished; he became the first in his class, and here learned the art of debating, after Cordier had taught him the art of writing.

There were, indeed, bright sides to that stay at Montague College. Calvin formed the central point of a circle of sociable young men, among whom were the three young Montmors, the comrades of his childhood years, and the son of the celebrated King's physician, William Cops.

It is true Calvin did not mince matters; he was not afraid to express his opinions whenever his companions did things which were not in accordance with his serious views of life. But it was not censoriousness, and the Calvin of the legends flees to the land of mists and lies when we watch him in company with his friends. In him were united the energy of his father and the charm of his mother; his innate bashfulness gave him that nice modesty, which forms the ornament and the crown of a young man, while his great attractive power accounts partly for the wonderful influence, which at a later period he exercised.

He could laugh and jest; by his amiability he conquered hearts, and by his uprightness he retained them. His disinterestedness and unselfishness struck every thoughtful person; and the charm which emanated from this noble character was so strong, that it afterward induced the gray-headed Cordier to go and live at Geneva.

The young Montmors followed Cordier and so did the sons of Cops out of sincerest affection for the man, who has been done the most horrible injustice by the most scandalous falsification of facts.

Geneva in 1641

Chapter V

A BATTLE AND ITS CONSEQUENCES

A PERPETUAL treaty of peace, made at Noyon in 1516 between France and Germany, had become waste paper. And Calvin's peaceful studies were disturbed by the cries of war and the clash of arms.

Two young men with ambitious and passionate blood in their veins, had ascended the two most powerful thrones of the Christian West. One was Francis I, King of France; the other, the Emperor Charles V. The King was scarcely twenty-seven years of age when the war broke out; the Emperor was six years younger.

The French King, decked with the laurels of Marengo, where, seated on a cannon-carriage, he had drunk a cup of water mingled with dust and blood to quench his thirst, felt hurt and offended when he lost the German imperial crown. He never forgave Charles V, and the bloody strife of arms should decide who was the more powerful.

In 1521 the strife began, and in the middle of the war a pope came and died. He was the well-known Adrian VI, son of a common weaver and washerwoman from Utrecht; a modest, sober-minded, and sensible prelate, who was perfectly well aware of the corruption that had attacked the sheepfold of Christ, but lacked the energy to take the reformation in hand. Twenty months only did he wear the papal crown. His days were already numbered when his reign began. And while he gave nothing to true Christians but fine promises, he was mocked and laughed at by the Italians for the candid confession of his faith.

The energy which Adrian VI lacked Luther possessed in double measure. The monk's cowl he laid aside for ever and was as happy as a prince when Catherine von Bora gave him her hand and heart.

That joy, however, was not without alloy, for the clear water of the Reformation was in danger of being troubled by the storm-flood of Revolution.

In 1524, the same year in which the victorious army of Charles V drove the French from Italy, the German peasants rose up to wreak their grievances, real or imaginary, upon the nobles. These anarchists of the sixteenth century fought like wild beasts; the dames of the rebellion spread with the rapidity of a prairie fire — from the Alps to the Harz mountains and from the French frontiers to Bohemia, to be quenched in a sea of blood.

Horrible cruelties were committed in that peasant war. A German margrave had the eyes of eighty-five rebellious peasants put out because they had declared that they would never regard him again as their master. And from the devastated villages of the peasants rose up to heaven the blood-red flame with the lamentations of poor women and children. With the enemy at their heels, the remnant of the French army, led on by the Knight Bayard, fled to the French frontiers. A shot shattered Bayard's spine, and he died uttering the words: "I die in an honourable fight for my fatherland!"

And France and Europe bewailed him as their bravest warrior.

Yet when the Imperials had crossed the French frontiers, their glory waned. Attacked in their rear, the Germans and the Spaniards were sent home flying, after they had heroically and martially stormed in vain the walls of Marseilles. Decimated by continual skirmishes, hunger, and sickness, General Pescara led his wasted and beaten army back to Italy, without having fought a serious battle.

In Paris the greatest joy prevailed, bonfires were lit, and the good tidings from the South must have done the heart of young Calvin good. For he was a child of Picardy, of France, and never denied the national tie which bound him to his fatherland.

A bright smile passed over the face of Francis I, and the eyes of the whole French nation followed him, when, at the head of his army, he crossed the Alps at three points, and in ten days descended into the smiling plains of Lombardy. Without a battle or blow he reconquered the greatest part of his dukedom; on the walls of the capital, Milan, he planted the French standard, and the Imperial army would have been scattered like chaff had it been followed.

But Francis I wanted something else; the walls of Pavia were a hindrance to the King, and he led his army against the fortress. The fortress uttered a cry of distress, which was heard in Germany. The celebrated George von Freundsberg, the father of the young commander of Pavia and who had grown gray in arms, sprang up to save his son, and the town. He was the general who, patting Luther heartily on the shoulder at the diet of Worms, had spoken

these remarkable words: "Little monk, little monk! It is a dangerous game that you are playing today, but if you mean well and are sure you are right — then go on in God's name, and He will not forsake you."

By the beating of the drum, the gray-headed Freundsberg called together his faithful lancers, and when he appeared before the walls of Pavia with twelve thousand soldiers, he was sure of victory.

The French King was resting on his laurels; he set his soldiers the example of merry-making and carousing, and lodged in one of those Lombardian abbeys, where the monks, by their revels and drunkenness, had filled the soul of Luther with the bitterest indignation when he was on his way to the city of Rome.

It was on a gloomy February morning in the year 1525 that the Imperialists began the attack. The battle was excessively severe; the King fought with desperate bravery, but his bravery was of little avail against the well-disciplined troops so ably commanded by Pescara and Freundsberg. The French were not defeated, but crushed; their bravest soldiers covered the plain like corn-sheaves on the stubble-field in the time of harvest. Francis I handed his sword over to the Dutch general, Lannoy.

In one of the splendid rooms of the Palace at Madrid stood young Charles V, dressed in black velvet, waiting for tidings from the battlefield.

The Emperor was of medium height; his forehead was broad and imperious, and his dark blue eyes, full of majesty and benevolence, gave a certain lustre to that plain face, of which the ugly, misshapen lower jaw was an inheritance from his fathers.

The Emperor was thinking of what Pescara had written: "We will conquer or die." And his face trembled from anxiety and painful impatience, when a courier, who had ridden his horse half dead, appeared at the gate of the palace. "Where from?" asked the porter. "From Lombardy!"

The courier was immediately admitted. And his tidings seemed somewhat like those of Cushi to King David: "*The enemies of my Lord, the King, and all that rise against thee to do thee hurt, be as that young man is.*"

Motionless as a statue stood there the great grandson of Charles the Bold. The blood seemed to congeal in his veins. He spoke not a word; no one spoke; in silence his courtiers stared at him. Then the Emperor fetched a deep breath and muttered: "The King of France my prisoner!" He then disappeared in his bedchamber and threw himself on his knees before the image of the Virgin Mary, while words of the deepest gratitude flowed from his lips. To his astonished eye unfolded a brilliant future. His imperial hand was to be stretched out protectingly over the Roman Catholic Church, which was being threatened by a late monk, was to plant the cross on the mosques of Constantinople and reconquer the holy sepulchre.

If Charles V were thinking of the Sultan, the captive King of France was thinking of the same man. Taking the gold ring from his finger he whispered to one of his confidants: "Let the Sultan see this ring!"

But the Sultan was far away, and Margaret of Valois, the only sister of the King, knew of better help. She sent the King St. Paul's Epistles, and wrote: "These will be your deliverers!" There are two persons, who in the French Reformation tower far above the others, a queen and a plain son of Picardy. Margaret of Valois was one; John Calvin the other.

We mention the royal lady first. Margaret Duchess of Alençon was the most charming and witty, the most intellectual and amiable, and if we except her daughter — the greatest woman of her age. She was the sister and mother of kings, afterward herself Queen of Navarre and the grandmother of the man who is called France's greatest King.

The seed, sown by old Le Fèvre, had, in the case of the Duchess, fallen into good ground, and pure and undefiled in the midst of a corrupt court she had, in her quiet enthusiasm, set about the salvation of her brother. She had flattered herself that her work would not be in vain; a change had already taken place in the King's heart; even the blind eyes of her mother, the bitter and notorious Louisa of Savoy, seemed to open to the gloriousness of the Gospel.

But the war came and passed like a hurricane over the young blossoms, while the Duchess referred the King, who looked for help from Turkey, to the Pauline Epistles.

But Margaret of Valois did more. When she heard of the disastrous result of the battle of Pavia she could not rest, but started at once for Spain to see her captive brother. Her mind was a prey to the most violent emotion; her brother, of whom she was passionately fond, was for her the symbol of beloved France, of the Reformation, of liberty. This King was then in the hands of a powerful Emperor, who was surrounded by such advisers as the Duke of Alva.

It was a long and tedious journey, and sometimes she thought she would succumb from very weariness. Yet like a heroine she rose up again, and seated in a litter, passed through the fields of Catalonia.

On a Wednesday the Duchess reached the Spanish capital. The Spanish grandees uttered a low cry of admiration when they saw that eloquent and lovely face. The Emperor took her reverentially by the hand, and led her between two rows of courtiers to the apartments of her brother.

The King had become seriously ill: he was grieving about the hard conditions of peace which the Emperor had imposed upon him. Yet at the sight of her, the pressure of her hand, the look of her eyes, his hope revived.

Margaret did not come alone. She brought with her France, his native land, the charm and solace of home, and the sweet remembrances of his childhood years. Her love, her devotion, and her faith triumphed. She frowned a little when she saw the treatment of the ablest court physicians and prescribed another mode of cure, and watched like the most faithful nurse at the bedside of the hero of Pavia.

Did the Duchess make use of those silent hours, as ministering sister, in the double sense of the word, to attack Rome?

Even in the days of her greatest zeal for the Gospel she never did so. While she believed in the suffering and death of the Saviour as an expiation for sin, her piety remained shrouded in the mists of Rome. She was a spiritual daughter of Le Fèvre; her hand was more fitted to heal wounds than to deal them. She had set herself the impossible task of reforming the Church without destroying its unity.

It was an error of judgment, not of that noble heart, in which there was the deepest love for the Saviour of sinners. She spoke to her sick brother of that love. She urged him to celebrate with her the Lord's supper, and together they knelt down and received the bread and wine in remembrance that Christ died for them.

The battle of Pavia, which had made the Spanish people tremble from joy, had plunged France into the deepest mourning. The flower of the French nobility had remained on the fatal plains of Lombardy, and the storm of the panic raged through the streets of Paris. When young Calvin came from the University, he could see groups of excited people standing at the corners of the streets, in the squares, and before the churches. They could not conceive of a French King being a prisoner — it was a thing unheard of; the Parliament called all able-bodied citizens to arms, and while the Imperial eagles were expected before the walls, command was given, that all the gates of the city except five should be walled up.

A reaction soon followed this terrible calamity.

The leaders of the people asked themselves what terrible crime the French nation had committed, that her army was annihilated. The fiery partisans of the Roman Catholic Church knew of no other reasons than the weak, irresolute attitude toward the Lutherans. And they considered it their duty to avert by bloody sacrifices the wrath of heaven, which had been kindled by the Protestant heresies.

The persecutions had begun some time before; in the same month in which young Calvin started for Paris, a Norman hermit had been burnt there on the Pig-market.

Yet the Royal Court had had no mind for these persecutions; the influence of Margaret of Valois stood the Protestants in good stead; and not till France was in danger of succumbing to her misfortunes did the hour strike for fire and blood.

Many Protestants took to flight; Le Fèvre, the meek and gray-headed old man, who was placed on a par with Luther, and called the precursor of Antichrist, fled to Strasbourg with his sorrow and his burden of ninety years.

Johannes de Klerk was condemned to be whipped in public on three different days. Amongst the spectators was his own mother; her face shone with heavenly joy, because her child, whom she had brought with suffering into the world, was accounted worthy to endure reproach and pain for the name of the Lord Jesus.

"Keep up your courage, my child!" she said consolingly. And when the red-hot and hissing irons pressed the brand of infamy upon his forehead, this Kenau Hasselaar[2] of the Huguenots, cried out: "Jesus and His standard-bearers shall live!" In April (1525)

---

[2] A famous Dutch woman who led about three hundred women to defend the city of Haarlem during the Spanish siege of 1572-1573.

De Klerk went to Metz, where, three months before, the body of a confessor of Christ was consumed by the flames. There he found a great number of kindred spirits, who received him with open arms. William Farel pressed his hand; the brand upon his forehead stamped him in the eyes of the Evangelists as a chosen one among the chosen. Yet, his days were numbered; his impetuous iconoclastic zeal brought him speedily in conflict with the Government, and in July he was led to the place of execution to be burnt. He was made to sit on sharp nails; and afterward bound with iron chains.

Compassionate voices among the crowd cried out: "Pray to the Virgin Mary!"

But De Klerk shook his head, for he would not pray to the Virgin.

"I do not despise the Blessed Virgin," he said, "but I cling to the Lord Jesus Christ, who died for me."

When the executioner with his red-hot tongs wanted to pull off his nose, De Klerk, who was looking in a different direction, involuntarily turned his head away from the heat of the iron.

By this movement his lips were burnt off to the teeth, but then he understood what they wanted to do and bore the cruel mutilation without uttering a cry of pain. The executioner then drew three circles around his head with the burning iron, as a punishment for having damaged the crown on the image of a Virgin Mary. His right hand was then torn off, and the faggot-fire was lit.

In the midst of the smoke and flames his face shone like that of an angel of God; Christ, who knows His own, had spread His hands over him to bless, and amidst the crackling of the wood, there rang forth from the lips of the dying man these words: "Their idols are silver and gold, the works of men's hands. They that make them are like unto them, and so is every one that trusteth in them. O Israel, trust thou in the Lord; He is their help and their shield!"

Pauvan, a young clergyman from Picardy and countryman of Calvin, was burnt alive on the *Place de Grève* in Paris.

Much had happened before this.

When the officers of justice had seized him, he was frightened to death. And to save his life he had followed the example of Peter and denied Jesus.

The clerical authorities were satisfied, and the scaffold was altered to imprisonment.

Yet in the gloomy vaults of that subterranean prison the look of Jesus penetrated, and the apostate wept bitter tears of repentance. He was deeply moved; no monk crossed the threshold of his prison to whom Pauvan did not proclaim the Gospel.

The clerical authorities were informed that the prisoner had lapsed into his former errors ten times worse than ever before. And to burn out this pestilential bacillus by fire, Pauvan was led to the *Place de Grève*.

It was perfectly black with people when he appeared at the stake; there was a look of blessed peace upon his face, and when the flames rose up, he spoke to the people in the strength of the Holy Spirit.

William Joubert, a young man of twenty-eight and of good family, began to search the Scriptures, and once said at the office where he was engaged: "Neither Geneviève nor Mary — the Son of God alone can save!"

It was a bold declaration; the young man was put under lock and key, and the anxious father hastened from La Rochelle to save his child. He did everything that could be done — went from one judge to the other and promised heaps of gold if the life of his son were spared.

But it was of no avail; William Joubert had to mount the dust-cart which was to convey him to the place of execution, and the people who came streaming up saw how the executioner bored through his tongue, bound him to the stake, and then set fire to the faggots.

And the poor father turned and headed for home — a broken old man!

It was a very serious and earnest matter when the proclamation of the Gospel was opposed through the use of force. In the squares and on the street-corners in the capital city, there was an announcement made with trumpets that all French Bibles would have to be turned in. And in the future no printer would be allowed to print as much as a single book written by Luther.

A horrible time had begun. The heavy bells of Notre Dame were sounded, and the reddish glow of a fire lit up the square in front of the church. The pale, serious son of Noyon could see the bleached skeletons of the holy martyrs being shaken this way and that in the wind as they dangled from iron chains.

The enemy was triumphing now that Margaret, the noblewoman who had undertaken to protect freedom and the Reformation, was on the far side of the Pyrenees Mountains. The storm of persecution was separating the wheat from the chaff.

The abbot Briconnet, who had for years been a friend of Le Fèvre, was part of the chaff. How was it possible? The Evangelicals had built on this man as though he were a rock. Less than a year before he had threatened the Royal House with the wrath of the Almighty in case it did not use its influence for the sake of the people's welfare when it came to the naming of bishops.

Because he was frightened by the change in public opinion and by the turn which events had taken, he slunk like a beaten dog to the feet of the children of Belial, who now wielded the power. He begged the court to undertake an investigation into the heresies and abuses in the dioceses under his jurisdiction. The commission of inquisitors went to work and discovered that an edifying book written by Le Fèvre had been circulated among the people.

Béda got a copy of the book in order to sort out the truth from the lie. He did not need to spend much time looking through it before he began to discover heresies.

"If someone preaches something other than the Word of God and Christ," he read, "he is not a faithful communicator of the Divine mysteries but a deceiver." What was that other than an accursed heresy?

"We must simply believe the Word of God in accordance with the view of the Holy Spirit and not in accordance with our own view. And we may not mix our own foolish opinions into the Word." Another heresy!

The king of inquisitors raised his eyebrows angrily as his inquisitive cat's eyes discovered no fewer than forty-eight heretical claims in one simple little book.

"It is full of devilish heresies and heretical lies," said the man. "The writer is a heretic, and whoever reads his book is also a heretic. All such heretics deserve to be burned at the stake and to have their ashes scattered by the four winds of heaven!"

Briconnet would have to come: he would have to take responsibility in this matter. This apostate signed everything that was placed before him. He called Luther's doctrine a plague and poison; it was a poisonous plant. He saw it as his obligation to help to root it out in the field entrusted to his care.

His obligation — yes, that's what it said . . .

No help could be expected from the court; the barometer indicated that there was a storm brewing. In Louise of Savoy, who was ruling in place of her imprisoned son, the old hatred flared up when, at the Sorbonne, she raised the question: "What means can we use to uproot the teaching of Luther that has been condemned?"

Béda did not have a hard time coming up with the answer: the bloodiest persecution was, in his judgment, the tried-and-true means.

Dark clouds began to gather above those who considered themselves Evangelicals. Their enemies would no longer stand for anything. They seized the nobleman Berquin of Artois, who was a friend of Erasmus and the Duchess Margaret.

Two years had passed since Berquin had become acquainted with the men of the tribunal and of the Sorbonne. He had already been condemned on that occasion, and his life would have come to an end if the powerful hand of the King had not opened the door of his prison cell.

In the eyes of the Sorbonne Berquin was a monster and an evildoer, for he had studied the Bible, had translated some religious books from Latin, and had called the monks foolish donkeys.

The danger that had come so close to him, threatening him, only served to purify his heart and to increase his zeal. Berquin was a forerunner of those noble figures who were to come down from the high citadels into the plains, leading the valiant Huguenots who drew their swords for freedom and righteousness!

He persuaded Artois to preach that the soul could be saved only through Christ. Neither simple huts nor palaces were passed over. With the Bible under his arm, he spread the divine seed on the picturesque banks of the Somme, on the open squares in the towns, and in the isolated dwellings of shepherds. He surprised his old friends with the new ideas about grace and reconciliation which his eloquent lips developed.

The Bishop of Amiens did not know what to do. All of the north was astir. Béda was summoned to help.

The right man had been found. For this man, who was an inquisitor by nature, it was a mere triviality to find all sorts of heresies in the writings of Berquin. And while Berquin, with the simple joy of a Christian and the uprightness of a child, continued to spread the seed of life, it was decided that he must die.

Even his goods were demanded by the servants of the court. But those servants would have been torn to pieces by the farmers on Berquin's lands if Berquin had not intervened. He surrendered voluntarily. With firm footsteps and head held high, he walked across the threshold of the prison.

Now the last hopes of those who were being persecuted were fixed upon God and upon the Duchess of Alençon.

The Duchess had heard the death-cries of the martyrs, and the image of the poor exiles who wandered far from their fatherland followed her like a sombre spectre right into the glittering palace of Charles V. She had four thousand gold coins distributed among the poor fellows and redoubled her efforts to open her brother's eyes to the truth. Her hope and courage did not forsake her; her love made her cling to the firmest expectations. "I began," she wrote, "to make the true fire flame up in his heart."

The true fire — how could the Duchess say such a thing?

She was blind. Her love had made her blind. Francis I was a character full of contradictions — frivolous, fickle, and untrustworthy. Under the slightest pressure he would show himself willing to break the oath to which he owed his freedom.

Even so, the holy unselfishness of his sister moved him. She had given him back his courage and life, and so, to demonstrate his gratitude, the King wrote from his prison to the French parliament, that the persecutions against the Evangelicals were to be halted until such time as he returned.

To be halted? The high priests and Pharisees in Paris were surprised at this. They asked each other whether a king who wrote such foolish letters could be taken seriously. It appeared that his long imprisonment had damaged his brain. They thought the best thing for them to do would be to continue vigorously with the uprooting of heretics.

But then Margaret appeared on the borders.

She was warned that the Emperor, who had begun to fear her more than an enemy army, would lock her up along with her brother as soon as his imperial guarantee of safe passage had run out. And there was indeed reason not to ignore this warning. The cold, silent prince (Philip II) who was making ready to ascend the golden throne of Charles the Great was capable of almost anything.

Now, Margaret had not made her journey to the powerful capital city of Spain in vain. With her she brought a document to the fatherland that counter-balanced the battle that had been lost — the abdication of Francis I! Armed with this document, the Duchess would redouble her efforts from France to rescue her brother from his Spanish purgatory.

It was high time for her to think of returning. At six o'clock on the morning of the last day of her free passage, the brave princess jumped into the saddle and galloped off at full speed toward the border. In one day she covered as much territory as would normally take four days. The officials of the Emperor had no choice but to report that the Duchess had crossed the border just an hour before her guarantee of safe passage ran out.

A sunbeam of hope and courage spread light on the path of the poor persecuted people when they heard the news that the Duchess had left the sickbed of the French king in order to rush to the sickbed of the suffering Evangelical people of France.

She was firmly resolved to save the King and the Reformation. She would have liked to spread the wings of her love over both, and she said that heaven could not be satisfied by scaffolds and burning pyres but only by sinners returning to the Saviour.

If the coming of the unusual princess to Madrid shocked the leaders in Spain, her departure shocked them even more. And all the events came together in such a way that the peace that people yearned for could be obtained.

It appeared that the war would end with a wedding, as in an old-fashioned novel, and that the Emperor had no objection to seeing the imprisoned King become his brother-in-law — on the provision that he was willing to accept the strict peace conditions by swearing an oath.

The King was prepared to do so. But in place of swearing one oath, he took two.

The first oath he swore in the presence of his servants. After calling on the name of the Almighty in a solemn way, he declared that he accepted his obligation to abide by none of the conditions which the emperor had stipulated. And hardly an hour later he swore, with one hand on the Bible, and without as much as a muscle twitch on his face, that he would fulfil the peace conditions with unimpeachable faithfulness.

The Emperor was satisfied, and the King was a free man.

When the Pope got to see the peace treaty, he smiled and said: "Excellent! Beautiful! As long as the King is so sensible as not to observe these terms!"

And of course the King was so sensible — why else would he have perjured himself?

Margaret was frightened at the thought of what would become of Berquin. She threw herself down at her mother's feet and begged for his life. Louise of Savoy, whose frivolous nature the King had inherited, was just as susceptible to momentary impressions as her son.

She feared for the flood that threatened to sweep across France like a storm. Being deeply moved and emotional and not knowing what to do next, she commanded that the process that was underway be halted until the coming of the King.

This decision produced a tremendous shock. The leaders of the movement against the Protestants got tremendously indignant at the thought that Berquin would slip through their fingers again. They regarded it as necessary that he die, for, like Erasmus, he was an apostate and deserved no better lot than his books — to be burned in the flames!

And so the balance that would determine life as opposed to death tipped this way and that in the little house. Margaret fought her heavy battle that could lead to a Protestant Pavia if there was no powerful help and support forthcoming.

The path which Margaret had followed had taken her right past the Emperor's throne when Charles V asked for her hand.

Charles' youth made the marriage impossible, and so she married the Count of Alençon, who, in his entire life, had nothing else to boast of except that his cowardice had caused the terrible catastrophe of Pavia.

He was a prince of the blood, which did not mean that he could not be foolish, rough, and fainthearted. He fled from the field of battle in order to save his life, which was a futile effort on his part: shattered by scandal and shame, he died shortly thereafter.

And then there was the young Henry Albret, King of Navarre, who was an entirely different sort of man. He had fought bravely to the bitter end and had been taken prisoner with Francis I. The supporters of the Emperor had locked him up in a strong castle, high up in a tower. The whole castle was encircled by a deep moat. But even if the tower had been ten times higher, the King of Navarre could not have been held within it. In the pitch black of the night he climbed down a small rope ladder; and if there was anything unusual going on below, he made sure to cling to the wall in such a way that he looked like a gigantic bat. Without incident this daring climber reached the ground. He even managed to get to French soil in time to celebrate Christmas.

With the liveliness that was part of his nature, King Henry knew how to tell the story of this glorious event in his own life. But there was a second reason why he had appeared at the court.

With the clarity of vision that is typical of a woman, Margaret had understood this reason at once, but she would not consider a second marriage as long as her brother, who in her eyes was the sun of France, had not yet celebrated his joyous return.

How her heart leapt with joy when, shaking the Spanish dust off her feet, he returned to her beloved France!

Henry Albret greeted the French King as his Jonathan. Yet this Jonathan had no desire to give his sister to the man of Navarre, and Charles V, whose eye had also rested on Margaret, was not to have her either.

It was a time in which the Protestants could again breathe easily. The Emperor had placed himself at head of the Roman Catholic Church. There was a general feeling that Francis I would become the leader of the Protestants, and that these two mighty rulers would fight out the great difference of the age.

The French sun which had risen behind the Pyrenees now let some joyful light fall on the path of those who were being persecuted. With him the King had brought hope, freedom of conscience, and the Gospel. Martyrs — people whose names were already being struck from the roles of those still living — were led forth from the prisons. Warm tears of joy and loud cries were heard, and the people of the Lord saw in the King the deliverer sent them by God.

The waves of excitement spread all the way to the German city of Strasbourg. It had become a free city for the exiles who had been driven across the borders on account of their faith. Now, with homesickness in their hearts, they gazed at the Vosges Mountains.

In Strasbourg was the gray prophet Le Fèvre, whose recollections reached back to the Middle Ages. The pious Roussel was there as well, at the head of a long list of excellent men. And William Farel had come from Montbeliard in order to bind together these brothers in the dispersion.

The hour of their deliverance had come! With loud cries they parted from their friends in Strasbourg, who had become so precious to them. The Lord had made all things well! That was what they felt within their souls. In their last gathering in the old imperial city, they reminded one another of what Isaiah had said: "And the ransomed of the LORD shall return, and come to Zion with songs and everlasting joy upon their heads: they shall obtain joy and gladness, and sorrow and sighing shall flee away."

Like a peaceful pleasure garden in the middle of green countryside lay the Castle of Angoulême, where Margaret of Valois was staying. That was where Le Fèvre and Roussel directed their steps, in order to express their heartfelt thanks to this noblewoman.

To them it seemed as though they had reached an antechamber of heaven itself. Those who had been exiles could now pour out their hearts. They told about the things they had experienced in Strasbourg, and about the comfort which their soul had received in their suffering, and about the brotherly unity which had bound them together in such a mighty and heartfelt way.

Margaret listened, with the quiet joy of the soul of one who has been chosen by God for eternal salvation. And under the sweet intoxication of a glorious future which, in her eyes, lay ready for the Gospel, she might well have cherished the thought, for a moment, that she was perhaps destined to be the one who would lead the Reformation in the French-speaking countries.

Yet this thought was an illusion, a phantasm of the brain, for the glory that goes with the throne is not helpful for the work of reformation. In the atmosphere of a royal court, the plant of reformation withers away.

Who was it, then, that was destined by God to lead His elect?

Was it Le Fèvre? The old man shook his head. He was old, and he had gone to France in order to shut his weary eyes there. And even if he had been a half century younger, he still would have missed the fire of battle that is needed if one is to storm the enemy phalanx. He was not a Luther, not even a Melanchthon. He was a man with a most noble nature, the kind of man we love because of his character and esteem highly because of his principles, but he did not possess the powerful wings of the eagle. Such men remained pioneers who might show the way in advance, but they cannot become leaders of the people.

Roussel was a spiritual son of Le Fèvre. He had a pious nature like that of the Apostle John, but without the holy deliberation possessed of the Apostle. Repeatedly he felt his conscience stirring in him, prompting him to rise up and utter a powerful war-cry that would arouse those who were asleep. But he never quite got to the point of taking action. The muscles of his wings were just too weak. And not being strong enough to overcome his human fear, he was upright enough to utter the bitter cry of distress: "Miserable man that I am! Who will deliver me from this misery?"

Was there then no leader, no head, to be found for the struggle? What about William Farel, that son of thunder, who had made the Alps resound with his lion's voice?

William Farel — surely he was the one! He was flesh of their flesh and blood of their blood. The French Protestants could not desire a more suitable man as their leader.

Farel was ready. He stood stamping his feet with impatience because he was so eager to get back to France. And when his impatience subsided, he was overcome with sadness because for his friends a barrier had gone up that separated them from the fatherland, and he was left behind alone.

Roussel comforted him with encouraging letters and opened the prospect that his exile would soon end. Those words gave Farel fresh courage, for he had turned his back to Switzerland, and he saw that the fields of his beloved fatherland were white with harvest. The calling of a servant of God beat strongly in his chest. The zeal of the Lord consumed him. This strong and courageous reformer, this Knight Bayard of Protestantism, shed warm tears at the thought that he might become a useless servant.

But while he was staring himself blind at France, a letter reached him from Bertholt Haller, the reformer of Bern, with the plea: "Come over and help us!"

He understood this plea. France had scorned her greatest son, but Switzerland wanted him. So now, turning his back to his Fatherland, the pilgrim headed for the mountains of Switzerland.

But at the very same time a speedy messenger from Roussel was on his way toward him. The exile was ended — finally! And now a royal letter appealed to him to come back at once.

There stood Farel — what was he to do?

He remembered how fervently he had prayed on his knees for this result. But now that it had come, it was too late!

It was a heavy temptation, but Farel withstood it in a heroic struggle. And like a despised schoolmaster he began, with the blind obedience of the true man of battle, to undertake the task that was to lead him to the glittering heights of a reformer.

Farel was lost for France, but in the very same month in which he headed for Switzerland, the prison doors opened before Berquin, and he stepped out to embrace his freedom.[3]

Was Berquin the designated leader for French Israel?

The Protestants believed it. Berquin began to believe it himself. For the second time he had been delivered from the fierce mouth of the Sorbonne lions by the highest King. Enjoying a rare popularity, he was firmly determined to resume the struggle at once.

Erasmus advised him to enjoy some sweet rest on the pleasant banks of the Somme. But Berquin was no Erasmus. How was he supposed to rest while Satan was in the harness day and night?

---

[3] November 1526.

How was he to rest now that a new age was beginning and the society that had been made dark by the night of the Middle Ages had begun to breathe freely again? He saw victory as a shining possibility in the distance. Spiritually ripened by his time of imprisonment, he moved forward in the power of the Holy Spirit.

Such, at least, was the thinking of the people.

Yet this thinking was a new mistake, for his brow was to receive not the crown of the reformer but the crown of the martyr.

The time of a new persecution had not yet begun. There was rest and peace; the Word of God was increasing, and the proclamation of the Gospel was advancing to the farthest corners of the land.

The gentle way of a woman had won the victory. Margaret of Valois had triumphed in her struggle against the Sorbonne, against the spirits from the abyss and against the Pope, while she extended her hand to the joyful man from Navarre.

With trumpets and drums the wedding feast was celebrated. The glittering night of the celebratory games lasted an entire week, and King Francis I made the most solemn promises to Henry Albret, while remaining firmly resolved not to keep them.

Chapter VI

THE GLIMMERING LIGHT

WHAT a strange peculiar being is man! Gérard Cauvin (Calvin) had spared no pains to ensure his son a clerical career, and now that his ideal was about to be realized, suddenly came his order: "Don't do it! Stop! Go and study for the law, John!" But yet it is true, that unless the Lord give His blessing, our labour is in vain. Gérard Cauvin had toiled and moiled to get on in the world, and yet nothing that he did prospered. The neighbours of Corn Square, Noyon, said that he had buried his prosperity in the grave with Johanna le Franc, and although he married again the grim spectre of financial difficulties overshadowed his life.

From one misfortune another was born. As *procureur* he could not properly acquit himself of his duties; as testamentary executor of a chaplain's bequest, he delayed to render an account; again and again he came into conflict with the Church authorities, and angry and embittered, he bade his son lay aside theology and study for the law.

But would Johannes obey his father's command?

He was then a young man of eighteen, with a determined, independent character and an opinion of his own, and was apparently qualifying himself with great zeal for his future career. His father's idea, that the law paid better than the Church, left him entirely cold; he had a sovereign contempt for gold; and the world of historic materialism, sketched by the socialistic democrat Marx in such brilliant colours, was for him nothing but a visionary region.

Johannes' answer pleased his father. It never entered his mind to disobey his command. His father wanted him to go to Orléans and study law. And he said, "Very well, I will go."

Indeed Johannes did not find it very hard to have to come to this decision; the nimbus that surrounded his church had, in his eyes, lost much of its lustre; and in the silent hours of night he began to study the Scriptures, called by the Sorbonne *a pest and a curse*, and by Olivetanus, *a source of Divine blessing*.

Olivetanus was a Picardian; a son of Noyon and relative of Calvin. And while this defender of the truth was destined to become the heroic missionary of the Waldensian Alps, he guided Calvin into the path that was to lead to the highest seat in the most remarkable Republic ever known in profane history.

Untiring assiduity, the most dogged perseverance and a talent, brilliant and genial, combined to forward Calvin with giant strides. And to his great cheerfulness, his retentive memory, his perspicuity, he added a amazing aptitude for clothing the lectures of his teachers in an agreeable style, full of sensible and witty conceits. He was animated with a deep and earnest desire for knowledge; and even then he showed that almost anxious love for order, which he retained all his life. This same precision he expected from his friends; he did not like parting with a book that belonged to him, and would ask for it back, although he did not want it, simply not to be vexed at a gap in his bookshelf and the lack of scrupulousness in his friends.

He began then to study divinity, and Thomas Aquinas was his man. This thinker charmed him; and had he remained in the Roman Catholic Church, then he would have become a follower of Aquinas. And he raised scholasticism to the queen of sciences.

It was the time that the breath of the Gospel passed over France like the smell of spring; the names of Le Fèvre and Erasmus, Luther, and Melanchthon filled the air; and the new idea that nothing but grace can save man found its way even through the strong walls of the cloisters.

Olivetanus professed this doctrine and Calvin contested it. He regarded it with aversion, for its novelty hurt him, and his pride could not bear the thought that he had erred like a blind man. He trembled for the fate of his cousin Olivetanus, who had dared to touch the fathers, the priests, the holy Church with his heretical hands, and he invoked the saints to bring back the lost sheep to the true sheepfold.

But was Olivetanus a lost sheep?

Calvin began to doubt; disquietude filled his soul, and the bright ray of light that flashed through him revealed to him his sins. He was the pilgrim who was portrayed a hundred years later in the immortal book of John Bunyan; there was a mountain of sin, which threatened to crush his weak shoulders, while all his good works and all the saints, with the queen of heaven at their head, were powerless to help him.

Then a shudder went through his soul; the thought of God frightened him, and he cried out, "O God! Thou holdest me hemmed in as though Thou wouldst dart Thy lightning on my head!" By the advice of Olivetanus he began to examine the Bible, and wherever he opened the Word of God — he saw the crucified Saviour. Then he began to dry his tears; he took heart, and the Lord *passed by him with a still small voice.*

"O Father!" cried he in adoration; "the sacrifice of Thy Son has turned away Thy wrath; His blood has washed away my sins; His cross has borne my curse!"

But with strong ties he was bound to the Church of his fathers; there was a mist before his eyes, although above the mountains shone the light. He stood in the midst of the movement, in the turmoil, in the surge; more than once he looked with perplexity about this turbulent world, and while Olivetanus had become his friend, Béda, the fanatical pioneer of the Jesuits, was his teacher.

THE JESUITS!

When in 1528 Calvin left the capital to take up his abode at Orléans, a dark Spaniard entered the gates of Paris. He was a man of middle age. He was on foot, and drove a donkey, which carried his books, while his purse was filled with gold pieces, given him by rich and charitable people.

It is possible that Calvin and the Spaniard met each other in one of the tortuous streets of Paris such as it was then; that the Spaniard asked the way, and that Calvin with his inborn willingness showed it him.

That man, that Spaniard was — Ignatius Loyola! Strange! Amazing! Extraordinary!

Calvin and Loyola were to be the armed leaders of two principles, who were to strangle each other in a deadly and desperate struggle. Their names express two world-ruling thoughts. Calvin was the embodiment of the Reformation, Loyola of the Roman Catholic Church. And while Calvin was to become the father of the Huguenots, and Loyola the father of the Jesuits, the children of Rome collected together to defend to the uttermost the authority of the Pope.

Chapter VII

THE CAPTIVE POPE AND THE TRIUMPHANT GOSPEL

YET the Pope and Rome no longer existed. At least, the affrighted burghers told one another so. What had happened?

The Imperial army had marched to the South to punish Pope Clement VII for an act of perfidy. The dreaded German lansquenets formed the kernel of that army; booty, glory, and honour were promised them, and Bourbon, who commanded them, had said: "Look, soldiers, yonder is rich Italy! It is for you — take it!" And they took it.

In the month of May, 1527, the Imperial army reached the city of seven hills; it was in the evening; the sun had just gone down.

The next morning the attack began; the scaling ladders were made fast to the walls, and the Duke of Bourbon was the first to climb to the top. He received a shot right in his breast. His fall made his soldiers mad with rage; nothing could resist the impetuosity of their attack, and they poured into the streets of the eternal city like a torrent that cannot be turned aside.

Then from the city there went up a long cry of grief; like Vandals the soldiers made havoc of everything; the most splendid works of art were destroyed and the archives plundered.

In the Pope's vestry, the cavalry horses were stalled, and as there was a scarcity of straw, the lansquenets collected all the valuable documents they could find there, and tearing them to pieces, strewed them under the horses like straw.

The despoilers kept holiday; they got down into the graves of the Popes and stole the ring from the finger of the dead body of Pope Julius II. A booty of more than ten million guilders was taken, and the soldiers gambled for gold, as silver and copper had lost their value.

It is said that the German lansquenets were the leaders, and this opinion is founded on the fact that the majority of those soldiers were Lutherans. And yet it is true that the Roman Catholic Spanish soldiers far surpassed the Germans in roughness and cruelty, and in the desecration of churches and graves could not be matched.

The Germans indulged in their love of ridicule to their hearts' delight. They were seen on donkeys riding through the streets of Rome in red clothes and with cardinals' hats on their heads. One of the troop was dressed up like the Pope and adorned with the triple crown; he was conducted to the front of the Angel's Tower, where he was done homage to; and the soldiers shouted so loudly that Clement VII could hear them: "Luther shall be our Pope!"

Clement had fled to the Angel's Tower, while for a whole fortnight the city was given over to the wild licentiousness of a rude soldiery, who no longer recognized any leader. They had become one vast concourse of shameless anarchists. General Lannoy was driven away, and it cost Philibert of Orange no end of trouble before he succeeded in restoring anything like order.

Clement VII relied on the help of Francis I, but that man was like the reed which pierces the hand. And while the allies left him in the lurch, he was obliged by hunger to make terms with the Imperial troops of Charles V, in the same year in which, in honour of the Pope, the flames of the torturing fire rose up in Prague and Munich.

It was, indeed, a strange world in which the Emperor Charles V lived.

His ambition was flattered by the thought that the Pope was then compelled to make the ignominious journey to Canossa. On the other hand, he feared that the anger and indignation of the Roman Catholics would not fail to procure him many a bitter enemy, and raising his voice, he expressed his Imperial displeasure at the scandalous conduct of his own troops.

To mete out the full measure, the Emperor commanded public prayers to be offered up in the churches for the deliverance of a Pope, shut up by his army; these prayers did not, however, prevent him from making good use of the holy father's imprisonment, and to get out of it all that he could.

The ruins of Rome sent a shudder through Europe; for the Roman Catholics it was a time of sadness and ignominy, while the burghers of Geneva said: "It is the beginning of the end." These brave, self-conscious citizens asked themselves, of what significance it could be to their town that Charles V had treated the Pope so roughly; and staring at the illustrious Imperial example, they were surprised that they had not yet shaken off the yoke of the weak Bishop, Pierre de la Beaume.

Geneva began to declare for the Reformation. Zwingli, the Swiss Reformer, had seen, as in a vision, the eternal light of the Gospel, shining above the lake of Geneva, and he wrote to his friend, Thomas Hofen, who was getting ready to fulfil a diplomatic function at Geneva: "This mission may, indeed, prove of extraordinary use to the citizens of Geneva, recently received into the confederacy of the cantons."

In these words, Zwingli expressed perfectly the thoughts of Hofen. And while the latter fulfilled his political task, he did not delay to make good use of his spare time, and in all simplicity to disseminate the word of the Lord. He found a point of contact in the desire for liberty, which descended from the tops of the Alps into the hearts of these children of the mountains, and the free spirit of the citizens of Geneva listened willingly to his amiable words as long as he confined himself within the limits of neutrality. Yet when Hofen laid his finger on the sore, censured excesses, and began to complain about the crying religious abuses, they turned their backs to the man, whose new ideas surprised and troubled them.

Hofen was not a Zwingli; he was soon depressed; he had a feeling such as Jonah had, when the gourd above his head withered away. And in the dejection of his soul he poured out his heart to Zwingli.

With frowning brow Zwingli read the despondent letter, but the Reformer was far from sharing in that despondency. He did everything in his power to strengthen his weak brother; and he made an appeal to the political freedom so longed for by Geneva, to throw the gate wide open for the Gospel.

According to Zwingli, a people could be governed only by the Bible or by the sword. There was no middle way. And where there was no holy fear for the Majesty of God, the cowardly fear of man would dominate the heart.

In those letters to Thomas Hofen you hear the rushing of the democratic Swiss blood.

M.HULDRICUS ZUINGLIUS,

"O my dear Thomas!" thus wrote Zwingli from Zurich; "there is nothing that I desire so much as to see the doctrine of the Gospel flourishing in the Republic of Geneva! Where this doctrine triumphs there the audacity of tyrants will be suppressed!"

Hofen felt his heart relieved when he had read this letter. This noble and amiable soul, so quickly depressed, so quickly elated, set to work again with enthusiasm, redoubling his zeal, till a second storm burst upon him, more violent than the first.

The numerous priests and monks of Geneva arranged themselves in close battle array against him. They reviled him in the streets; they went from house to house warning the people against the heretical infection exhaled by that envoy. The doctrine taught by him was, according to their inward conviction, a cursed doctrine, and the town would become like Sodom and Gomorrah if they listened to this dangerous Berne fox.

Then Hofen was crushed, annihilated; his task was done, and within a few months he was to travel to that land where all tears are wiped away from our eyes.

During his stay at Geneva as envoy, Hofen undoubtedly often came in contact with Besançon Hugues, the Nestor of the Geneva citizens, who was ready to lay down his life and all that he had for the liberty and independence of his native town. Hugues was a powerful personality, a Roman figure, whose eloquent tongue ruled the assemblies of the people; a born diplomatist, who knew how to move the stern old men of Berne to tears by his recital of his country's misfortunes, and as Captain-General was one of the most redoubtable defenders of Genevan freedom.

Hofen had undoubtedly placed his hope in this honest, noble patriot; but Hugues was a good Roman Catholic, and it must have been a bitter thing for the gray old patriot, when, by the force of circumstances, he was placed in the painful position of having to make his choice between the liberty of his town and the belief in the Church of his fathers.

But the choice had to be made; the seed, watered by Hofen's tears, had sprung up, and next to the old patriots who clung to Rome, a new party, with *Freedom and the Reformation* inscribed on their banner, soon gained ground. This party stood strong, by showing that the authority of the Pope and the freedom of Geneva were irreconcilable. And in league with the Government they propelled the ship of state vigorously on in the direction of the reformed waters.

Amazing! — while a destroying army was forcing its way through the gates of Rome, the Gospel was triumphing at Geneva. And while the shameless and riotous conduct of many of the clergy filled the citizens with grief and aversion, the leaders of the new movement cried: "What have we to do with the Prince Bishop de la Baume? To your tents, O citizens of Geneva!"

Chapter VIII

THE ASHES OF THE MARTYR

THE Pope's throne, however, stood firmer than rash Protestants supposed, and when Johannes Calvin took up his pilgrim's staff to walk to Orléans, persecution entered the streets of Paris.

Nobody had expected this. A sunny peace lay spread out over France; the Royal Court was transferred to Fontainebleau, so much beloved by Francis I, in order to afford a worthy reception to Hercules II, the young Duke of Ferrara, who was about to marry Renata, the daughter of Louis XII.

Margaret, the new Queen of Navarre, was there too, and the Pope's ambassador, who paid particular attention to her, was so much struck by the harmonious blending of majesty, purity, and lovingkindness that characterised her attitude, that he could not refrain from expressing his unconcealed admiration. She was constrained to take part in the noisy festivities given by her brother; but amidst all the contamination she kept her garments undefiled and testified to the godliness of the Gospel.

During these festivities there came suddenly like a flash of lightning from the clear sky — the news of the unheard-of scandal, that on Pentecost Sunday, May 30, 1528, in the night, the image of the Virgin Mary, at a corner of the street in the district of St. Antoine, Paris, had been shamefully disfigured.

The festivities were immediately stopped; in this desecration the King saw an attempt upon his kingly majesty, and, furious, flew to Paris, to find out the culprits. He offered a reward of a thousand gold crowns to him or her who could point out the culprit, while the police searched every house in the district, without discovering any trace of the criminal.

The capital was in a state of great excitement. Processions were organized to the mournful spot, where the Queen of Heaven had been insulted; five hundred students, with lighted wax candles in their hands, went to the place of disaster; the whole Sorbonne was there; the children of Paris went through the streets in long processions, singing their most beautiful hymns in honour of the

Holy Virgin. Thither repaired the princes of the Court. It was quite a pilgrimage. The sound of clarions and trumpets filled the streets, and bareheaded, the burning torch in his hand, the King knelt down to present to the Virgin Mary an image of gilt silver.

This was not sufficient; more had to be done; only by blood could the abominable insult be wiped out. And the Sorbonne, the Parliament, and the King joined hand in hand to root out French Protestantism. The red glow of the funeral pyre again lit up the *Place de Grève* in Paris, but the death of a few insignificant and unknown Christians was not sufficient. Nobler blood must be shed; a victim of some repute was longed for; the name of Berquin was mentioned.

Erasmus trembled for the fate which threatened Berquin; the old Rotterdammer could not understand how any one could court martyrdom, and he wrote warning letters to his friend to urge him to flee.

Yet Berquin did not flee, because in his eyes it would have been a shameful act of cowardice. His thoughts were full of victory, and in the strength of his belief he said: "God helping me, I shall triumph over the monks, the University, and the Parliament even."

Things, however, became serious; the Queen of Navarre received the ominous news, that Berquin had been seized and shut up in a strong castle, while she was powerless to save him.

Her brother had turned his face to Rome, and her mother, who, six years before, had in her enthusiasm exclaimed: "My son and I are beginning, by the, grace of the Holy Spirit, to know the white, black, gray, brown, and all the colours of hypocrites!" had again joined those many-coloured hypocrites, in order to persecute God's chosen ones.

Budé, one of Berquin's judges, watched with bleeding heart the course of the prosecution. His whole soul rose up against the murderous plan that the Sorbonne and the Parliament were concocting against the man who was as dear to him as his own life, and the thought that he was as powerless as his friend, who sat there on the criminals' bench, pained him beyond measure.

He did everything he could to save Berquin. He visited the accused in prison, sat down by his side as in the days of old, and was full of sadness when he perceived that his friend turned a deaf ear to all his plans to save him. Then Budé adopted other tactics.

If Berquin could be persuaded to give way a little, if it were but an inch, a jot, then much had been gained. It was, he pointed out to Berquin, in the true interest surely of the good cause which he had espoused, that by making some concession, he spared a life that still might be productive of so much happiness and blessing to others. There was still such a glorious prospect for him, such an excellent field of labour, such a noble task!

Budé became more and more pressing; it was the voice of friendship, the truest affection, which whispered into Berquin's ears. And while the Protestants awaited the issue with abated breath, came the mournful tidings that Berquin had fallen from the faith.

He had fallen; his eyes were darkened, and thinking to serve Christ, he had denied Him.

With relieved heart Budé hastened to the judges to tell the great news, that Berquin had expressed his readiness to publicly ask God and the King for pardon in the great castle-yard. Yet at the same moment the heart of honest Budé shrank back; he was frightened at the victory which his eloquent mouth and his friendship had obtained, and in his soul there rose up a mournful thought, that Berquin had served his life at too high a price.

Budé was right. Berquin's peace of mind was gone; fear, self-reproach, the bitterest remorse took possession of him, and when Budé entered the prison again, Berquin said in a firm voice: "I will retract nothing — I would rather die first!"

That decided his lot; Berquin was to die; the King, who had twice saved him, did not interfere. One April morning,[4] early, the ministers of justice entered the gloomy cell in which Berquin was shut up. He had expected them, and fetched a deep breath when he came out.

The birds were singing in the trees, and the young, fresh lenten green refreshed his eyes. It was noon before the mournful procession reached the *Place de Grève*. It was black with people, the unusual spectacle of witnessing the head of French Protestantism die, had brought the people together; a brisk trade was done in letting rooms and windows to those eager to see.

A dungcart, surrounded by a great number of armed men, conveyed the martyr to the place of execution. Berquin had donned his most costly clothes; a velvet mantle hung from his shoulders;

---

[4] April 22, 1529.

thus arrayed he wished to meet his King, who invited him to the wedding.

He was a model of Christian resignation when he left the cart, and his face reflected the quiet peace of a good conscience. Calmly he ascended the fatal steps of the scaffold, and he turned to the people to speak about Christ, for whom he was then about to die, when a wild shout from the hirelings of the Sorbonne drowned his voice.

The hangman approached; Berquin bent his head, and with the rope that was put around his neck, one of the noblest men of France was throttled on the stake.

His corpse was cast into the flames, and the little weak community of Protestantism saw the man on whom their hope was built, consumed to dust.

Throughout the whole land there was great dejection amongst the Evangelicals, when the sad news reached their ears. It was a blow at the heart of Protestantism; no one had expected that the nobleman who stood so high in the favour of his King, would end his life as a criminal at the stake.

Others followed Berquin to death; the fearful crept back to the feet of the priests, while God's children comforted themselves with the heavenly light that even above the gloomiest gallows did not lose its splendour.

In France there was great sadness; a long cry of grief rose up to heaven; and the Queen of Navarre was the saddest of all.

She was bitterly disappointed; her ideals had come to nothing, but she put her trust in God and thought of the words: "*And shall not God avenge His own elect, which cry day and night unto Him?*"

She was comforted, and taking her harp, sang: "O Lord God! Thy child is passing over the brink of death to come to Thee, his God, his Strength. O Lord God, awake! And be present everywhere to avenge the death of thine own!"

The Sorbonne had triumphed. The once defeated Béda sat with a grim laugh of satisfaction again in the exalted seat of the judges, and with Berquin's death the Evangelical belief was reduced to dust.

So at least thought his enemies and rejoiced, but God had ordained otherwise, and from the scattered ashes of the noble martyr was to arise the mighty Reformer of France.

Chapter IX

AT THE FEET OF THE LAWYER

FROM Paris to the town of Orléans, with its forty tennis-courts, was a great change for young Calvin. In the sixteenth century Orléans was the most illustrious town of France; Paris was called the capital, but Orléans the heart of the beautiful French country.

It was, indeed, a place of merriment and joy!

There in the shadow of the gigantic gilt bronze cross, erected in honour of the Maid of Orléans, they skipped and danced to the measure of the merry song of hundreds of students, who had flocked here together from the four corners of the globe. Hungarians and Portuguese, Italians and Englishmen here met one another. Moreover, there were numbers of Germans, who from over the mountains had brought with them their language and their Lutheran ideas.

And in this town at this University, at the feet of Pierre de l'Etoile, the king of jurisprudence, sat Calvin with his burning desire for knowledge.

Calvin was much impressed by the acuteness which characterised the great master. De l'Etoile was a sun, by whose brilliant light the lustre of other scientific stars waxed dim. He was of an upright character and amiable disposition, and to the inexorableness of the law he united the tenderness of a mother.

He was a faithful son of his Church, and had vigorously opposed the new ideas which he called heresies. This did not prevent him, however, from conceiving real friendship for the young student, although his Evangelical opinions troubled him, and with his large, loving heart he remained Calvin's friend to the end.

Calvin, indeed, at once attracted attention. The sprightliness of his wit, the strength of his memory, and his remarkable style were the sparks of the genius he displayed, while his amiability and the gentle, irresistible charm which he exercised, soon gained for him a large circle of friends.

Amongst those friends whom he found on the pleasant banks of the Loire, Melchior Wolmar must be first mentioned. In his house a young, winning boy of ten, named Theodore Beza, attracted Calvin's attention.

Wolmar was wondrously skilled in Greek. And as Calvin had to thank Cordier for his Latin, so he would have to thank Wolmar for that admirable Greek, by which he afterward became the unexcelled exponent of the Holy Scriptures.

Wolmar was something more than a great Hellenist — the was a true Christian. And to Calvin, who burned to know the truth, Wolmar showed the sum and substance of the Pauline Epistles: *the doctrine of imputed righteousness out of pure grace.*

Yet this heart, thirsting for happiness, had another teacher — that was God. And Calvin began to evince strange and far-reaching ideas, which called vividly to remembrance the heretical opinions in this same town five centuries before. We mean the eleventh century.

The year 1000 was awaited in breathless anxiety. In desperate fear the months, the weeks, the days were counted that still separated the world from the year 1000, that terrible year, in which the end of all things was to come — the unravelling of the world's history; the dreaded Last Judgment; the Terrible Day of the Lord.

Yet the year 1000 had come and gone; the drooping spirits had revived; and the millions, who had walked in the shadows of death, trod again the sunny hills of life.

Twenty-two years afterward, in this very Orléans, to which the Emperor Aurelianus had given his name, strange doctrines were proclaimed, doctrines which were strikingly like the utterances of this young man from Noyon. The proclaimers of these doctrines were then condemned to death, but people asked one another whether after five centuries the rise of these heresies was to be commemorated.

Again Calvin knew not what to do. Hot as a furnace, he was, however, taught in the way of righteousness, and the day was not far off when, with the strength of a Samson, he would break asunder the bonds which had bound his hands. Then he voluntarily renounced the world, in order to possess the highest good, and the world paid the man out by hating him most bitterly.

Calvin at age 24

The mystery of salvation was revealed to him; he had looked into God's loving heart and was saved.

"O Christ!" he exclaimed, "Thou hast manifested Thyself to my soul, and from now on all that blinded my eyes has disappeared . . . Naked and possessing nothing, I come to Thee."

On his seal he engraved a sacrificed heart, with the following marginal inscription: "O Lord! As an oblation, I offer Thee my heart, sacrificed for Thee!"

This was his motto, and he remained true to it all his life.

At the same time, in the Imperial Chapel at Augsburg, the Protestants of Germany handed over to the Emperor the twenty-eight chapters of their Augsburg Confession (June 25, 1530). In breathless silence the Confession was read aloud; and when the reader, the doughty Pontanus, had finished, he said: "Most Gracious Emperor! This is a confession of faith, which with God's help is proof against the gates of hell!"

"Sire," added John the Steadfast, Elector of Saxony, "that is also my confession of faith, from which I will not budge one hand-breadth — God do with me what He will!"

Those were the men who had already quenched their thirst at the eternal fountains before they had been discovered by Calvin. They defied the power of the Emperor, the anathema of the Pope, the anger of the world, because their guilty souls had found forgiveness through the blood of the cross.

And standing on the dazzling mountain pinnacle of faith, while angels and devils listened, Luther sang his spirited triumphal Psalm, to the glory of God:

Ein' feste Burg ist unser Gott,
Ein' gute Wehr und Waffen;
Er hilft uns frei aus aller Not,
Die uns jetzt hat betroffen.
Der alt' böse Feind,
Mit Ernst er's jetzt meint;
Gross macht und viel List
Sein grausam' Rüstung ist:
Auf Erd' ist nicht seins Gleichen.

Yet Calvin did not neglect the study of the law, and made such astonishing progress, that he was no longer regarded as a student, but as a master. One day, Pierre de l'Etoile asked him to give the Professor's lecture, and this young man, who was scarcely twenty years of age, discharged this honourable but difficult task with such clearness and acuteness, that he was looked upon as the worthy successor of De l'Etoile. The doctor's title was even offered him, and that he did not accept it was due only to that rare modesty which distinguished him all his life.

The seaman's blood surged in his veins. From Paris he had gone to Orléans, from Orléans to Bourges. There he received the tidings that his father was seriously ill, and he hastened to Noyon to watch by the death-bed of his father.[5] Did a beam of the eternal light refresh the failing sight of Gérard Cauvin? We do not know; the whole scene lies veiled in mournful vagueness. Moreover, the body could not be buried in consecrated ground, as Gérard Cauvin had failed to give a satisfactory answer to the questions put to him by the Church. For the sensitive heart of Calvin it must have been

---

[5] Gérard Cauvin died May 26, 1531.

a terrible martyrdom to think that the awful ban of the Church rested on the cold corpse, and much must have gone on in his heart while he stayed in the death-room, and his brother Charles was pleading in the Chapter-house for the Christian burial of his father.

Calvin took his father and the laws of Justinian to the grave. His ideal was a quiet little corner in the wide world where he could continue his studies undisturbed and unearth the golden treasures from the Holy Word of the Lord. He was no man for the Bar; his heart was too tender for the rude attacks of enemies, and while he wished to live as a quiet, forgotten citizen, God had ordained that he should die in harness.

His delicateness and sensitiveness were not less great than his tender-heartedness. That went too far, and his friends took advantage of it. His heart was full of affection and gratitude, gratitude for the smallest token of friendship. His friendship was very exacting — it is true — yet was not that exactingness a proof of its sincerity?

Furthermore, he was almost too particular in the discharge of his duties, in the execution of a commission entrusted to him by a friend.

A whole afternoon was spoilt if he had neglected to bow to an acquaintance, and the forgetting to send a greeting in his letter caused him a sleepless night.

There were two things which frightened him: poverty and riches. Pecuniary difficulties worried him as those little poisonous gnats worry us in summer; and the fear that he would not be able to meet his obligations made him feverish from anxiety.

When he had left the house of death at Noyon, Calvin had gone to Orléans, via Paris, where the loss of two crowns worried him beyond measure. Those two crowns were to pay a debt with, and not knowing how to get them, he sent in great distress of mind the following letter to a well-known friend:

DEAR NICHOLAS,
It is only necessity that compels me to ask a favour of you — a favour which, I fear, will be inconvenient for you just at present to grant me. But I knew I could

speak to you open-heartedly, and as I have a good opinion of your readiness to help, I apply to you.

My brother, who, as I know, has received the money, which my debtors have sent him, has, with his usual carelessness, disappointed me. I am, therefore, in difficulty and cannot wait a day, even an hour, longer. If you help me you will relieve me from an anxiety, of which you can form no idea, unless you yourself have experienced it. I want two crowns. Cop would have lent them me, if he had not spent all his money in the purchase of furniture for his room. My other friends are too far away, and I should have to wait too long for their answer. Farewell!

At the end of the week I hope to pay you back the money.

Calvin was nervous and irritable, easily put out and passionate. Yet his heart was characterised by an almost womanly tenderness, and he could with truth say to Viret, who knew him better than any one else: "You know the tenderness or rather the weakness of my heart."

This sounded like a lament, and was it not so?

Chapter X

THE CAPPEL TRAGEDY

When Calvin had followed his father to his last resting-place, Ulrich Zwingli stood with a friend at night in the cemetery of the cathedral at Zurich, looking at the sky.

They were looking to the west of the firmament at a dreadful comet, with an unusually long tail and of a pale yellow colour, which stretched out in a southern direction. Just before it disappeared especially the atmospheric phenomenon made a great impression on them, as it then appeared to glow like a furnace.

Zwingli looked long at the star and seemed to be deep in thought; then he said: "That ominous comet will light up my way to death."

The number of the forebodings increased. People told one another that above the Brunig two flapping standards had been seen high in the air. At Zug they thought that they had caught sight of a flaming shield in the sky. Loud mysterious peals of thunder were heard. Above the lake of Vierwaldstädter a fleet, manned with armed soldiers, was seen in the air.

Amidst the general dejection, which precedes an impending civil war, Zwingli remained perfectly calm and collected. His mind, it is true, could not shake off the phantom of those forebodings, yet with the far-reaching eye of the Reformer he could see beyond them all, and it comforted his soul to know that the King of Kings would at last accomplish His sacred object.

In the firm conviction of being a soldier of Jesus Christ, he looked with undaunted eye at the black thunder-clouds which were gathering above the lofty summits of the Alps, and was certain of his blessed immortality were the lightning to strike him dead.

Zwingli was a man of the sword and of the Bible. In him rushed the blood of the old crusaders, and he felt but little for Luther's fervent wish, that the strife for truth might be decided without the shedding of blood.

Zwingli's opinion was, that a war, carried on in the strength of the Lord for the most sacred of all beliefs, was good and glorious; he lived in that conviction, and that conviction drove him to the fatal pear tree at Cappel, where he fell like a hero.

The five Roman Catholic cantons[6] were now quite determined on war. It was a religious war — the bitterest war that is waged on earth.

Zurich was warned of this, yet the majority of the people did not show much alacrity, and hesitating and irresolute, a little army was got together.

At ten o'clock in the morning of October 11th there were only seven hundred men around the standard of Zurich; the shadows of a terrible disaster fell across the hearts of the brave Zurichers; there was no order, no discipline, no arrangement, while the Job's tiding, that a strong force of the enemy was approaching, multiplied.

In the midst of the terrible confusion Zwingli was asked for, and the council appointed him chaplain of the forces.

Zwingli was ready to go. At eleven in the morning he came out to mount his horse. All eyes were fixed on him; his face looked as resolute as ever, yet in his eyes there was great sadness.

And it was no wonder — Anna Reinhardt was a part of his life. She was not only a faithful wife, but an unexampled help in his pastoral work; generous, hospitable, full of love for the sick, a refuge for the poor she never denied; the home of Zwingli was filled with sunshine by this excellent woman.

When strangers asked who that quick, busy woman could be, the answer was: "That is Dorcas of the Scriptures." But Zwingli called her his apostolical roe.

The Sunday afternoons were most pleasant. Then the clergymen's wives met at the house of Zwingli, and there they deliberated how they could best serve the Lord and help the poor. If the clergymen were not prevented by duties they joined this circle, and with a loud voice they sang the hymns composed by Zwingli, to the glory of God.

The Reformer thought of all this when he left the threshold of his house.

"We must part," said Zwingli, with choking voice, to his wife Anna, who stood there speechless from grief and her face pale.

---

[6] Uri, Schwitz, Zug, Lucern, and Unterwalden.

"God wills it — His will be done! May He be with you . . . with me . . . with us all!"

Then Anna lifted up her tear-dimmed eyes to him and asked with a choking voice: "Husband, shall we meet again?"

"Wife!" was his answer, "if it please God!" But Anna knew that a fortnight before he had from the pulpit foretold his speedy death, and the thoughts of death cast their gloom over his open Swiss face.

The Reformer sprang into the saddle and cast a last melancholy look back at the house, where he had enjoyed so much love, consolation, and happiness. Then, with the grieving multitude following him with their eyes, he gave reins to his horse and rode away to the battle and to death.

So he reached the standard of the city of Zurich, but it hung drooping down, and the little army gathered around it in the autumn air, like a mournful funeral procession.

When the troop had crossed the bridge at Adliswil, under which the mountain torrent rushed madly along, the first cannon-shot was heard, about halfway from Cappel.

So the battle had already begun; their brothers who stood in the vanguard, were in the fight, and as though struck by an electric shock, they hurried on to take part in the strife.

Near the inn, *The Beech Tree*, at the top of the mountain Albis, they halted. What an impressive panorama lay there unfolded to the eyes of the Reformer! He saw the beloved city with its many roofs; the Zurich lake with its pleasant banks; the meadows, the vineyards, the fruitful orchards; and before him, at the foot of the mountain, rose up the gray walls and the spire of the old abbey of Cappel, then the centre of a bitter strife.

"Let us wait here for the reserve!" said Toning, the captain of the sharpshooters.

"That would be wise if we could hope for an army," replied Lavater, the commander of the troop.

Zwingli's heart beat loud and vigorously. He thought it an unheard-of thing to remain standing there idle, while their brothers had such need of their help, and he sprang forward to share like a good shepherd the fate of his sheep.

The gray-headed banneret Schweizer, who bore the standard, said that Zwingli was right. The cannon in the distance was calling them; it would be an indelible disgrace, if like cowards they remained behind.

So the men of Zurich descended the mountain, and it was three o'clock in the afternoon when Zwingli and his party joined the little troop of the vanguard, just as the Waldstädters were advancing with an overwhelming force.

"Well, Master Ulrich!" said a Zurich citizen, who had never been a friend to Zwingli; "what do you say now? They'll dust your jacket nicely for you overt there."

"There are here brave men enough," was the calm reply, "who know as I do that they are in the hands of the Lord, and therefore are not afraid of the odds against them."

The Zuricher repented of his harsh words, and replied: "I am ready to lay down my life as well as the others." And the man kept his word.

It was now four o'clock; the autumn day was already drawing to a close, and the thought became stronger that the Waldstädters would postpone the decisive attack till the following morning. But while the Zurichers were about to take up new positions, they were suddenly attacked by a murderous fire from the sharpshooters, who had concealed themselves in a little wood, which they had left unoccupied.

It was a moment of terrible confusion, yet Lavater, who knew fear only by name, seized a lance, and, springing before his men, cried out with his lion's voice: "Men of Zurich! Fight for the honour of God and for the honour of our masters!"

With his helmet on, his sword by his side, and his halberd in his hand, Zwingli stood there gloomy and silent.

"Master Ulrich!" cried a citizen, "speak to the men and encourage them!"

Then the great Reformer spoke of God Who never forsakes His people, and of the lawfulness and justice of their cause, although they should suffer defeat.

His eye saw the great inevitable disaster rapidly approaching, but the Lord God was his refuge.

Trust in God! He alone can save! Those were the last words which his fellow-citizens heard from him — they were his testament, which he left to his beloved Zurich.

Then the battle raged. The Waldstädters fought with the courage inspired by victory, the Zurichers, with the desperation of a man who will sell his life at the highest price only.

Hot and fierce was the contest around the great banner of Zurich.

Old Schweizer held it clutched in his wiry hand above the field of the dead, where the brave Zurichers lay felled like cornstalks on the stubble field at harvest-time.

"Stand firm, comrades!" cried the banneret in a loud voice; and undaunted he kept his ground till he fell — with the standard so gloriously defended, still in his hand.

Then the enemy gave a triumphant shout, but the standard did not fall into their hands. The conspicuously heroic courage of a Zurich citizen saved the banner — it was the soothing balsam on the smarting wound.

For the sword of the Waldstädters, who were worked up to madness, did fearful execution! The flower of Zurich's citizens lay strewn upon the battlefield. Toning, captain of the sharpshooters, forfeited his life; seven members of the Lower Court, nineteen members of the Supreme Court of Justice, and 482 citizens of Zurich and the environs were all slain.

There lay the father among his strong sons; the rich merchant beside the poor workman; and the evening breeze blew plaintively over the field of death.

Twenty-five Protestant teachers lay there dead amidst their slaughtered flock. Like bloodhounds, the Waldstädters sought for the preachers; they thirsted for their blood; the world's history knows of no battle in which so many shepherds and teachers were slain.

Striking and touching was the death of Ulrich Zwingli.

He hastened up to give the consolation of the dying to a citizen, when the latter, bleeding from thirteen wounds, had fallen prone on the ground. A heavy stone struck the Reformer on the head and he fell down senseless. After a time he got up to fall again, wounded in two places. With a great effort he rose up again, only however to succumb as before. And when he got up for the fourth time he received a fierce thrust from a spear.

Then Zwingli could do no more. He lay on his knees, but no longer had the strength to rise, and he saw his life's blood flowing away from his gaping wounds.

"It is nothing," he whispered in a faltering voice; "they can only kill the body, but the soul they cannot hurt."

Those were his last words. He fell back and lay there with clasped hands, his eyes, over which the film of death was stealing, fixed upon the everlasting stars. He lay in a meadow close to the high road under a pear-tree, which was afterward called Zwingli's pear-tree.

Two plundering soldiers of the Waldstädters found him dying, but did not recognize him. They asked him if he would not have a priest. "And if you are unable to speak," they said, "then commend yourself to the mother of God and call upon the saints."

But Zwingli shook his head and then the soldiers began to curse, while one of them turned the Reformer's face to the light of a watch-fire that was burning there. Then he recognized Ulrich Zwingli and was frightened. But a captain, who had served under foreign flags, no sooner heard Zwingli's name than he swayed his broad two-handed sword and killed the Reformer, crying out, "Die, hardened heretic!"

"Thus," writes the chronicler, with affecting brevity, "was Ulrich Zwingli, a faithful teacher of the Church of Zurich, done to death in the midst of his flock, which, like a true shepherd, he had not forsaken till death. He died by the hand of a mercenary, for the confession of the true faith in Christ, the only Redeemer and Mediator, the only Intercessor of the faithful."

A council of war was held over his body. Noble-minded Roman Catholics cried: "Let the dead rest! Let God be their Judge!" But their voices were drowned by fierce shouts; the body was quartered, and the parts thrown into a great fire, while the ashes were mingled with those of a swine and scattered to the four corners of the earth.

Zwingli was scarcely forty-eight years old; it was all over, and with him a great and glorious light in the community of the Lord had gone down.

Anna Zwingli had now become a widow in mourning; all Zurich went into mourning for its heroes, who had fallen there at Cappel.

But none were more deeply afflicted than Anna Zwingli. Her stepson was dead; her son-in-law, her brother-in-law, the husband of her so tenderly beloved sister; her best friends. And she, with her little children, was left behind alone.

It seemed all over with the glory of the Reformation. Zurich had to make a humiliating peace, and popery began to regain its old influence in Switzerland.

"Alas!" said a teacher in Basle: "Is Zwingli then, whom I so long loved as my right hand, fallen beneath the cruel blows of the enemy?" It was the voice of the worthy Oecolampadius, who was consuming himself in the service of the Lord. He had become worn out by the wearisome contest, and in little more than a month after Zwingli's death he followed him to the grave.

"Rejoice!" he said to his friends, when death was stirring in his veins, "I am now going to the land of everlasting bliss!"

He was then only forty-five years old. In ideas he stood between Zwingli and Calvin, but his gentle, peace-loving nature was more than once carried away by the turbulent blood of the Reformer of Zurich.

When he was dying he sent for his three children. It was a mournful sight — the eldest was scarcely three years old. He clasped the little children's hands in his and said: "Love God. He will be a Father to you!" And then he blessed his little ones.

His death-chamber presented the sublime spectacle of one of the Lord's elect going to his Father. Ten brother-workers were present.

"What news do you bring?" said the dying man to a friend.

"I have no news," was the answer.

But the dying man had news — he would soon be with his Saviour.

When they were about to open the window to admit more light, he said, laying his hand on his heart: "Here is light enough!"

That was a different expression to the dying cry of the great German poet Goethe: "More light!" When the sun rose in all his glory, his first beams fell on the closing eyes of the John of the Reformation, and mourned by his whole congregation, he passed away to enter into the joy of His Lord (November 21, 1531).

Chapter XI

WANDERINGS

While the sun, red as blood, went down over the smiling valleys of Switzerland, Calvin was writing his first work. And in the spring of 1532 it was published. It was an exposition of Seneca's celebrated work, *Meekness*.

It had made the writer nervous. It gave him no rest; "the die is cast," he wrote. And the doubt of success, which a writer feels who appears for the first time before the public, caused him no little uneasiness.

The word Calvinus, the Latin for Cauvin, appeared on the title-page for the first time. And the Reformer was from then on to be known under that historic name.

The book was printed at Calvin's expense; it was a great venture for an author who possessed little, and the worst was, that the printer's bill far exceeded the estimate.

In order to push the book, he had prevailed upon some teachers at Orléans, where he was then staying, to use it when teaching; to please him, a friend at Bourges promised to speak about it in his lectures. He wrote long letters about it to Daniel, and proposed sending him a hundred copies.

Calvin was often pinched for money. "I must contrive, some way or other, to get back the money that the publication of my book has swallowed up," he wrote to Daniel. "Yet I should be very glad if you would first write to let me know whether my book has been favourably received."

An exposition of a book by a heathen Stoic — how in the world did Calvin get the idea? It was so thoroughly out of keeping with the burning question of the day; in writing this book Seneca had dared to make a noble effort to crush the bloodthirsty feelings that began to rise up in the youthful Emperor, Nero. And then, when the French prisons were teeming with Protestants and the flaming faggot fires were burning to ashes the elect of the Lord, Calvin published his exposition of a heathen book!

But yet there is connection. One can scarcely repress the thought, that Calvin was thinking of Francis I as Seneca thought of Nero, and that these theses on gentleness written in elegant Latin with powerful eloquence were an appeal to the heart of the French King to govern with clemency.

The writer of twenty-three felt as Moses did when he saw the cruel oppression of his people; it was love for his weak fellow-believers that was powerfully awakened in him. In publishing this book he had in view, as appears from his letters, the prosperity of his country which he loved.

With a boldness, which is surprising to us, he expresses, amidst observations on language and antiquity, his thorough disapproval of the political abuses of his time, the lack of good legal administration; he makes special reference to the principles of absolute government, and reminds the monarch that the greatest safety lies, not in armies and gold, but in faithful friends and the love of subjects.

In this first book even, he takes his firm stand against the tendency of the Stoics' ethics, and this is the more remarkable, as during his whole life he had to defend himself against the imputation of being a thorough Stoic.

"This is the gist of the problem," he says; "the Stoics reject compassion as a sickness of the soul." And to this he replies: "No one can be good who is not compassionate. It matters little what the dull sages say in their darkness. In any case, I do not know whether they are wise — all that I know is that they are not men."

To these principles of compassion, sympathy and pity, Calvin remained true, and with all the earnestness of a feeling heart he defended the right of crying eyes at the very time in which he was accused of the greatest hardness of heart.

As a young man of twenty-three he defended the humanness of sorrow, and in the last edition of his chief work, the *Institution*, these words were to be found: "If all tears are to be disapproved of, what then shall we say of the Lord Jesus, from whose body dropped tears of blood?" So we see again, that the Calvin of reality had a different heart and a different pulsation to the Calvin of the legend. He was a man of flesh and blood, and had thickly underlined the words of the text: "Blessed are they that mourn, for they shall be comforted."

At the corner of De la Poterne Street is to be seen the gable of a remarkable house with a pretty enclosed balcony, where Calvin after close study loved to rest. The neighbours said that it was no wonder, for the eyes of Françoise Daniel, the daughter of the house, had bewitched him, and kindled another fire in the young man's breast than the fire of knowledge.

Whether that is true or not, who can tell? So much is said to which no importance can be attached. While Calvin was preparing for his examination as Doctor of Law, there was a merry wedding in the house of the Daniel family, but Françoise was not the bride nor Calvin the bridegroom, though it may well be supposed that he was among the wedding guests.

Five months afterward Calvin was again in Paris, and the letter which he wrote from the capital to his friend Daniel, spoke of something else than young love and myrtle wreaths.

During Lent, Gérard Roussel, under the powerful protection of Queen Margaret had preached to a congregation of four or five thousand people, whereupon the Sorbonne had made a vigorous attempt to incite the people against the Evangelicals. Yet it got nicely paid out; the head authorities of the Sorbonne were imprisoned in their houses, and King Francis got so angry that he banished the fanatical Béda thirty miles from Paris.

The atmosphere was as full of electricity as the air is on a hot summer day, when the thunderclouds gather in the south; the excitement increased every day, and one lampoon appeared after the other. The heads of the Sorbonne considered the Queen of Navarre the cause of their trouble. They were furious, and proposed sewing her up in a sack and throwing her into the deepest part of the Seine.

Calvin wrote about all this. He had already become mixed up in the fray, and espoused the cause of the Reformers.

So the morning of All Saints dawned on November 1, 1533. The Rector, Nicholas Cop, the friend of Calvin, had to deliver the solemn address for that day before the University.

He had requested Calvin to prepare it, and Calvin had replied: "Very well — I will do it." The text was taken from Matthew 5, "Blessed are the poor in spirit."

It was a piece of startling audacity; never had Roman Catholic France heard anything like it before. It was a manifestation, a demonstration, the voice of Protestantism, the loud echo of Luther's battle-cry of seventeen years before.

It was the voice of Calvin, but the timid student had become the bold Reformer, whose eagle's flight upward, past the saints and the holy Virgin, astonished everyone.

The unsought-for opportunity had been seized to give civilised and lettered France a fearless explanation of religious principles, which, at the same time, meant an ultimatum, a declaration of war to the Sorbonne.

The Sorbonne at least had regarded it in this light, and trembling from rage, it would not have rested till Cop had been cast into prison, had he not saved himself by flight.

Francis I was then staying at Lyons. And the Protestants, who built their hopes on him, were then to find out that he was the reed of Egypt which pierced the hand that leant upon it.

On the head of Cop a prize was set of three thousand livres; the persecution burst out; people said that the King had sworn to destroy Protestantism, root and branch, and Calvin had to make a rope of the sheets to escape with out of the window.

"Calvin, who had fled out of the window," an historian tells us, "made his way with all speed to the suburb of Saint-Victor to the house of a vinedresser, dressed himself in his coat, threw a linen wallet around him, put a mattock on his shoulder, and then made his way to Noyon."

Political considerations prevented, fortunately, the French King from cooling his passion on the Protestants, as he had intended, and Calvin, who had escaped through a window and narrow streets, was soon seen again in Paris and in broad daylight. But the air was not yet free from storm, although the youth of Noyon was received by Queen Margaret with great honour, and presented even to the King.

Of this, no one was more firmly convinced than Calvin; again he took his pilgrim's staff in his hand and went to Angoulême, there in peaceful seclusion to continue his studies.

The town of Angoulême is built on a plateau, a sort of rock which suddenly, to a height of more than sixty metres, rises up above the valleys. You still find there the old fortifications, which have been converted into boulevards, while the frowning battlements are transformed into smiling parapets.

In this fortress Calvin was to be found; in a dark, narrow, angular street, where he had taken up his abode with his college friend, Louis du Tillet, pastor and canon.

People asked who the pale young man was, and the pastor answered: "Charles d'Espeville." But then they were no wiser than before, for who had ever heard of D'Espeville!

But that did not matter; it was Calvin's fictitious name and for D'Espeville the house of the kind pastor was a cave of Adullam, where he could prosecute his studies undisturbed.

He had now learned to live from day to day. Experience had taught him to do so. For he had learnt this: if he had looked for rest, dangers had risen up like mountains, and if his soul had shrunk back frightened, the hand of the Lord had prepared for him a peaceful resting-place.

His heart had become quiet like the heart of a child comforted by his mother. The twenty-third Psalm was his portion, and though scarcely twenty-five years old, he seemed already ripe for heaven.

One thing only caused Calvin much grief — his slowness. Yet this slowness consisted in his working at night because he found the days too short. The library of Du Tilly with its three or four thousand volumes was the forge on which this new Vulcan, in the most brilliant French, wrought his religious conviction, and the weaving-room where the great master, in midnight meditations, wove the powerful work of the *Institution*.

As the work advanced, Calvin communicated the results of his inquiry to a few learned men in the neighbourhood. A prior, who bore the strange name of Pope of the Lutherans, belonged to this club, and this amiable "Lutheran Pope" offered his house, outside the gates of Angoulême, as a place of meeting.

"Let us find the truth!" Calvin would say every time that he opened a book.

"Not look for, but find," Calvin used to say. "The truth that we are seeking for is to be found." At the request of Du Tilly he also wrote sermons and Christian arguments, in order to give the people a taste for the true and pure knowledge of salvation in Christ Jesus. And whenever he preached, these significant words generally formed the conclusion of his discourse: "If God is for us, who shall be against us?"

Yet Charles d'Espeville did not remain under the hospitable roof of the prior of Angoulême. He turned his face to Nérac, then a distinguished place, and called the haven and refuge of all the comfortless. For there Margaret had taken up her residence. She was again overcome with a feeling of compassion, had made Nérac a free town for Protestant Israel, and, like a cluck-hen, which protects her brood of little ones, had spread her royal wings over the poor exiles, who by terrible sentences had been driven away from sunny France.

She had then made the mournful discovery that her marriage was hopelessly miserable, yet the misery which wrung her heart, made her exactly fitted to become the queen of the wretched. She was good and kind to all. With the learned she could carry on able discussions, for she was learned; in theology she was at home, and those same fingers, which could execute the finest tapestry work, wrote sweetly flowing verses. She made the best use of her time; when travelling she wrote pamphlets, and seated in her litter, a court lady held for her the inkstand.

To the Court at Nérac Calvin turned his steps, and there he met Le Fèvre.

Amazing! At the very time that the active old man published his excellent French translation of the Bible,[7] and whetted the Reformer's sword with which, in the name of the Lord, it was to achieve great deeds, Calvin appeared there.

The old man, who was already breathing the air of eternity, looked at the youth, laid his hand upon his shoulder, and said with the sacred enthusiasm of a seer: "You will be the instrument by which the kingdom of heaven shall be established in France!"

Le Fèvre seemed to be immortal; he was a hundred years old, yet his eyes were not yet dim. And stretching out his arm to the East, he exhorted Calvin to listen to Melanchthon. He thoroughly expressed Le Fèvre's opinions. There was a mental affinity with the German Reformer; Le Fèvre was the French Melanchthon.

---

[7] The French translation of the whole Bible was published at Antwerp, April, 1534. At the request of Philip II and the Duke of Alva it was placed on the list of forbidden books.

Yet this chosen one of God got into Satan's sieve before his little barque had anchored safely in the harbour, and the words of comfort and consolation: "All is grace!" once spoken by him to Farel, seemed to have lost their force.

The fears of hell assailed him; the Almighty stood before him as a wrathful judge, and to Roussel, who exhorted him to take heart and put his trust in Christ, he replied: "We are doomed; we have concealed the truth, which we ought to have confessed and borne witness to before men." It was an affecting scene; none of his friends doubted the sincerity of his piety, but he himself knew it, and saw the abyss before him.

Once he was sitting at the royal table and suddenly burst into tears.

Queen Margaret was much affected, and asked him what it was that made him so sad.

"Madam!" said the old man plaintively, "how can I stand before the judgment-seat of God? I have in all sincerity preached the gospel of His Son to so many people, who thereby have suffered death while I have sought to avoid it, and that at an age when far from fearing it, I ought rather to have longed for it."

Then the Queen comforted the good man, who, for his faith, was an exile at her Court. Again he took heart, heaved a deep breath and said: "I must go to God, for I feel that He is calling me."

Then he turned to the Queen and said: "Madam, I make you my heiress; my books I bequeath to Gérard Leroux, give my clothes and all that I possess to the poor, and commend the rest to God."

A slight smile passed over the noble face of the Queen, and she replied: "But what do I get then, Dear Master, of the inheritance?"

"Madam," replied Le Fèvre with French wittiness, "the care of dividing my goods properly amongst the poor!" Then great weariness came upon him.

"Adieu, gentlemen!" said he to his table-companions. Then he laid himself down to rest, and the Lord closed the tired eyes of His servant.

His friends made no noise for fear of disturbing him in his sleep. But it was the eternal sleep. He had reached the blissful Zion after a pilgrimage of a hundred and one years.

MARGUERITE DE VALOIS

That Calvin was eager to visit his friend Roussel in his abbey at Clairac, can be understood; in August, 1534, he is said to have gone there, and the stranger is still shown the old round tower with the strong walls covered with ivy, where nearly four centuries ago Roussel and Calvin talked together about the momentous interests of their fatherland.

Calvin had something to say to Roussel, and so he spoke. And about what would he have spoken with greater force and more serious warning than about the false mysticism that he could not tolerate in his friend?

Roussel has been called Le Fèvre's most faithful pupil, but yet it is true that he deviated from the lines mapped out by his great predecessor, and landed on the cemetery of passiveness.

Nevertheless, there ran through his doctrine the golden vein of the Gospel, and while he adorned his confession of faith with good works, Roussel showed the remarkable spectacle of a Protestant priest in a Romish frock.

Le Fèvre and Roussel displayed the same characteristics, though the former went farther than the latter. And the death of the hundred and one years old pioneer placed a barrier before the progress of the Reformation.

Le Fèvre was for purifying the temple, on the foundations of which Calvin wanted to erect a new building. Le Fèvre, like Roussel and Queen Margaret, longed for mediation, but they did not serve the Roman Catholic Church. This would have no transactions, no reconciliation, no healing of the breaches; in the logic of her iron consistencies, she collided with Calvin; and condemning Le Fèvre's writings to the flames, she was vexed that with the books she could not throw the writer in too. The honour shown to the saints was not sufficient; the Virgin Mary was to be exalted as the supreme Queen of heaven, and the Pope regarded as the true representative of Christ.

So the Church was bent on war; what would not bow to her should break. The days of patient waiting were past; the gates were thrown open, and the battle was to rage along the whole line.

With bleeding hearts Le Fèvre and his adherents had supplicated for the unity of the Church, and mockery and scorn had been their recompense. Now it would be war to the glorious end, and singing their immortal Psalms the serried ranks of the Huguenots, with Calvin at the head, came out of the gunpowder smoke.

Chapter XII

IN THE FIERY FURNACE OF PERSECUTION

YET the head of the Huguenots was then sitting behind the prison-bars at Noyon, his native town. What had happened?

He had gone to Noyon to renounce his clerical appointments; his chaplaincy and the pastorship at Pont l'Evêque which had been offered him some time before. He was now twenty-five years of age; the period at which one has either to serve the Church in reality or give up the emoluments connected with it. He felt in his heart compelled to come to the latter decision — certainly a strange feeling to Marx, the apostle of historical materialism, who thought he could explain all the impulses of the soul by the materialistic key.

There at Noyon he was confined in the prison, on account of an unseemly uproar caused in the church on the day before Trinity Sunday.

That tumult was, no doubt, a device, or at least a pretext, to get hold of the dangerous heretic; for a week Calvin was in prison and then discharged.

Yet two days afterward, the servants of the law again laid hands on him, and they would certainly have kept him had not the motives for his imprisonment been disputable.

From Noyon Calvin journeyed to Paris, and there in the capital he met the restless spirit, Michel Servet, who had imposed upon himself the task of rooting out the doctrine of the Trinity, on Protestant territory.

In Paris the signs pointed to dangers; nevertheless, Calvin was prepared to risk his life in order to win Servet for his Saviour.

He suggested an interview; the place even and the hour were arranged. Yet Servet stayed away — a fact the more to be regretted, since Servet died at the gloomy stake on Champel Hill.

The capital could not hold Calvin; he longed for a quieter place, and already saw the dark clouds gathering, which would obscure the light of France's sun.

So he then went to Poitiers, accompanied by his faithful friend, Du Tillet, and reached the flat heaths of Poitou, where many a bloody battle has been fought.

At Poitiers Calvin unfurled the flag of the Cross; he longed to win souls, and spoke with an open heart about Christ and the great eternity. He was at once surrounded by a select circle of hearers and friends, and preached with the burning zeal of his soul on the great salvation in Christ Jesus.

But the meeting-place was too dangerous, and to escape the spies, Calvin and his friends went outside the town and met in a large cave.

That is Calvin's cave, and is so called at the present day. It has now become a place of shelter for the sheep; then it was a place of refuge for the sheep of Christ. There Calvin preached, and he invoked the Holy Spirit to descend upon the little flock assembled there in Jesus' name.

The Reformer was wont to stand on an elevated spot; the listeners leant against the rocks. Amidst deep, mysterious stillness the words of life flowed from his lips and he generally ended with an impressive sentence that stirred all hearts.

When he spoke he carried everyone away with him, and the flush of enthusiasm tinged his pale cheeks. Suddenly he was overcome by an irresistible impulse at the thought of man's need. He fell on his knees under those solitary roofs; the whole assembly followed his example, and heaven seemed to descend into that cave.

Calvin spoke with fire against the mass.

"That is my mass!" he exclaimed, laying his hand on the opened Bible. Then he bared his head, threw his cap on the table, and raising his eyes heavenward, said in a touching voice: "O Lord, if at the Judgment Day Thou wilt punish me because I have spoken against the mass, I shall answer Thee. O God, Thou hast not commanded me to celebrate it. Here is Thy law — here is Thy holy word!"

From that time a strong desire was awakened to celebrate the Eucharist according to the Lord's institution. The many ceremonies, the incense, the choristers — all that had lost its value; a plain, real communion with the Saviour was yearned for, and the first Lord's Supper was celebrated by the French Protestants in Calvin's cave.

Yet Calvin could not remain at Poitiers, for the odour of heresy issued from him, and from the dark clouds, which his eye had seen, the first lightning flashes were already darting forth. His fatherland, whose reformer and benefactor he wished to be, gave him no resting-place for the sole of his foot, and he had to cross the frontiers to escape the French stake.

But in all that was the hand of the Lord, for Calvin was not destined to become the martyr, but the reformer of his country, and from Geneva this powerful patriot sowed in the furrows of his beloved France the seed soaked in blood and tears.

The most fickle king whom France has ever known, could not make up his mind how to act toward his subjects of the Reformation. Policy was his compass, and the equipoise had leaned first to one side then to the other. Béda went to prison, and when the doors were opened for him they were closed upon Roussel.

Amongst the Protestants themselves there were two parties, the moderate and the extreme. They could not agree, and sent an apothecary, a simple-minded, pious, and sensible Christian, to Switzerland to ask the advice of Farel and other distinguished exiles.

Farel had his answer ready. He drew up a powerful poster written with burning zeal, the preamble of which ran thus:

"Truthful articles respecting the terrible, great, and infamous abuses of the Popish mass, diametrically opposed to the Holy Sacrament of our Lord Jesus Christ, the only Mediator and Redeemer."

The document was printed at Neuchâtel; the sheets were concealed in bags, which were firmly bound with linen and string, and these clerical dynamite-bombs reached Paris uninjured.

Thoughtful men shook their heads, but their warning was like a word spoken to the deaf, and on the appointed historical night of October 17 to 18, the dangerous posters were stuck on the walls of Paris and Orléans, and even by a daring hand on the door of the King's bedroom.

Paris seemed as if struck by a fit of apoplexy; fierce fanaticism awoke, and the furious King hastened to his capital to defend it against the heresy which had entered its gates. Solemn processions were organized. On the heads of the Protestants a price of a hundred crowns was set, and the prisons were filled to overflowing.

Yet these measures were not sufficient to allay the indignation, and the insult committed against the Church could be wiped out only by blood.

The shoemaker Milon, lame and paralysed, enjoyed the high distinction of being delivered up first to the stake (November 13th, 1534).

He could not be accused of having stuck up the posters, for he was unable to walk, but he had been found in possession of them, and for that reason he was condemned to the flames. The jailer lifted up the victim in his arms like a child and put him into the cart which conveyed him to the *Place de Grève*. So he rode past his home greeting it with a smile, and he was slowly roasted to death in accordance with the demand of the King's advocate.

The rich cloth-merchant, Du Bourg, was a different person. Not as a martyr, but with the proud attitude of a warrior, he strode on between his executioners, the halter around his neck, the torch in his hand. The hand, with which he stuck up the accursed poster, was cut off, but he bore the cruel mutilation with the firm courage of an old Roman. And so he breathed out his heroic soul — amidst the flames, which were kindled on the great fish-market place.

A mason, named Poille, was the third of the martyrs. He spoke of Jesus Christ, for whom he was ready to shed his last drop of blood, which so embittered the executioners that they bored through his tongue and fastened it to his cheeks with an iron pin. But he still spoke — with his eyes, from which shone the heavenly joy of a Stephen; and amidst a low, smothered cry of fear from God's children, who surrounded the scaffold, Poille was burnt alive.

From this time the death sentences followed quickly one upon the other; the murderous lust which slumbers in the heart of man awoke, and the terrified Protestants fled to the four quarters of the horizon, like a flock of sheep attacked by wolves.

For Queen Margaret the time had come to unburden her distressed mind by silent tears, and her grief moved the King to release her three friends, Roussel, Courault, and Berthaud, from prison and send them to a monastery. Roussel, the weak reed, bowed his head, remained with the Church and went to his abbey. The terrified Berthaud died a monk, and only the old half-blind lion Courault persisted in his faith. Despising the coarse monk's gown and rosary, he escaped from the thick walls of the monastery and fled to the land of liberty where Farel lived.

Yet with this last favour shown, the King's mercy came to an end. He solemnly declared before a select assembly that he would not hesitate to destroy every heretical member of his family, in order to prevent the others from becoming affected by the same pestilence. Accompanied by his three children, he went bareheaded, with burning candles in his hands, from square to square,[8] rejoicing to see how six of his most faithful subjects were being burnt to death amidst the demoniacal shouts of an excited populace. The Order of the Jesuits was founded, and the man who was destined by God to become the leader of French Protestantism left the country as a refugee.

---

[8] January 21, 1535.

Chapter XIII

THE WHOLE ARMOUR

MEN are getting bad, it is said. Were they better in former times?

Two fugitives were making for the French frontiers; with them they had two servants, who knew their misery, their grief. One of the fugitives — according to a Romish historian it was Calvin — could not suppress his emotion at the thought of France having ejected the Protestants. And notwithstanding this, one of the servants was bad enough to rob the fugitives of the leather bag with all their money, and to gallop off with it. They would then have been in the sorest need, had not the other servant, out of his own pocket, lent them ten crowns. And so at last, downcast and oppressed, they reached Strasbourg.

Noble men they were, whom Calvin and Du Tillet met there!

Bucer, who, in the spirit of wisdom and meekness, lectured on the books of the New Testament, must especially be mentioned. Calvin admired the upright heart, the amiable disposition, and the keen intellect, ever busy, of this excellent preacher.

Yet he was rather afraid that Bucer, whom he subsequently called his father, was playing a part which he would too quickly renounce, and concede too much to Rome, in order to preserve peace.

Calvin did not remain long at Strasbourg. He feared that the clerical trend in this new Jerusalem might work unfavourably upon the wavering character of his friend, Du Tilly.

It might have done. Moreover, he longed for the quietness of his study, and hoped to find it in Basle.

In this hospitable town, which ten years before had welcomed Farel, he found the resting-place so longed for, in the house of a well-to-do lady; and thirty years afterward this excellent woman would tell about the life and studies of the celebrated Reformer.

Here he met Nicholas Cop, his bosom friend, from Paris. How glad must Cop have been to see that pale, never-to-be-forgotten face again in his room. And how much they would have to tell each other!

The tidings from France were sadder and sadder. They heard of the end of the cripple Milon, of Du Bourg, and many others. Calvin knew Du Bourg. How many times he had partaken of that good man's hospitality!

A few months later, an old man, almost blind, hobbled into Calvin's room. It was Courault. And when this faithful witness told Calvin about the persecutions, a deep sigh escaped his breast.

It was really terrible. In the spirit Calvin saw the gloomy strappado, which plunged God's children into the flames, raised again, to cast them anew into the blazing fire, and he cried out: "O with what furious rage are God's enemies filled!" Then, however, a strange story was told inside the walls of Basle. King Francis, who had frightened his subjects by his barbarous cruelty, was now to show that his hypocrisy was equal to his hardness of heart. He had amused himself with the charred bodies of his Protestant subjects, but it had suddenly occurred to him that he could not do without the support of the German Protestant princes in his ambitious policy against Charles V, and he made a vigorous effort to justify himself for the murder of his subjects. In a detailed manifesto addressed to the German Protestant princes, the King tried to make them believe that the persecuted were dangerous revolutionists, and to get over the difficulty of lack of proofs, the King made this strange assertion: "I have preferred to bury their peculiar theses in the darkness from which they sprang, rather than to send them to you, who are the light of the world."

It was a cunning trick, for since the Peasant War, the German princes were terribly afraid of the revolutionists, while Communism had again broken out under the leadership of the notorious John of Leyden, who had made the town of Munster the earthly Zion, and paid for his crime on the scaffold.[9]

A cunningly devised plan, that of Francis I. Yet there was one man who watched over the unsullied banner of French Protestantism, and whose soul was set on fire with zeal for God,

---

[9] Munster was taken by the allied princes, and John of Leiden beheaded on January 22, 1536.

when his brothers, who were chased like wild beasts of the field, were so shamefully vilified by the King.

Then appeared his *Institutes.* The work was the solemn and impressive protest of a heart moved to tender and sacred pity for those persecuted for their religious belief, and of a conscience trembling with anger and indignation at the shamelessness of a crowned hypocrite.

Yet for a youth, timorous and but little known, it was a bold deed to apply direct to a mighty monarch. The need, however, was urgent; the flames of the funeral pyre, which consumed the martyr, hew in his face, and it would have been cowardice had he not made use of the only weapon he possessed — the pen — to try this last resource.

The need was urgent. New flames were shooting forth. A godly farmer was brought before the tribunal, dragged to the place of execution on a sledge and burnt alive. A barber at Santerre suffered the same fate, and it was probable that many others would follow.

Yet Calvin espoused their cause; he put his sharpest arrows to his bow and then shot them at the conscience of the King.

"Sire!" said he, "you yourself are witness how greatly our doctrine is slandered every day. Indeed, they tell you that it has no other object than to destroy all power and authority, to disturb peace, abolish the laws, to do away with seigniories and possessions — in short, to bring everything into confusion. And yet you hear only the smallest part of these slanders. Fearful reports are spread about it, which, if they were true, would condemn us, and justly too, to thousands and thousands of gallows."

It was not his object to secure for the Reformation a certain right to stand beside the Roman Catholic Church — he did not supplicate for pardon for the Reformation. How could he ask for pardon! It would be a violation of the truth the Reformation brings, indeed, the true light — that shining upon the path of princes and subjects would prevent them from stumbling.

He drew himself up to his full height in a hopeless attempt to soften the King's heart.

He cried aloud — he shouted in the ears of the King: "Sire, I consider our case from all points of view. We are persecuted; some of us are kept in prison; others are flogged; some again forced to make a public confession of their guilt; others are banished or escape by flight . . . We are oppressed, insulted, and inhumanly treated; regarded as an abomination and a curse — and why? Because we place our hope in the living God, and believe that eternal life consists in the knowledge of the one true God and Jesus Christ, whom He has sent." Writing the *Institutes*, he stood upon the lofty watch-tower, and at those solemn moments his soul was stirred by the furious struggle between truth and falsehood, which disturbed the world. He saw the calamities; the mournful sound of the death-bell rang in his ears, and the echo of Jeremiah's lamentations was heard in his words as he wrote: "Many seas of disasters overflow the earth; many new pestilences ravage the world; all falls to decay. One must despair of human affairs, or bring order into them, even by forcible measures."

And yet men rejected the remedy. "O forsooth! God's eternal truth must be alone heard in the Kingdom of God!"

The letter to Francis I, which forms the introduction to the *Institutes*, contains a series of the most brilliant sentences that ever flowed from the pen of the Reformer. It is pent-up anger that speaks from them; Calvin did not for a moment forget that the crowned hypocrite was king by the grace of God, and with undaunted courage he stood up for the truth.

But he was the son of the sixteenth century, and defended the truth but not liberty; and while he did not deny the authorities the right to kill heretics, he simply demonstrated that his brothers in belief were not heretics.

At the end of the letter he made a direct appeal to the heart of the King, and finished his incomparable argument, that was read probably by millions besides the man for whom it was intended, with the following words:

"If the slanders of the malevolent at once stop your case, so that the accused have no opportunity to defend themselves, and, on the other hand, if these turbulent, malicious creatures, without your authority, go on showing their rage, by imprisoning, flogging, and torturing by fire and sword, we shall in sooth, like sheep devoted to the slaughter, be driven to despair; but yet we shall possess our souls in patience, waiting for the strong hand of the Lord. He doubtless will reveal Himself in His own good time and come armed to deliver the poor from their oppression, as well as to punish the scornful. May the King of Kings confirm, mighty and illustrious King, your throne in righteousness and your rule in fairness!"[10]

Sharper, more biting language against the officials of the Roman Catholic Church and her sins has but seldom been used by a Reformer, and never was the exaltation of the Church of the sixteenth century defended with such strength of inward conviction, with such thorough knowledge of the Church's past, and with such fire of eloquence, as in this address to the King, Francis I.

The *Institutes* were written in Latin, that they might be accessible to the whole civilised world. The volume was octave, and contained little more than five hundred pages, and yet it may be said that the publication of this book indicates a new chapter in the Church History of the West.

The *Institutes* expanded; Calvin worked nearly all his life at them. The first edition, a book of only six chapters, had increased in the last edition to four books with eighty chapters. Yet the sentences which underwent alteration can be counted; the substance, the contents, the trend remained the same, and the old man put his seal to what the young man wrote.

The book did not work like the swift, impetuous cavalry attacks which Luther made use of to harass his enemies, but like the slow, irresistible onset of a Macedonian phalanx.

The sales increased from year to year; the editions followed one upon the other; the book became for France what Luther's translation of the Bible was for Germany. It was translated into almost all European languages, and no writing of the Reformation period was more vigorously opposed, more fiercely attacked, or more feared by the Roman Catholics than Calvin's *Institutes*.

The contemporaries of Calvin spoke of a gesture which he often made while speaking; how for instance he raised with one hand his black cloth biretta, and with the other pointed upward.

Sometimes he gave force to that gesture by the words: "All for the honour of God!" And people had become so accustomed to the expression, that it was understood although unuttered.

---

[10] From Basle, August 23, 1535.

All for the honour of God — that expression embraced the whole life of the Reformer, and his *Institutes* were the result of it.

The *Institutes of Christian Religion* are the chief work of Calvin; as in a golden temple, the great thoughts on the redemption are therein laid down; the *Institutes* were Calvin himself.

He wrote them in defence of his brothers in Christ, whom he loved; yet in defending them, he explained and justified the Reformation. He was as scriptural as Zwingli, but Zwingli was exegetical and Calvin dogmatical. Like Zwingli, he had an aversion to traditions, which was not shared by Luther, and while Calvin agreed with Luther in the doctrine of the redemption without works, the latter maintained that we are justified by faith, and the former by God, as saving through the sovereignty of godly grace.

The substance of the *Institutes* was Predestination. On that Predestination the Reformed Church of France was founded as upon an impregnable rock, against which the gates of hell should not prevail and the furious attacks of Satan would break like impotent waves.

While France and Germany stood aghast at the unparalleled boldness with which the *Institutes* were written and new controversies against Popery occupied his mind, the writer, with his friend Du Tillet, was toiling over the snow-covered mountain paths, in order to reach sunny Italy.

What were the thoughts that filled Calvin's mind when his eyes looked upon the eternal glaciers in their snow-white garments? Must not this man, who had to fight out his great inward battle with innate sin, have then thought of the words: "Though your sins be as scarlet, they shall be as white as snow!"

The desire of his heart drove him to Italy, to the place where the Pope ruled; to the land of arts and sciences, of heroes and martyrs. There superstition reigned; well then, those who were sitting in darkness should know that Christ — and He alone! — is the hope of a poor sinner.

Calvin's mind was deeply stirred, when from the last hill he looked down upon the smiling plains of that Italy where rose the city built on seven hills: the proud, riotous woman, the great Babylon that was shedding like water the blood of the Lord's beloved children!

With that Babylon, with that mighty Goliath, he went to do battle. For his weapon he had nothing but a sling, but in that sling lay the word of God that overthrows the mighty.

Ferrara was the first place they stopped at, and farther than this Calvin never got.

When Duke Hercules, with his youthful consort, Renata of France, was celebrating his return to Ferrara (December 1, 1528), the city had just been grievously visited. The plague had decimated the population; twenty thousand people had been buried in the cemetery; the shops were closed; the voice of lamentation was heard in every house, and the lecture-rooms of the University were desolate and forsaken.

Yet the Duke, who was celebrating his joyful return, wished to see joy and not sadness. The wearing of mourning was forbidden; the church bells had to send forth merry peals, the shops to open, and the lectures at the University to be resumed when he came. And this was done.

In bright festive garments the people went out to welcome the Duke and his consort on the pleasant banks of the Po; the cannons were fired, from the houses flapped the flags, red, white, and green, and the Duchess Renata was borne in triumph through the gates in a litter.

She was arrayed in a superb dress of gold cloth; on her head was a glittering crown; a procession of four-and-twenty pages in crimson surrounded her; before her went the clergy with the professors of the University, while the envoys of France, Venice, and Florence followed.

The historians vie with each other in praising Renata of France on account of her brilliant qualities, the nobility of her soul, the energy and intrepidity of her mind, her clear judgment and her fine sense of justice, as one of the most remarkable women of her time. From her father, the excellent King Louis XII of France, she had inherited her taste for arts and sciences; this taste was strengthened by her communication with Queen Margaret of Navarre, while as a daughter of France she had brought with her to the Court of Ferrara her undestroyable love for her native country.

Yet her husband was a grandson of Pope Alexander VI; a man who by inclination and policy was a furious opposer of

Protestantism. Hercules II excelled others in knightly games, in his hatred against the Reformation, and in the writing of elegant Latin verses. He was a great, strong man; a conspicuous figure at the tournaments; his religion consisted in a fanatical superstition, which did not, however, prevent him from keeping mistresses and bastards.

At Ferrara was the little sensitive poet, Marot, who, on account of the sensational posters, stood number 7 on the list of those suspected; number 22 was Cordier. In the city there were also many French fugitives, and as Queen Margaret had made Nérac a free place for the persecuted, so Ferrara, under the management of the Duchess Renata, became the cave of Adullam for the oppressed and sad at heart.

In this city, at this Court, appeared two noblemen, one of whom called himself Charles d'Espeville. He was dressed entirely in black velvet, and on his head was a doctor's biretta of the same material.

He wore a broad white collar and a gold ring. He looked tired — tired from mental exertion; nevertheless, his face was as noble as it was severe, and he possessed those distinguished manners which rendered him fit to move in the cabinets of kings.

Renata introduced her two compatriots to the Duke as literary men, who had come to visit glorious Italy, and the Duke, apparently flattered by their coming, gave them a hearty welcome. For he was fond of literature and science, and was not displeased to see the circle of literary men, who had gathered around his young and intellectual wife, increasing. It flattered his pride; it enhanced the lustre of his Court, and there seemed to him but little that was suspicious in the religious trend which characterised their meetings.

Yet there had been reasons enough to make the Duke uneasy, for the air of Italy was filled with the germs of reformation. In the very shadow of the Vatican were found men of high culture and deep study who, as watchmen on the lofty tower, looked eagerly for the joyful morning which would raise the Roman Catholic Church from her ignominy, her misery, her decline, and give her a new, prosperous, and God-glorifying life. A secret correspondence was carried on between Rome and Wittenberg; under the very eyes of the Pope, as it were, letters were written to Luther, Zwingli, and Melanchthon. A society, which before everything appealed to the testimony of the Holy Scriptures, was spread over the whole of Italy; it confessed the doctrine of justification by faith, and had sixty members in the city of Rome.

Yet this movement sided more with Le Fèvre, Roussel, and Erasmus than with Luther and Zwingli. It shrank from a rupture with the Church; the venerable cathedrals of the Mother Church prevented their eyes from seeing the dazzling mountain-tops of the Reformation; and they shuddered at the thought of stretching out their hands to seize the crown of the Pope, the anointed of the Lord.

The Capuchin monk, Ochino, was the celebrated speaker of this society. When he appeared in the pulpit the people flocked to hear him; the largest churches were too small to contain the hearers, who hung upon his words. And when he, the man of self-chastisement, whose thin face told of his continual penance, spoke in the Cathedral of Ferrara with burning eloquence, of the glory of the heavenly Paradise and the all-surpassing love of the Blessed Redeemer, the Duchess was melted to tears of penitence and earnest longing.

Yet behind the brilliant eloquence of this celebrated Capuchin monk lay concealed a lacerated heart. He stood with both feet in the stream, which, thundering down from the heights of the world of thoughts, stirred up the age. He could not remain there; he must advance or go back; he had to choose between his Church and the Reformation. And his followers — the Duchess Renata in the first place — had to make the same great and difficult decision.

Then Calvin appeared; he obtained permission to preach in the private apartments of the Duchess. From his own lips Renata heard the powerful discourse which, setting aside the regulations of the Church, pleaded only for the Gospel. He announced absolute, complete justification by faith, but that demanded also an undivided and total surrendering to God, to live and die for Him in perfect self-denial and so to come to that inward feeling of personal communion of life with God by which one is conscious, in loving, burning consecration, of being entirely His, the chosen of His almighty love. The embodiment of this conception was the incomprehensible doctrine of election; it was the profound expression of that all-penetrating, mysterious in-dwelling of God in man — for his salvation, his everlasting bliss.

Was the preaching of predestination on the lips of the youthful Reformer an incitement to meekness? By no means — he preached obedience to the Divine will, the severing of bands which bound one to Baal, the deliverance, the bold deed which would make one tread, with heroic steps, the path mapped out by God.

Calvin spoke plainly and to the point; with a perspicuity and acumen such as had never before been heard in Ferrara. He declared that the priest as mediator is superfluous, as Christ is the great Mediator; that the absolution of the minister can be dispensed with, as God gives it. He rejected the intercession of the saints, the reconciling power of the Sacraments, and made an urgent appeal to personal responsibility. He wanted Christianity in its entirety — belief with works; and one's whole life had to be a Christian life, a growing up to the stature of Christ.

In Ferrara there were many things of great interest to Calvin, but his life's vocation was the preaching of the Gospel, and in the Duchess he found a soul that was hungering and thirsting after righteousness. He had many an interview with Renata; the Bible formed the chief topic of their conversation, and the Divine Word was the lamp that illumined the dark path of the Duchess. She followed the advice of Calvin to follow that light steadfastly, and a Roman Catholic writer has said: "Calvin infected Renata so much with his errors, that one could never get the poison, which he had made her drink, out of her heart again." Yet for the diligent Evangelist of Noyon it was not sufficient to win a woman, although she wore a ducal crown. He thought perhaps of something else — he dreamt, maybe, of conquering the whole of Ferrara.

Already there was a great movement at the University, the minds of many were greatly agitated, and it would have been nothing to wonder at if Calvin had in Ferrara thought possible what was subsequently accomplished at Geneva.

Yet these ideals would burst like soap-bubbles when the Duke showed himself in his true character.

So long as the meetings were confined to weighing and considering, to speculating and comparing, he had remained neutral, but when this strange fanatic from Noyon insisted on one being not only a Christian in name, but also in deed, he became uneasy in mind. And the approval with which Renata listened to the bold preacher confirmed his uneasiness.

It was but a year ago that he had gained the ducal crown and he did not mean to vex the Pope and risk the possession of a dukedom.

With a zealous hand he began to weed out heresy from his dominion; many men with a leaning for the Gospel received commands to leave his dukedom. And with regard to Calvin, the Duke said with threatening gesture: "That man, that Charles d'Espeville, shall, as soon as he is discovered, appear before the court of justice to answer for his religion." The Duke's decision struck Renata like a flash of lightning from the clear sky. She felt herself at once deserted by her truest friends, that she would have to remain behind alone with priests who did not understand her and with monks of whom she had a horror.

Calvin, who had been scarcely two months in Ferrara, fled at the very moment that the Inquisition was about to seize him. His departure grieved Renata deeply, but the bond, which bound her to the Reformer, remained unbroken. She continued to look upon him as a chosen instrument of the Lord; she was continually in correspondence with Calvin, and this correspondence lasted thirty years, till his death.

When the pen slipped from his trembling hand, he dictated to his brother his last letters, intended for the Duchess. To them he added a medal struck by King Louis XII during his conflict with Pope Julius II, on which was engraved the famous saying: "I will destroy the name of Babylon."

So Calvin then turned his face to the North. The sower had gone out and come back, after having scattered the seed in the furrows. A harvest of blood and tears ripened, and the prediction of the seer of Noyon to one of his spiritual children in Italy would be fulfilled: "He who in this land and at this time will lead a Christian life, let him prepare to die!"

Chapter XIV

BATTLE AND DEFEAT

IT was on an evening in the month of July, 1536, when a stranger arrived at Geneva. He was a young man of seven-and-twenty, of scarcely average height, with a black pointed beard, a high thoughtful forehead, a stern, quick eye, and sharp, regular features.

He came from France. His object had been to reach Strasbourg by way of Lorraine, but the roads were full of soldiers, for a new war had broken out between the French King and the German Emperor, and the traveller had taken a circuitous route to the south, in order to reach Strasbourg via Geneva.

It was Calvin. After many a long wandering from Ferrara he had at last reached the French capital, but as it was not safe there, he had formed the plan of settling at Strasbourg.

It happened that Du Tilly was then at Geneva; he discovered Calvin and made his discovery known to William Farel.

Farel was aroused when he heard Calvin's name mentioned. He had read the *Institutes*, and in the author of this remarkable book had recognized the keenest intellect and most powerful writer of the age.

He sprang up as though he had received an electric shock; he was a most impulsive man, and the thought flashed through his mind, that this John Calvin was the man sent by God to help him in his difficult reformatory work within the walls of Geneva.

The meeting between Farel and Calvin under the humble roof of the inn, where Calvin had alighted, deserved to be put on canvas by a painter.

Calvin, shy by nature as he was, stood astonished and hesitating before the impetuous Farel. He had totally different plans; he longed for a quiet spot, where he might receive instruction instead of giving it. Bucer and Capito attracted him. No, he was not the martial hero to try conclusions with the untamable nature and rebellious spirit of the formidable men of Geneva.

There lay the town stretched out before him; the noise in the streets reached his ears. The town was full of light, joy, and merriment; above it was the blue firmament, which was reflected also in the clear mirror of Lake Leman below, while the Rhine flowed rapidly past.

Geneva was the cross-point of four high roads; they led to Savoy and Lyons, Switzerland and the Jura. Everything passed along these roads; new faces of merchants and travellers were constantly to be seen; the sharp practices of trade prevailed in the great market squares; it was a town of priors and monks, of knights and barons, and Farel's voice seemed powerless to drown the light-hearted cry of the worldly-minded: "Let us eat and drink, for tomorrow we die!"

And in this town was Calvin to cast anchor?

The bare thought sent a shudder through his frame; for himself he knew no more unfortunate resting-place on the face of the earth than this.

"I am timorous and shy by nature," he exclaimed. "How then shall I be able to fight against those raging waves!"

But Farel, who never gave up, was not going to give up this time either. He expressed undisguisedly his bitter contempt for the servants of Christ who shrank from the strife; he reminded him of Jonah, who had the temerity to disobey the Lord's command, and for his disobedience was cast into the sea.

His short form grew taller; that angular, ugly, sunburnt face with that bristly hair and that red beard was lit up with the glow of a holy zeal.

Like a prophet, he stood before Calvin, and fixing his flaming eyes upon the young man, he cried out with his voice of thunder: "You think of nothing but rest; you trouble yourself about nothing else than your studies. Well then, in the name of the Almighty I tell you, that unless you give ear to His call, your plans He will not bless. May God curse your rest — do you hear what I say? May God curse your studies, if in such urgent need you dare hold back and refuse to give help and support!"

Calvin had found his man; he bowed his head; from now on his life was to be bound up with that of Geneva!

Who could withstand William Farel? This iconoclast, this Vaudois could be turned aside by no one. His motto was: "If we can't convince the Roman Catholic heretics, yet we can tell them the truth plainly to their face, as Jesus did to the Pharisees."

Erasmus had trembled in his presence.

"Never in my life have I seen so bold a man," said the savant of Rotterdam.

Farel's strength lay in his manner of acting. During a procession he had snatched the relics from a priest's hand and thrown them into the water. For the Roman Catholics there was no name more detested than that of William Farel. He defied prison and ill-treatment; covered with wounds, dripping with blood, he appeared before the people to preach the Gospel, and to assure them that the Pope was the first-born son of Satan. Wherever he appeared, strife and disturbance were unavoidable; the enthusiasm of the Crusaders, who stormed Jerusalem, was in his heart; he forced his way into Roman Catholic churches while the priest was celebrating Mass, and mounted the pulpit, drowning the uproar with his lion's voice! Yet this man was humility itself; he requested that no titles should be put on his letters, and this bold heart was so sensitive, that Calvin afterward wondered more than once, how greatly that Farel could be affected. Such was the character of William Farel, who drove the Protestant plough through the soil of Geneva.

But why had Farel come to Geneva? On a splendid October day in the year 1532, while the autumn gossamer threads hung in the air, Farel and his fellow-combatant, Sonnier, had in their wanderings, discovered in the distance the three old towers of the cathedral of Geneva. Thither they turned their steps and visited Olivetanus, Calvin's nephew,

Olivetanus was greatly rejoiced to see the energetic Farel. He stood in urgent need of help. Farel appeared to him the right man in the right place. And while Farel immediately began to preach the Gospel, he pledged his life, that he would make true his words.

His appearance roused a perfect storm; the women cried after him and Sonnier: "There go the dogs, the rascals!"

Farel wanted to argue, but the priests found it wiser to fling invectives at their heads, whereupon Farel, with his usual boldness, answered: "I have not disturbed the world, nor this town, but you and yours have disturbed the whole world by your traditions, your inventions, and your dissolute lives."

But for the seven hundred priests, who lived at Geneva, this was too much.

"Into the Rhone with him!" was shouted. He was kicked, trampled on, and would have lost his life had not the authorities interfered. And early the following morning Farel and his companion were conveyed across the lake in a rowboat.

A few days afterward, when the waves of excitement were still high in the town, a strange kind of poster was stuck on the walls.

The passers-by stopped, pointed out to one another the great advertisement, and read the following: "A young man just come to this town will give instruction in the reading and writing of the French language, to all who will, big and little, men and women, even to those who have never been to school. If within a month they cannot read and write he wants no money for his trouble. He is to be found in the Great Boytel Hall, near the Molard, where the Gold Cross hangs out. He also cures many sicknesses for nothing."

The philanthropic teacher of languages, who came with such alluring proposals, was called Antoine Froment. He was a young man of twenty-one, a cowled Gospeller and secret envoy of Farel, who, by stratagem and address, was seeking to win Geneva over to the Gospel.

The new teacher of languages was successful; people praised his ability, his zeal, and while he gave instruction in French he did not delay in giving instruction also in the New Testament. The results were surprising. With the keen insight, peculiar to Farel, he had seen that the fields were ripe for the harvest. Conversions took place; the number of Protestants increased every day, and at the same time, the same confession of faith as Froment's, was heard from the lips of a Franciscan monk.

On New Year's Day, 1533, the rush to hear the remarkable French teacher of languages was so great, that Froment could not reach his own room. There were crowds of people who tried to get to the steps, the passage, and the stairs, and suddenly the cry was raised: "To Molard Square!" Molard Square — the forum of Geneva! There your ears were deafened by the cries of the hucksters, the din of the market and the fair. There stood the booths, and in the immediate neighbourhood of the well-known inn, the *Golden Rose*, where Servet lodged before he was arrested, the farces, in which the people so delighted, were acted.

To enliven the festivals, firelocks and cannons were discharged; and whenever quarrelling and discord prevailed in the town, the pugnacious citizens repaired to this square to settle a bloody reckoning with the opponent. Here the Protestants and Roman Catholics glared at each other, pale with rage and excitement, the women with the claw-hammer under their skirts; and here the prior Werly, who so zealously defended his church, received on May 24, 1533, the fatal sword-thrust that ended his life and the band which bound Geneva to the Romish Freiburg.

It was, however, not yet May, but a cold New Year's Day, and in triumph, Froment was borne along to the square. He was placed on a seat, and these people, thirsting after the righteousness of Christ, cried out: "Preach to us the Word of God!"

Then Froment spoke, and the words of his text were: "Beware of false prophets."

Yet the rage of a fanatical crowd, with armed priests at their head, came like a tidal wave to vent itself against him. He had to flee, and took refuge in the house of an apothecary well disposed to Protestantism, but the man's windows were smashed and Froment left the town at the dead of night.

Yet although Froment had fled, the Gospel remained. Powerful Protestant Bern supported the movement and wrote to the Council of Geneva: "Let truth, your Excellencies, have free course!" No one knew what would be the result; bitterness had reached an unknown height, and the alarm-bell called the citizens to arms (March 28, 1533).

The Roman Catholics took a laurel-spray as their badge; they organized an army, and while fearful cries of murder and destruction rent the air, and the loud ringing of the bells filled the streets, they rushed down the heights of St. Peter's to crush the Protestants, who had occupied Molard Square.

The Protestants numbered 2500 men, without the women, old men, and children. Their cannons stood ready to fire, and any moment the battle might begin.

Yet the burgomasters tried to calm the minds of the Protestants, while the Roman Catholics of Freiburg did the same good work amongst their fellow-believers. The Lord blessed their united efforts; a compromise was effected, and the Reformation went on quietly with its work within the walls of Geneva.

The warlike Farel entered the city again in triumph, with his inseparable companion, the pulpit, which could be taken to pieces and was fastened together with straps.

Froment followed; the Reformed Church was founded, and Viret, who in his back bore the deep scar of a lance-thrust dealt him by a priest, baptised for the first time.

Calvin, Farel, Viret — these were afterward called the trefoil. Two Frenchmen and a Swiss, for Viret was a Swiss. Of these three heroes he was the most distinguished for his meekness; in a period of strife and dissension he showed the most lovable side of the Reformation; by the tenderness of his love he had freed himself from the shackles of his age and he once saved the life of a Jesuit, who was on the point of being hanged. He embraced his enemy; he heaped coals of fire on the heads of his opponents, and that they resisted this fire was a proof of the hardness of their skull, not to say of their heart.

In those days the monks made this rhyme:

> *Farel will fight,*
> *Viret will bite,*
> *And Froment will rave,*
> *But us our God will help:*
> *Let them the devil have!*

A woman of the inn, where the preachers were staying, confirmed the last line by asserting, that through a chink in their bedroom door she had seen how the devils, in the form of black cats, had sprung about under the table and were fed by the heretics.

But not every one seemed to be certain that the devils would soon fetch them, and a poisoner determined to help them. She was a servant in the house where the preachers were staying, and she bought the poison at an apothecary's and sprinkled it in their soup.

Farel did not eat any of it, he had no appetite. Froment was about to begin when he was called away, as his wife and children had just come. Viret ate of the poisonous soup under the eyes of the servant-girl and became very ill, without, however, dying from the effects. And the servant, who had fled to the cellar of a prior, was sentenced to death.

Then the issue approached with rapid strides. Farel, who expected much from debates, had pressed for an argument with the Roman Catholic divines, and in this argument, which lasted four weeks, Farel came off victorious.

To the beating of a drum the people raged and stormed against the worship of images; with deafening shouts Farel was conducted to St. Peter's Church, the principal church in Geneva, to preach the word of God,[11] and the Roman Catholic worship was no longer tolerated publicly at Geneva.

The priests could smite their breasts and say: "We are guilty; we have contributed to the Protestant victory, by our ignorance, our dissolute life, our deep debasement!" And having carried on

---

[11] July 23, 1535.

the contest to their shame, they left the town as cowards, seeking for consolation and help in the tents of the enemies of Geneva.

The contest against the Bishop de la Baume and his ally, the Duke of Savoy, then became a struggle for life or death.

Baudichon was made captain-general of the Geneva forces; he had four hundred Volunteers under his immediate command, and these stood ready day and night to prevent an unexpected attack, while even a small fleet was equipped to support the defence.

Farel stood there in the midst of the anxious multitude like a seer of the Old Testament, and he prophesied victory at the very moment when the bravest citizens expected the capture of their fortress.

For no one could deny that the position was critical; the strength of the enemy was overwhelmingly great, and the cool, enigmatical attitude of friendly Bern awakened uneasiness.

The men who ruled in Bern were first-class diplomatists; they said that charity began at home, and thought of the difficult political circumstances in which Bern itself was placed, while the terrible disaster at Cappel was not yet forgotten.

Yet all at once when there was great danger of Geneva going over to Francis I to escape falling into the snare of Savoy, the Bern bear made his war-cry heard. It sent a chosen body of men, under command of the celebrated General Nägueli, to relieve the distressed town; the flames of the castles set on fire, in which Geneva had been besieged for two years, were the signs to the town that the deliverers were approaching; the strong gates of the castle of Chillon opened when Nägueli hammered against them with his stronger fists, and a little Geneva fleet, which had rendered powerful assistance to the men of Bern, brought Bonivard, who had been prior of the Abbey St. Victor and for six long years in the subterranean vaults of Chillon had sighed for the liberty of Geneva, back to the city in triumph.

The hand which had defeated the Savoy foe was then stretched out to receive a proportionate reward, but Geneva was willing to be the friend but not the vassal of Bern, and the perpetual peace which was made with Bern fully answered the wishes of the Geneva Government.

So after a struggle of thirty years Geneva was placed on the list of the free states. But owing to the disquietude of the times prosperity had sadly retrograded; many houses stood empty; commerce and industry had been seriously affected. Multitudes of strangers streamed through the gates to occupy the empty places, but there was chaff amongst the wheat. Moreover, many Roman Catholic elements had remained behind in the town, while licentiousness had become a deeply rooted national sin.

Yet Farel was not discouraged. With a gigantic task before him, which would have made the stoutest heart shrink back, he boldly faced it; day after day his thin long face was seen in the pulpit, exhorting and comforting, reproving and praising, and announcing to the godless that they were quickly ripening for eternal doom.

He thought out a new code of morality, called the monks shaved robbers, and with almost scrupulous solicitude took care, as all Reformers do, that the minds of the people should be properly developed by education.

Farel lacked fellow labourers. Viret bade him farewell and went to Neuenberg and Lausanne; Froment backed out. But Farel lacked more, and for the first time in his life the undaunted conqueror of Geneva discovered with tearful eyes his lack of organising talent.

Force his way, storm, pull down the old mouldering building with his sinewy hands — that he could do! But to build up, to put brick upon brick, to see with a clear eye, whether the wall was in a line with the plummet — that was more than he could do. For this he lacked the calmness and the tact, the clearness and the depth, the creative power. In the midst of victory he felt himself alone and forsaken with his few colleagues, and while he was in danger of succumbing to the heavy burden, God made use of the French King, to bring Calvin and Farel together.

For the army of Francis I formed an iron barrier, which prevented Calvin from reaching Strasbourg by way of Lorraine; with a disappointed heart he turned to the south, knocked at the door of a Geneva inn and met Farel.

That was the hand of Divine providence; Farel saw it with the eagle's eye of a prophet, but the son of Noyon would not see it, till his resisting heart, hungering for rest and quietness, was crushed as it were by William Farel's voice of thunder.

All opposition was frustrated; Farel, who had triumphed over Geneva, then triumphed over Calvin, and hand in hand they were from that time to found the community of Christ and storm the strongholds of Satan.

"To further the cause of the Reformation in the Vaud," says Doumergue, "Bern had determined to resort to the means that had there met with such good results and been of such great utility to Farel, i.e. the holding of a great public disputation at Lausanne."

There Calvin and Farel went, and there they met Viret. With the loud beating of a drum the disputation was announced at the corners of the streets. It lasted a week. Three hundred and thirty-seven priests were invited to this great duel; four hundred and seventy accepted the invitation, but only four could be found to defend their belief.

On Monday, October 31, 1536, in the morning at seven o'clock, Farel opened the disputation with a discourse to the innumerable multitude which had filled the cathedral. In the middle of the church, places were kept open for the speakers, the four scribes, the two presidents, and the five government commissaries of Bern, who were recognisable by their black doublets, the red stripes in their hose, and the fluttering feather in their broad-brimmed hats.

On Friday, after a Roman Catholic divine had come with a cleverly worked-out argument to refute the theses of Farel and Viret, Calvin came forward with an elaborate speech, in which he quoted the principal church fathers to prove the fallacy of the Roman Catholic assertions. He spoke extemporaneously, quoted from his wonderful memory passages from the church fathers, and inflicted a really crushing defeat on his opponents.

In breathless anxiety the people followed his brilliantly lucid argument, and at the end a Franciscan monk sprang up to do homage to the doctrine expounded by Calvin, as the only true doctrine. He asked forgiveness of God, against whom he had so grievously sinned, of the people whom he had misled, and he cast off the garb of his order to go and live as a Christian.

There was a rich harvest for the Evangelical doctrine. The most inveterate opponents became fellow-workers; others declared themselves won over; in the three following months more than one hundred and twenty priests and vicars and more than eighty monks embraced Protestantism.

Houses of ill-fame were demolished; the immoral women were driven from the town, while from Bern came the order to remove all images and altars from the churches of Lausanne without tumult, and to abolish the Roman Catholic service.

Without seeking it, without even wishing it, Calvin became the generally acknowledged leader. And at the great Swiss synod, which was held in those days at Bern, and where two hundred and ninety-six parishes were represented, this leader appointed by God, already raised his voice to plead for the amalgamation of the different national churches.

In the beginning no great expectations were entertained of Calvin. He was unknown in the town; to this was added his timidity, his weak, pale looks — no, expectations were not great.

But the work which he did in conjunction with his colleague Farel soon showed what a gigantic intellect dwelt in this frail earthly temple.

For the organisation of the Church and Church discipline, a memorial was submitted to the authorities for approval; therein the right of cutting off was assigned to the Church, while the authorities might inquire further into the matter afterward. These articles spoke also of church singing, to put heart into the prayers and awaken zeal.

Besides these articles the Catechism appeared: a short and easy summary of the Christian faith for the young, and a confession of faith which all citizens of Geneva had to swear to. All who refused to take the oath were to be banished — a strange measure, resulting from the unfortunate misconception of the rights of Church and State.

At the appointed hour the Secretary of the town appeared in the chancel of St. Peter's Church to register the oath. Calvin maintained that the people were as ready to take it as the authorities were to impose it. This was true as far as it concerned the inhabitants who had assembled in the church. But many had remained away, and although the majority of the people took the oath, there was still a minority who impatiently looked forward to the day when they would drive Calvin and Farel out of the gates.

In the meantime, however, it was a happy beginning for the Reformers; the churches were regularly attended, and Calvin often looked back afterward with joy to this period of promising blossom.

The attention of Europe was attracted to the light, which began to beam forth from Geneva; thither from England repaired young men in order to meet Calvin and Farel, and had not the Anabaptists come with their strange doctrines, then, in spite of the innumerable cares and the hot strife, this period might have been reckoned the happiest of Calvin's life.

In the spring of 1537 two Dutchmen applied to the Geneva authorities with the request to hold a disputation with the Geneva preachers.

It seems that these foreigners scarcely mentioned adult baptism, from which they derived their name; circumstances induced them to speak rather on behalf of their heretical opinions concerning the corporality of the soul, the freedom of the flesh, and the abolition of all civil and spiritual order. And these anarchists of the sixteenth century found at Geneva, with its easily moved population, thirsting for freedom and licentiousness, a fruitful soil for their heretical and dangerous opinions.

The disputation was held; and again Calvin showed what a master he was in defeating his opponents, but the Anabaptists were not divines, nor the hearers either, and in order to prevent the discussion from confusing men's minds the Council put a stop to it. The Anabaptists were expelled from the town, so that danger from this quarter was averted. But some of their partisans remained behind in the town, and the storm was already gathering that would crush Calvin and Farel.

After the Anabaptists came Caroli. He was Doctor of Divinity, Prior of the Sorbonne and Canon. He belonged to the first priests who had been won over to the Reformation, but he brought his character with him to the Protestant soil, and showed that the laying aside of the Prior's garb is no proof of a real change of heart.

This man now slung an accusation into Calvin's and Farel's face, which for a moment struck Calvin dumb with astonishment.

He was beside himself; his honour as an orthodox teacher, his whole work, everything was at stake. "This Satanic deceiver," thus he wrote to his friend, "has cast a slur upon me which cannot be tolerated."

Caroli had asserted that Calvin denied the doctrine of the Holy Trinity — that was the accusation.

Calvin asked for a synod to settle the question; he therefore went immediately to Lausanne, and did not even mind a journey to Bern.

The synod was held, and never did Calvin contend with such vehemence as he did against this man. In his written defence he called Caroli an impudent liar, an apostate, a scoundrel, who richly deserved hanging, and Viret besought him in vain to moderate these sharp expressions.

But it must be added, that Caroli was, indeed, a man of thoroughly bad character, a dissolute wretch, who on more than one occasion had imposed upon Calvin, and had the blood of two holy martyrs on his conscience.

Then Calvin's passionateness, the fire that burnt in his inmost soul, were manifested, and he literally crushed Caroli under the weight of his proofs.

Calvin and his friends went out free; that they had denied the Holy Trinity had been nothing but a slander, and Farel gave Caroli the *coup de grâce* by unmasking him to the whole assembly.

So then at the highest Church Congress Calvin's honour was vindicated, but it is not easy to hush the voice of slander, and the authorities at Bern continued to be suspicious of the restless French stranger.

The disquietude spread even to Basle, Zurich, and Strasbourg. Bucer wrote to Melanchthon about the matter in such a way that he could not but help thinking that the Church of Geneva had gone over to the Arians, and the names of Servet and Calvin were coupled together. For the Reformer it was like a blow in his face, and by the inexorableness with which he afterward acted toward Servet, he wished expressly to show that he had never had anything to do with this heretical Spaniard.

There were other disquieting phenomena. The cunning Bonivard, who had a sharp nose for finding out which way the wind lay, joined the enemies of Calvin and Farel.

The great Council came to an end,[12] so that their opponents got into office, and although these men had not forgotten the heroic courage which Farel had displayed during the heavy siege, yet he and Calvin were urged to be moderate above all things. It was reported that the two reformers wished to found a new Popedom at Geneva; against Calvin's front door blows were dealt with the butt-end of muskets; in the evening crowds of people jeered before his windows, crying out: "Into the Rhone with the traitors!"

But they stood like rocks in the midst of the surge.

Blind Courault was taken into custody, and his colleagues went to the Council to protest against this violation of liberty.

It was in vain. They were forbidden to mount the pulpit on the following Easter Sunday, but they did so nevertheless, surrounded by their friends and their enemies, while knives were drawn.

The storm-clouds kept gathering more and more ominously over the heads of the two Reformers; among the Council of the *Two Hundred*, the question arose, what one had to do with those two disturbers of the peace, and with a great majority of voices it was decided to banish Calvin and Farel from the town within three days.

Then Calvin gave the following famous answer: "Let it be so! If we had served men, then we should have been badly rewarded, but we serve a great Master, who will reward us!"

So they went, leaving a place which, situated on the frontiers of the French and German world, seemed fore-ordained for a far-embracing, international field of reformation labour. One would have said that Calvin and Geneva were fitted the one for the other; it had appeared that this little corner of land on Lake Leman was to become the fruitful field for the development of Calvin's far-reaching reformation thoughts.

But had not that been a chimera? Did not Geneva drive her reformer away from the land like a leper?

"Come!" said Farel in a resolute tone, "it is well! Let us go in God's name!"

So they went, leaving a great work behind them. But their hearts were strengthened in God.

---

[12] February 3, 1538.

Chapter XV

IN THE SHADOW OF STRASBOURG CATHEDRAL

FAREL went to Neuchâtel, Calvin to Basle, where the plague had entered.

A nephew of Farel was smitten by it. Calvin nursed the man and another. And yet it was afterward said that Calvin fled away on account of the plague.

When Farel's nephew died Calvin paid the doctor's bill and the burial expenses. Yet it was afterward asserted that Calvin held his purse-strings tight.

In Strasbourg, however, they knew him better; he received urgent invitations to serve the Church there; and as he had remained at Geneva against his will, so he then went against his will, but with the blind obedience of a brave soldier, to Strasbourg, and said to Bucer: "Here I am."

Bucer, the reformer of Strasbourg, was a strange phenomenon.

He was short of stature like Zacchaeus, but of powerful intellect, with a great head on a muscular neck. Bucer was organiser, orator, exegete, divine, the model of a father, and a staunch advocate for the marriage of priests.

He usually had a bitterly small income: half of what a day labourer now earns. Yet his hospitality was proverbial; no poor man was sent away by him, while his uprightness was above all suspicion.

He dared without scruple tell his friends the truth. At a glance he saw the weak side of the Geneva fugitive.

"You are an irritable man," he said to Calvin, and Calvin accepted the remark with the meekness of a Christian.

There were other excellent men in Strasbourg, with whom Calvin was to become acquainted.

There was Capito, the man of the clerical aristocracy; Jacob Sturm, a son of the Patricians, the friend of the Landgrave of Hesse, and the best statesman whom Strasbourg ever had; John Sturm, the printer, who gave a model school to Strasbourg: a man distinguished for piety and knowledge; the preacher Zell, as amiable in character as he was indomitable in courage.

With these excellent men Calvin came into contact, and had daily communication, after the storm of adversity had driven him from Geneva.

As soon as he arrived at Strasbourg, he went to Capito; he lodged with Bucer; he held conferences at the house of Zell; John Sturm and Jacob Sturm saw him frequently at their houses.

So Calvin settled at Strasbourg. And in order to get the right of citizenship, he had himself enrolled on the guild of tailors.

Three long years Calvin stayed at Strasbourg. It was the practical school where he was formed to become subsequently crowned the King of French Protestantism. There was no more excellent training school to be found for Calvin; the Swiss called Strasbourg the Antioch of the Reformation; it was a second Wittenberg on the frontiers of France, a watch-tower, from the pinnacles of which the course could be seen of the strife that was disturbing men's minds and making the earth tremble.

Here in the old German Hanse-town Calvin could find out the faults which he had committed at Geneva, and exercise the tact to avoid them in the future; his sphere extended far beyond the borders of the surrounding lands; his knowledge had deepened, and he was made proficient to become the celebrated law-giver of Protestant Sparta.

Blind Courault, who had been banished with Calvin and Farel, had in the meantime reached the end of his hard life, and his blind eyes then saw Christ, whom he had so faithfully served.

With Du Tilly things had turned out quite differently. He had gone back to Rome, to which he had once turned his back, and he wrote long letters to Calvin, to persuade him to do the same.

He belonged to the class of the three friends of Job, who were poor comforters, and he asked the Reformer whether, in the adversities and misfortunes which he had experienced, the chastising and wrathful hand of the Lord was not to be seen. His old friendship for Calvin was not yet dead, but it wanted to drive him to a corner, where an abyss yawned before his feet, and to the money which

Du Tilly offered to Calvin in his financial difficulties, a condition was attached which the latter would not have accepted, even if he had had to die of hunger.

In Geneva Calvin had been pastor and political leader. In Strasbourg his work was confined to the office of shepherd and teacher. He preached four times a week, and proclaimed the Gospel outside his French Church, to the Anabaptists, with success and blessing.

He made serious efforts to maintain discipline, substituted clerical inquiry for confession, and showed himself in stormy weather the resolute helmsman who held the rudder firmly to guard Christ's little ship against shipwreck.

He was animated by an all-prevailing desire to promote and confirm the peace of the churches. He gladly overlooked minor points of difference, in order to preserve unity, and his soul longed for brotherly love and harmony.

The work of the Reformer grew heavier; he was overwhelmed with labour. To his four sermons a week were added three lectures, for which, as professor (after May 1, 1539), he enjoyed a salary of fifty-two guilders a year; he had to fight many a battle with the heretics, who, from all parts, poured into the hospitable Strasbourg, and in lengthy dissertations he gave his decided opinion about marriage.

This was indeed necessary, for eleven years before no one less than Luther had in his sermons on the book of Genesis, asked the question: "Must a man have more than one wife?" and given the answer: "It is not forbidden; I could not now forbid it, but I will not recommend it." The opinion of Melanchthon and other reformers was to the same effect, but Calvin thought differently. And his deeper insight into the Scriptures induced him, on the authority of those Scriptures, to condemn all polygamy as sin.

Now it is very probable that Bucer, who was such an enthusiastic lover of home, said more than once: "Calvin, why don't you look out for a wife yourself?"

And in sooth, marriage plans began to hit through the learned brain of the Reformer. He wrote about it to his bosom friend Farel, and enumerated the virtues which he expected in his future wife.

These were no small matter. He mentioned modesty, willingness to help, simplicity, economy, meekness; beauty of face was a matter of minor importance, but, on the other hand, he hoped that she would look well after his health.

A few months afterward he could have made a brilliant marriage with a rich young lady of title. But there were two things which made Calvin look serious; the young lady seemed to be proud of her position, and was unacquainted with the French language.

Calvin wished expressly that she should learn the French language, while with his habitual hastiness he already asked Farel to marry him.

But after all nothing came of it; the little ship suffered shipwreck before it reached the harbour, and instead of an invitation to get ready for the journey, Farel, to his great astonishment, received a letter from Calvin containing the following communication: "I shall not enter into this marriage, or God must deprive me of my reason!" In the meantime he was in the greatest pecuniary difficulties, and in order to secure himself against pinching want, he was obliged to take boarders. But these pupils were, as a rule, as poor as himself, and in these straitened circumstances Calvin learned the struggle for life.

Yet he did not give up his marriage plans, and in Idelette von Bure he found the woman, who was ready to marry him for better or for worse.

Idelette was a widow with two children; fortune she did not possess, but gentleness, piety, and captivating amiability formed the dowry which she brought with her.

For Calvin it was enough, and seven long years they lived happily together.[13]

Idelette's beautiful face made one think of Calvin's mother; she was still young and dark-eyed. The happiness was great for the poor wanderer, who had never known what it was to possess a roof of his own; it was indeed too great, and God quickly tempered their joy, as Calvin expressed it, lest they should overstep the bounds. He fell ill; Idelette fell ill too, and the Lord showed the two young people how frail all earthly happiness is.

---

[13] They were married in the beginning of August, 1540.

Idelette was the model of a Christian wife; the lovable side of the Reformer; the soothing hand, which healed the wounds inflicted by his sharp reforming sword.

She visited the poor, watched by the bedside of the sick, threw her doors wide open to strangers, and accompanied her husband in the few walks which he took. She comforted him when he was altogether disheartened; she rejoiced like a child when a cheerful smile lit up the serious face of the Reformer, and lay on her knees in the sitting-room when the sound of tumult was heard in the streets and cries of murder were raised against the Protestant preachers.

Idelette has been described as a shy, submissive wife, but she proved that she was a resolute, energetic woman, who inspired even the dying with courage. The marriage was blessed with a child. It was a son. But it was a premature confinement, and in the perplexity of his fear Calvin wrote to Viret: "God have pity on us!"[14]

The mother got well again, but the child died when it was about a fortnight old. And then it was not fear, but deep sadness which caused Calvin to write: "God has indeed dealt us a heavy blow by the death of our son, but He is our Father and knows what is good for His children."

Calvin never had any more children. And a Jesuit was only too ready to cry out: "Do you see! That is the curse which rests upon Calvin; such a scandalous man was not allowed to have children." But Calvin answered, that in Christendom he could count his spiritual children by tens of thousands . . .

The visible form of this Christendom was the Church. And it is really interesting to see how Calvin arranged the services in this Church at Strasbourg.

On Sunday mornings the Confession of sins followed the Exhortation, as is the custom in French churches at the present day. After this, the minister spoke a few words of Scripture to comfort the conscience, and then the congregation began to sing the first five commandments. A short prayer from the minister followed, and then the congregation sang the other five commandments. Then came the sermon, a long prayer, a Psalm — chanted by the congregation, and the Benediction.

Calvin adapted himself at Strasbourg, as he did in Geneva, to the forms of worship that were customary there. In Geneva the Lord's Supper was celebrated three times a year, on festivals, and although Calvin was an advocate for monthly celebration, he nevertheless gave way, when he saw that it was impossible to bring the congregation over to his way of thinking.

Calvin believed that there was a place for absolution although he gave it another name. After the public confession of sins, he considered it desirable to pronounce a solemn promise of forgiveness of sin, in order to comfort the depressed in heart. And

---

[14] July 28, 1542.

that he did not do so arose simply from the desire not to hurt the weak. Calvin, moreover, felt strongly the desirability of administering the Lord's Supper to the sick, but in Geneva this was not the custom, and as it would have been regarded as a strange innovation, he left things as they were.

He attached much importance to kneeling in prayer; on his knees he had gained his victories, and his heart expanded when the singing of the Psalms pealed through the arched roofs of the church.

The Reformation brought congregational singing, and Calvin loved the Psalms. At first he had sought for other songs, but had not found them, and the Psalms with their sorrowful heart-cries and their unshaken confidence in God were indeed wonderfully adapted for the militant and suffering Church of the sixteenth century.

Luther wanted to retain the Latin in the Church, but Calvin, whose desire was to reach the whole nation, shook his head and said: "In the Church the common language of the people, and nothing else!" He needed thus translated Psalms, and the poet Marot, whom we met at Nérac and at the Court of Queen Margaret, afterward supplied these needs.

With the Psalms, the Church of Calvin grew up. The martyrs sang them at the stake; they have resounded in prisons and on the battle-fields; the body-guard of Condé sang them.

They have gone far over the frontier of France. The Beggars of the Netherlands sang them; the Roundheads of Cromwell sang them; they have re-echoed in the great forests of Poland. They have gone beyond the frontiers of Europe; they have been heard in the hinterlanden of Africa; they have sounded above the roar of the ocean, and this mighty choir was led by Calvin, the father of Psalmody.

Chapter XVI

A FRENCH VOICE
AT A GERMAN SYNOD

THE French Emigrant Church at Strasbourg, at the head of which stood Calvin, grew rapidly. It flourished and became a model for the other parishes, and from a distance of five or six miles the converted Anabaptists brought their children to be baptised.

Nevertheless cares continued to harass the Reformer, and side by side with spiritual needs, poverty began menacingly to raise her head. His books did not bring in anything like what he had expected; his publishers complained bitterly about the slow sale, and he had to borrow money to pay his rent. In the midst of the most profound studies, fearful cares oppressed him; they gave him no sleep, no rest. And while his brain was busy with world-reforming plans, he thought of the crown which, when he was better off, he had lent to the Vaudois brothers and then needed so badly.

But, on the other hand, it was a gloriously luminous point, that there at Strasbourg he was freer and more independent than he had been at Geneva, where he constantly came into conflict with the worldly power, while a rich spiritual blessing was a kingly recompense for his pinching poverty.

At Strasbourg Calvin came into contact with the great German world; one day Idelette had to pack his boxes, and he set out with his friend Bucer to the Diet of Frankfort, there, where the heart of the German people beat, to make serious studies of the German Empire, to meet the celebrated Melanchthon, and to beg the protection of the German princes for his persecuted co-religionists in France.

German Protestantism was then at the zenith of its power. In the north and south populous provinces had renounced the Roman Catholic faith; in vain had the Emperor's statesmen tried to oppose triumphant Protestantism; and the sharp eyes of Calvin, whose eagle glance nothing escaped, had noticed the confusion and dejection in the camp of the Roman Catholics.

Then the die had to be cast which was to decide the lot of Germany and Christian Europe. Like a general, Calvin watched the allied forces drawn up in battle array; he sifted the reliable from the wavering states and made calculations as to the future attitude of the electors. In his long letters to Farel he explained, with great acuteness, how the foreign complications of the Emperor Charles V would further the efforts of their Protestant co-religionists; he thought long and deeply over the strife in the Dutch province of Gelderland; after the sudden death of the Prince of Saxony he cherished the hope of bringing the whole dukedom over to Protestantism.

Although in his heart convinced of the power of the Gospel, he maintained that God works indirectly, and while his French blood distrusted Charles V, he advocated an alliance between Francis I and the Protestant princes of Germany. In spite of his democratic nature his eye was fixed on the kings, who ruled the world, and the political mind of Francis I rejoiced that the flames of his fires had never reached this formidable heretic.

Frankfort, Worms, and Regensburg saw Calvin; with restless zeal he worked to win all Germany over to the Gospel; and he wrote about Germany in language such as the German nation had seldom heard since the death of Ulrich Hutten. Melanchthon leaned on the giant of Noyon, but Calvin felt the cares of the strong man, who had to be responsible for everything. He saw a sad delay in the triumphant course of the Gospel; he was surprised at the compromises of the Wittenberg Reformer and angry with Bucer, who when at Worms wanted to mediate to a dangerous extent, although he was convinced of the good faith of both.

Wherever Calvin spoke he excited the surprise of the learned by the depth of his knowledge. But he cared not one iota about personal fame; and when the landgrave, Philip of Hesse, invited him to dinner and showed him every honour, he bitterly vexed the stern Puritan by his second marriage.

Calvin was indeed shocked at the terrible lack of Church discipline in Germany; in his eyes the German clergy lacked the independence, which as soldiers of Christ they should have had; in the Lutheran doctrine he saw remains of Judaism, while the lukewarmness of the German Protestant princes grieved him greatly.

This lack of congenialness of spirit was mutual. People called him the noisy, fanatical Frenchman, and his great reputation for learning was evenly balanced by the aversion which was entertained for the iron consequences of this stranger. Greatly depressed, he returned home, although his confidence in the ultimate triumphs of the Gospel remained unshaken, and he reached Strasbourg at the very moment that the prophecy pronounced by him respecting Geneva was on the eve of being fulfilled.

Calvin had prophesied a short triumph of his enemies at Geneva. The catastrophe of 1538 was a triumph. The Lord's Supper was to be celebrated with unleavened bread, as Bern, against Calvin's protest, had persisted in celebrating it, and the new preachers who had sold the right of the first-born had become the pliant, submissive servants of the authorities. But this revolution had brought the religious liberty of the Reformed churches and the political liberty of the town into danger; the Roman Catholics lifted up their heads; the Mass was again spoken of, and the former Bishop of Geneva, the unfortunate De la Beaume, wished to make an effort to win back lost ground.

A meeting was held at Lyons which was called a conference, but which in reality was a conspiracy against the independence of Geneva. And the sharp-witted Cardinal Sadolet was instructed to write to the citizens of Geneva.

The letter was received and handed over to the Council. It was in order. The Council acknowledged in friendly terms the receipt of the letter, and would answer it in due course.

The hearts of the Roman Catholics beat faster when they learnt that a learned priest had written a Romish defence against Protestant doings, and two days after Sadolet's letter was received, several citizens dared to appear before the Council with the request that the oath which was required of confession of faith might be withdrawn. But after this Roman Catholic assertion of strength, followed the Protestant reaction. Sadolet had to be answered; the Geneva clergy had neither talent nor mind for such an undertaking. The Bern bear[15] was heavy and slow — what else was to be done than request the exile of Strasbourg to reply?

---

[15] The Bernese have a bear on their arms.

In six days Calvin was ready with his polemic. It was an iron hammer with which the argument of Sadolet was smashed; and many of Calvin's former opponents exclaimed: "Blind that we were — how could we be parties to the banishing of this excellent teacher!"

Broils in the town strengthened the desire for Calvin's return; Johannes Philippe, one of the foremost citizens of the town, was, for high treason, led to the scaffold; France and Bern both threatened the independence of Geneva, while within the walls anarchy raised her head, and the different parties stood ready to tear each other to pieces.

There was no longer any choice; the staunchest patriots turned their eyes to Strasbourg, and cried out imploringly: "Come over and help us!"

Chapter XVII

ON THE TOP OF THE MOUNTAIN

CALVIN would not go.

Again and again he thus poured out his heart to Farel: "When I remember how unhappy I was there at Geneva, my whole body trembles and revolts whenever there is a talk about my being called back."

Like a martyr he had held out at Geneva till the people drove him away. And delighted that the heavy yoke was lifted from his shoulders, the Reformer shrank from venturing again into that warring abyss.

Like mountains the difficulties rose up before him; *he was wondrously perplexed*, as he expressed it; he feared the influence of Bern, while, on the other hand, he understood perfectly well that without the moral support of the Bernese, it would be difficult for him to maintain his ground in the unsettled city of Geneva.

Nevertheless his sincere love for the Church of Geneva was not yet dead, and the more his eye saw of the endless difficulties which awaited him at Lake Leman, the more he hesitated to make a decision himself. He did not trust his own judgment and called in the advice of his coadjutors, while he, choosing a middle course, expressed himself ready to reorganise the Church at Geneva without remaining there for good.

Then the impetuous Farel appeared before the footlights. Once by his passionate language he had seen Calvin defenceless at his feet, and that was to happen again.

For eighteen long months Calvin held out, afraid to come to a decision. Farel heaped the bitterest reproaches on his head. He asked him whether he wished to wait till the stones of Geneva called him; he reproached him for the haste with which he had left the city, and his tardiness in returning to that city.

Under these violent attacks, Calvin, with a self-denial which is the more striking in one of his irritable and passionate nature, offered up his heart. In extreme anguish of soul, he made the device chosen by him, a heart offering itself to the Lord, a reality; and he did not consult with flesh and blood when he turned his steps to the city which had expelled him from her gates.

Calvin was disarmed; he capitulated; and Farel led his captive to Geneva.

In the beginning of September, 1541, Calvin set out from Strasbourg. His way led partly through the same districts which he had once travelled as a pitiful refugee. Now it was a triumphal journey.

Amidst the cheering of the population he returned in joyful triumph; he excused himself to the multitude for his delay in coming, but they were too glad to make any complaint. They had got him back again — that was the happy event of the day! And they would keep him till death should part them. . . Where were Calvin's enemies? The four burgomasters who had worked together so zealously to banish him?

Two of them had fled because they had tried to create an uproar, and their death sentence lay already signed; the third escaped from the walls through a window, but was so much injured by his fall that he soon expired, while the fourth was led to the scaffold and beheaded by the executioner of Geneva.

That was the fate of the four magistrates, who, in the days of their prosperity, had poured out upon Calvin the vials of their mockery and scorn. And then Calvin's friends remembered the prophetic words which he had written on parting: "Let us humble ourselves and not resist when God humbles us. In the meanwhile we will wait for His time, for quickly shall fade away the crown of pride of the drunkards of Ephraim!"

"What a turn through God's appointing!" exclaimed the Prussian King Wilhelm I in 1870 on the battlefield of Sedan reeking with blood. Those same words Calvin might have uttered more than three centuries earlier.

Driven away with scorn, he now returned with the greatest honour to the place, which Farel, in the name of the King of Kings, had indicated to him; and the same people who had once cried "Crucify him!" now shouted Hosanna.

The Council had provided for the bringing over of his family. The town-herald, who had spent twenty-three days in fetching

Calvin from Strasbourg, received fifty guilders for his trouble; for Mrs. Calvin's journey, seven guilders and fourpence were disbursed, which was far too little, while for the furnishing of the house assigned to Calvin, a hundred and twenty guilders and two pence were paid.

The love and esteem for Calvin's person assumed a naive, almost childish character. One of the councillors had discovered, not without commiseration, that his gown was shabby, and immediately orders were given to a tailor to make him a new one. The minutes of the Council record the gown — eight gold crowns

were paid for it. Moreover, St. Peter's Church, at the request of Calvin, was provided with new seats, while against one of the pillars a brand new pulpit was placed.

The question of salary gave the Council much trouble, and at last it was fixed at five hundred guilders, two measures of corn, and two casks of wine.

There was much discussion about those five hundred guilders! Some said it was too little; others declared that Calvin could put by a nice little sum every year.

In reality Calvin got as much as a burgomaster, and twice as much as any other clergyman. But those functionaries were men who could put their arms up to the elbow in gold ducats, whereas the clergy were often in want.

Indeed Calvin had a modest income, but, considering what she had before, Idelette was suddenly enabled to live in comparative luxury; but that they did not do so reflects credit both on Calvin and his wife. For anxious in the poverty which had so bitterly harassed them, they were not less with the five hundred guilders which were paid to them every year. Their hospitality soon far surpassed the liberality of the town, and Calvin — a great honour indeed! — left no treasures.

How wonderful are the ways of God!

It was true that Calvin and Farel, when they left Geneva, had asked to be restored to their honour both in Bern and in Switzerland without being able to obtain a hearing. Their humiliation had been complete; their truest friends had deserted them; and not till the inflicted wounds began to heal, till German hospitality had welcomed him to Strasbourg, and he had experienced the pleasure of regular and undisturbed labour, did Geneva call him back.

But then his longing for Geneva was gone; he had seen the abyss which there yawned, and it was his fervent hope that the wish he once had to return to Geneva, might never be fulfilled.

Then, however, it was just the time for him, who by a amazing concurrence of circumstances had smoothed the paths for his return.

In these events Calvin felt and recognized the hand of his God, of his Father, and this timid, modest man, this child of Noyon, was appointed His instrument for realising in this little corner of the earth the programme laid down in the *Christian Institutes*, and to found there a community which should shine and glisten like a city on a mountain in the glow of the morning sun.

With the terrible earnestness of a prophet, Calvin appeared in Geneva, and the solemn pealing of the great bell of St. Peter's summoned the penitent children of the city to listen to the preacher.

The great church was filled to overflowing; there was a special celebration of the Lord's Supper; and one day a week was set apart for penitence and prayer.

Calvin worked with the strength of a Hercules. The first weeks of his new labour in Geneva belong to the most labourious of his labourious life.

The zeal with which the congregation of Geneva clung to the shepherd of their souls, has seldom been equalled in Protestant Churches. Not the little Council of twenty-five, not the great Council of two hundred, nor the General Council of voters ruled Geneva in those days. Calvin ruled; his will was law; he was the uncrowned king of the Republic. And the words that he had once spoken in the unshaken confidence of faith had been fulfilled: "Marching under the banner of Christ, we can return from the battle only as conquerors."

Calvin had learned much in those three years of his banishment. He had learned the prudence which characterised Joseph at the Court of Pharaoh, and he subdued the passion which may rightly be called his chief characteristic sin. He kept a sharp eye on the zealots of his own party, and showed a spirit of reconciliation that surprised them. They had fully expected that he would at least in his first sermon sharply attack his former opponents, but with a tact that commands our admiration he made not the slightest allusion to them. He had not come as the vengeful head of a party, for he had read in his Bible that vengeance belongs to the Lord, but as a true shepherd of souls, whose sacred avocation it was, to lead all sheep to the true sheepfold, that is Christ.

He had to speak but a single word to deprive the former teachers of their appointments, but with wise moderation he refrained from uttering that word, and this attitude must have made a great and deep impression on the majority of the people.

Meanwhile the times were serious. In the East glistened the crooked sword of the Turks, and the plague, that terrible scourge of the Middle Ages, rode on her pale horse into the towns of Western Europe.

With deep sadness, Calvin heard that that excellent man, Capito, had succumbed at Strasbourg to the complaint, and that

Bucer had seen his wife and six children laid in their graves before he was himself attacked by the fell disease.

Geneva was not spared; the angel of death stretched his hand over the city, and the death-bell was heard and the black biers seen in all the streets. Fear lay on every face; many fled; commerce and industry were at a standstill, and the courts of justice were closed.

The Council adopted stringent measures. All foreigners had to leave the city within three days on pain of the rack; nobody, who had the plague, was to go through the town before ten o'clock in the evening and after three in the morning without a flag-bearer; the militia festival was postponed; cats and dogs which might transmit the germs of the plague were killed, and the plague-stricken who were not looked after in the hospital received a hint to choose as their dwelling-place the huts in the direction of Champel Hill outside the town.

The clergyman, Peter Blanchet, offered to act as spiritual consoler to the sufferers in the hospital. He went as he had done the year before. But this time the doors of the hospital were only to open to let the dead body of the hero pass through, and the Council found themselves in the difficult position, whom to choose in his stead.

Many of the clergy showed their reluctance; the report was spread that one of them had used the expression, "better sit with the devil than in the hospital."

Calvin and his colleagues appeared before the Council, and the Council decided that Calvin, on account of the Church services, could not be missed. Therefore from among the other preachers a choice had to be made, but they had serious objections, for they thought of their wife and children, and candidly confessed that they had not the courage to risk their life in that terrible pest-house. Only one clergyman offered to undertake the deadly office, if the lot should fall upon him, and the Council accepted his proposal for the time.

The Council had weighty reasons for sparing Calvin. The Government does not place the general who has to direct the battle at the head of the attacking force. But the question may be asked, what the Reformer would have done had the lot fallen upon him.

The question had already been answered by Calvin by his attitude at Strasbourg, when, of his own accord, he had nursed two men suffering from the plague, and, moreover, by his remarkable letter to Viret,[16] in which the following lines occur: "The plague is already beginning to rage here more violently. Few of those affected by it recover. One of us has to be appointed to help the sick. When Peter Blanchet offered himself, we willingly let him go. If anything happens to him, I fear, after him, to have to incur the same danger. For we belong to all the members of the flock, and cannot hold back from those who, more than others, need our help."

This is Calvin as he lived and always was! No bragging, no vain boasting — he willingly let Blanchet go, because he saw the dark cloud of death above the terrible hospital.

But though his flesh shrank back and his soul trembled with fear, yet he would go if duty called him; under the law of that iron discipline which becomes a soldier of Jesus Christ. And he would have shut himself up in the hospital with the plague-sick, to die with them. . . In all this he had but one object in view. Luther had said: "War with Rome to the death!" Calvin's watchword was: "Order and discipline!"

And he girded himself in order to resume the great reformation work, that had once suffered shipwreck.

---

[16] October 1, 1542.

Chapter XVIII

THE GENERAL IN THE MIDST OF HIS HEROES

ORDER and discipline!

No, to these something else was added. Calvin's watchword was: "Liberty, order, and discipline!"

"Pretty liberty!" cried a woman from the populace; "once we were compelled to go to Mass; now we are dragged to hear the sermon!" But that woman did not understand Calvin's object. He meant the liberty to serve God according to the Gospel.

The people had to go to church — that is true. But the laws made by Calvin, and which at the present day seem to us like the despairing act of a tottering and decaying Church, God made use of to make the dew of the Holy Spirit descend on the hard Geneva furrows. Citizens who cared little about religion and went grumbling to church, were to become the pillars of the Church, which they had once despised, and the vigorous and muscular physiognomies began already to depict a future, when Geneva would be called the Pella, of sorely tried French Protestantism.

The ideal of a Christian Republic one began to think possible, and even before the authorities approved of the ordinances submitted by Calvin, he, like a second Savonarola, requested the Council to inscribe the monogram of Christ, the letters I H S, on the public buildings, the coins, and the flag of Geneva.

Not the cross of the Roman Catholic Church that had supplanted the true cross, but Christ, the Redeemer of souls and of nations, it should be.

The Council acceded to that wish, and the monogram of Christ should from now on be imprinted on the forehead of Protestant Rome.

Calvin went on the premise, that God is the Ruler of all, and that every other government can only exist by reason of His authority. His standpoint was, that all kinds of government can be good, although for Geneva he considered the republican form the most desirable; and on those foundations, laid by him, arose in the Netherlands and England, in Scotland and North America, the temple of liberty.

In the beginning, says the historian P. Henry, there were five pastors and three assistants, whose regular duty it was, among others, to hold public Bible readings every Friday. They also had to visit the sick and superintend the education of the young. Moreover, they formed, together with twelve elders, two of whom belonged to the Little Council, four to the Council of Sixty, and six

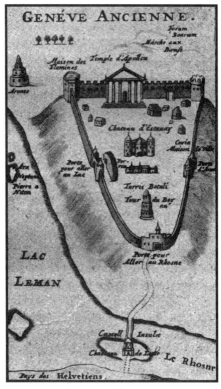

Ancient Geneva

to the Council of the Two Hundred, the Church Council, which met every Thursday, and whose chief occupation was to look after the conduct of the citizens. They had the right to call to account all who had transgressed the existing laws of order and discipline. This moral court of justice had an officer at its disposal to summon the offenders and bring them before it. For a first offence there was a serious admonition, for repeated offences a refusal of the Lord's Supper. If, however, the crime committed were of such a nature, that according to the laws of the State a fine or bodily punishment had to be imposed, then notice of this was given to the Government to take the necessary proceedings.

These laws breathe the spirit of the sixteenth century; the Church and State were firmly and closely interwoven; the idea was, that the Church embraced all citizens.

A stern spirit had got the upper hand of the merry, licentious life of Geneva. Gambling and wine-houses disappeared; dancing was forbidden; adultery, first punished with six days' imprisonment and a fine, was subsequently, at the express desire of the general assembly of the people, punished with death.

Only at five places, set apart for the purpose, might men amuse themselves with bowls; the wearing of showy dress was not tolerated; moderation in eating and drinking was prescribed, while the elders of this Protestant Sparta went from house to house once a year to convince themselves that the laws and ordinances were carried out.

The preachers themselves went out to induce the citizens to go to church; Calvin more than once made such an excursion on Sunday. But staunch advocate as Calvin was for forcing the people to hear, he was altogether averse to long preaching.

He could not stand it; it worried him, that Farel kept the people so long in church, and he considered it more effective to edify them by short sermons than to weary them with long ones.

It was in those days that Geneva lost one of her most excellent citizens by the death of Ami Porral, who, in 1532, converted to Protestantism, contributed incalculably much to the triumph of that religion within the walls of his native city.

In the great peril of 1536, when Geneva, threatened by Savoy, the Bishop, and France, was on the verge of the precipice, he did more than anyone else to secure the help of Bern. No one in the little Republic had seen better than he, how the independence of Geneva was strengthened by the Reformation, and he was in truth Calvin's right hand.

The death of this patriot was beautiful and affecting. Calvin stood by his bed and spoke of the only consolation in life and death.

"I am as sure of that truth," replied Porral, "as though it were brought me by an angel."

While the golden gates of the heavenly Jerusalem were opening to receive him he would no longer hear of enemies. He sent for them to his death-bed to make friends of them, and his lips whispered words of peace, love, and reconciliation.

At two o'clock in the afternoon Idelette appeared. He still recognized her kindly face. She spoke words of comfort, as a sister to a brother.

Then he cried in the words of Simeon: "Lord, now lettest Thou Thy servant depart in peace, according to Thy word: for mine eyes have seen Thy salvation."

"And shortly afterward," says Calvin, "he gave his pious soul into the hands of the Lord."[17]

A new chronicler was wanted for the town and the choice fell upon Bonivard, the Erasmus of the Geneva Reformation, who was then fifty-one years old.[18]

He accepted the appointment, and two years afterward married.

Calvin thought the marriage very comical. Bonivard was a widower and had fixed his choice upon a widow, who had two husbands in the grave already. Calvin wrote to Viret about it and told him that he had laughed immensely.

But the new couple did not laugh. They soon got to high words; Bonivard found out that his spouse was nothing like his first wife, and she in her turn bitterly bewailed being married to such a man. On a certain day she went off, and as she would not return, she was put in prison on bread and water, to teach her the duties of a wife.

The woman died and Bonivard married for the third time — a widow. It was quite an undertaking for the woman, for Bonivard was not a man of order; he knew nothing about economy, and his debts would have ruined him, if the Government had not come to his assistance again and again.

---

[17] June, 1542.
[18] The end of 1542.

When his third wife died, Bonivard, in his seventieth year, married for the fourth time; against his wish, but at the urgent request of the Church Council, as he had made promises of marriage. And the end was that the chronicler of Geneva was cut off as member of the Church.

So the people cried Hosanna to the Reformer, but there is only one step between adoration and revilement, and Calvin had already experienced how quickly the mind of the people can change.

There was something else: Luther could rely upon the vigorous support of powerful patrons; the noble elector of Saxony and the pushing Landgrave of Hesse would have drawn the sword for him, if necessary. With Calvin it was different; he had to depend on the favour of the people, which shifts like the sand on the seashore, while in secret a small but obstinate party schemed and drudged to throw him out of the saddle.

Moreover, what was Geneva, even though it offered him help? It lay on the junction of three roads, where three powerful Roman Catholic states met; it was a town of scarcely sixteen thousand inhabitants, with weak ramparts and weak walls, badly protected against a hostile attack. Calvin had to seek help from a higher source, from above, and from above he sought it. And his fervent prayer and the strong faith of his flock formed the firm, invisible wall against which all the force of the enemy would break powerless.

The glory that emanated from little Geneva shone forth as far as Poland. Geneva became the great central point, where the mightiest intellects met.

John Knox was there; Marnix of St. Aldegonde, the author of the immortal *Wilhelmus song*;[19] Cranmer, the reformer of England — three names which imply three revolutions.

Under the genial direction of Calvin, Geneva became the university, where the heroes and martyrs of Protestantism were educated. Here was their cradle; the Calvinistic view of life with its unshaken doctrine of predestination instilled steel into their blood. From this little insignificant spot of the world they went forth into the high road of life. No river, no sea, no mountain could

---

[19] The *Wilhelmus* is not only the Dutch National Anthem (about the life of William of Orange) but also a Reformed confession. It is published both in English and in Dutch in the back of W.G. Van de Hulst, *William of Orange, the Silent Prince*, Neerlandia, AB (Inheritance Publications) 1992. Fourth printing 2006.

stop them; they possessed the blind obedience of the Jesuit, without the gloomy heretical hatred which animated them. They ventured into England, where, under the rule of Henry VIII, no man's life was safe; into Spain, France, and Italy, where the scaffold awaited them. They were bound to the strangling pole, and there to die; the flames of the funeral pyre beat into their faces; they were cast into dungeons, where the light of the sun and the moon never shone.

John Knox

They were a chosen band destined by their blood to win nations to the Gospel. And this chosen band, although it died every day, was immortal, for the gaps in the ranks were filled up again and again by new heroes and martyrs, who, with sustained enthusiasm, fought and died for Christ.

Calvin was their teacher, their leader, their anointed king. He gave them his blessing when they went forth to battle, and without a muscle of his face moving, he heard of their sufferings and death. Only occasionally did he lose the iron self-control which becomes a general; then grief, dejection, sadness came upon him with the force of a mountain torrent, and in the bitterness of his soul he cried out: "They are led as sheep to the slaughter!"

So, many heroes and martyrs went forth from the city, but many exiles returned, who, on account of their belief, had fled from the land of their forefathers.

Amongst them were gray-headed old men, weak women, little children. Amid the biting cold of winter they wandered along the precipices of the high mountains, badly clad, benumbed, losing their way in the confusion of the snow-covered footpaths, perishing from hunger and cold.

Now and then they looked back, distracted by the fear that they heard the cry of their persecutors, and then they stumbled on, the poor oppressed flock of Christ, till suddenly, on the left of the last bend in the road, they discovered, afar off, a low cloud — the mountain pass.

Then the fugitives felt a strong, cold current of air, and Mount Blanc rose up before them, the mighty giant in his white, majestic snow-mantle.

A few steps more — and something glistened before their eyes — it was Lake Leman.

Then they quickened their pace; their weary eyes shone bright again, and along the rough slope, which amid a sea of fir trees went ever downward, their trembling eyes sought the horizon.

Suddenly they stood still; they stretched out their arms — and there! before them! rose the lofty towers of St. Peter's Church . . . That was Geneva, the Pella of tortured Protestantism, the town of Calvin!

The wanderers embraced one another, cries of joy, choked by tears, were raised, and greatly moved, they sang:

> *I love the* LORD, *the fount of life and grace;*
> *He heard my voice, my cry and supplication,*
> *Inclined His ear, gave strength and consolation;*
> *In life, in death, my heart will seek His face.*[20]

During a period of scarcely ten years, Geneva, which had less inhabitants than Zutphen,[21] had now received and housed four thousand refugees.

It was a heavy task that required great pecuniary sacrifices, and yet was accomplished with wonderful devotion.

Let us not forget — that the poorest part of the emigration came from France. Without shelter, without clothes, driven away

---

[20] Psalm 116:1 (*Book of Praise: Anglo Genevan Psalter*).

[21] At the time of writing this book, during the first decade of the 20th century, the Dutch city of Zutphen likely had about 10,000 inhabitants.

from their native land by the fury of persecution, they reached Geneva. They were shipwrecked men, who had been cast upon the shore of Geneva. And they brought nothing with them but distress, misery, hunger, and the wounds inflicted by furious, religious hatred.

New fugitives kept arriving; they spread about to make room for the next; it was an endless procession of spectres with lean jaws and eyes far sunk in their sockets — it was a procession of poor wretches, martyrs of the Reformation.

The Geneva houses were not large. Moreover, every family formed a little state in the state; and to their Puritanical austerity, the Geneva Protestants added a certain prudent reticence toward the unknown stranger.

But these characteristics were dissipated at the heartrending sight of the fugitives going through the streets deprived of everything. And with irresistible strength came another characteristic, compassion, pity for these poor creatures.

Beds were got ready — five, six in one room. Some houses had twenty-five beds. Quite a revolution took place in the regular course of housekeeping, and the good Geneva housewife, who up till then had done everything with the regularity of clockwork, showed her approval. She vied with her husband in works of Christian hospitality, and for the persecuted unlocked the holy of holies, where her children were not allowed to enter.

She cut up her clothes to help her sisters, she robbed her linen-press to protect the half-naked children from cold; she herself went without many things to feed them all; she refreshed the exhausted strangers with wine and herself drank water. O women of Geneva! O daughters of Calvin! Blessed shall your memory be till the end of time!

Chapter XIX

AS FOR MAN, HIS DAYS ARE AS GRASS

LUTHER could reckon on the support of influential patrons, but he no longer needed that support. And while gloomy and ominous sighs filled the air, he was to leave the scene of battle, where he had fought with so much honour and courage.

Luther at home

In his sermons, letters, and conversation, the old fire and energy of this heroic heart were still apparent, but a longing for the heavenly country was unmistakable. With trembling heart he also foresaw a religious war, and then thought of an old prophecy, according to which the lands of Germany were to be harassed with a terrible religious war.

His last sermon, preached at Wittenberg, was the farewell of a dying man. Every one felt it; every heart was moved. And from Wittenberg he went to Eisleben, his birthplace, there to die.

Properly speaking, he was ill only once in his life; that illness lasted but a day, and it carried Luther away to eternity.

In the evening he complained that his chest troubled him so, and thought that it meant death. Three times, shortly after each other, he said: "Father, into Thy hands I commend my spirit! Thou hast redeemed me, O God of truth!" Then he was still; the films of death were fast closing over his eyes.

Once more he awoke from his stupefaction. Then Dr. Jones turned to him and asked the question: "Reverend father, dare you die in the doctrine which you have preached?"

"Yes," replied Luther, with an astonishingly clear voice, so that all present could distinctly hear it.

That was his last word on earth. And he fell asleep that night[22] between two and three o'clock, sixty-two years of age.

As a benefactor to nations, he was conveyed to Wittenberg amidst the ringing of all the church bells, solemn dirges, and the lamentations of the population.

The young counts of Mansfield and fifty noblemen with their retinue, formed the procession of honour; in the evening Halle was reached; the people had poured out of the gates; all the clergy and the members of the Council had assembled at the gate. The body was placed in the vestry; the church was crowded with people, who, with weeping voices, sang the funeral Psalm.

The following morning the body was conveyed over Bitterfield and Kemberg to Wittenberg. Catherine von Bora, Luther's wife, and her three sons, followed directly behind the hearse; the earthly remains were, according to the wish of the deeply afflicted Elector

---

[22] February 18, 1546.

Catherine von Bora

of Saxony, John Frederick, to rest near the pulpit of the Wittenberg Schloss Church, from which the great Reformer had so often preached his soul-stirring sermons.

Melanchthon made a funeral speech; Bugenhagen too, spoke a few suitable words. And when he, overcome by sadness, burst into tears and exclaimed: "Who will be our shepherd now, who our teacher? We are forsaken, left orphans!" all the people burst out into one mournful cry of grief.

Luther and Calvin — two Reformers! But what a difference! Luther was bold, undaunted — the man of feeling; Calvin was sharp-witted, deeply sensitive — the man of logic. What the one lacked, the other possessed; they were Elijah and Elisha; and it was the Lord's gracious ordaining that Calvin should be the successor of Luther.

With what reverence did Calvin look up to the doctor of Wittenberg. "We say it frankly," he thus expressed himself, "that we consider Luther a great apostle of Christ, through whose mission and work the Gospel has, in our time, been brought back to almost its original purity."

He declared with all the earnestness of his soul that Luther had had to contend with no less difficulties than the Apostles had themselves, for he had to overthrow the Papal colossus, a power which had struck fatal roots firmly and deeply in the national life of the Christian West.

The angel of death, which had cut off the life of the German Reformer, appeared a year later at the immoral Court of Francis I, to summon the King before the Judgment Seat of God.

His throne was, to the topmost steps, bespattered with the sacred blood of the martyrs.

It was a year and a half since fourteen men, who would not deny their belief in Christ, were hanged and burnt on fourteen gallows placed in a wide circle on the great market-square of Meaux.

With their tongues, mutilated by the executioner, they praised God's grace and comforted one another with their last breath.

More horribly did the hirelings of Francis I act toward the Vaudois. The inhabitants of the town of Cabrieres, who, trusting to the solemn promises made in the name of the King, had willingly opened their gates to the French soldiers, fell under the sword-cuts of these soldiers, who had changed into executioners.

To extort confessions from the innocent, their feet were thrust into boots filled with burning lime. A barn full of straw, to which forty defenceless women had fled, was set on fire and the poor victims who tried to escape were caught on the pikes.

By hundreds the wretched Vaudois wandered about in the forests, there to die of hunger, or to be captured and dragged to the gallows.

The cries of distress uttered by the Swiss and German co-religionists reached the ears of Francis I, but he replied in a hard-hearted tone, that they should be sensible enough not to meddle with matters which did not concern them.

And this was the mournful end of a King's life, that was devoted to knightly pomp, thirst for fame and scandalous excesses.

Father of science, this man has been called; in the martyrology of the Reformed Churches he has another name. And he died unlamented.[23]

---

[23] March 31, 1547.

Francis I departed this life, but the sword that persecuted the French Protestants was not sheathed. The stream of fugitives that crossed the French frontiers went on, and among the wanderers who reached Geneva was a young man, who, by his tall, impressive stature, his distinguished manners and noble appearance, immediately attracted attention.

The pedestrians stood still and looked back at the Burgundian as he passed into Cannon Street and knocked at Calvin's front door.

The Reformer had seen this man several times before — fifteen years before in Wallmar's dwelling. And he gave Theodore Beza a hearty welcome.

Beza had gone through much in those fifteen years. This merry, life-loving poet, this brilliant, *fêted littérateur* could say with truth, that God had snatched him as a brand from the fire, that from now on he might devote his life to the service of the King of Kings.

But Satan had paid him out for leaving his service.

His future was blighted; the Parliament in Paris stood ready to burn the runaway heretic in effigy, and like a beggar, without money, without protectors, without prospects, he arrived at Geneva.

What was he to do? He did not know; Calvin, whom he asked for advice, did not know either; and his family refused all help.

For a time Beza thought, with the pecuniary assistance of a friend at Geneva, of starting a book-printing business. Geneva had no printing office; the plan seemed a good one, and business men were consulted about it.

But the Lord frustrated the plan, for He had already provided for the sorely tried Beza. Lausanne called him as professor to her University, and he was soon to shine there as a brilliant star in the scientific sky.

Before Beza left, his marriage with Claude Benosse was solemnized.[24] Merrily rang the bells of St. Peter's Church; Calvin performed the ceremony, and the congregation sang the comforting Psalm:

> *Those dwelling in the hiding place*
> *Of God Most High shall tarry*
> *Beneath the shadows of His grace;*
> *His goodness will not vary.*[25]

---

[24] October, 1548.
[25] Psalm 91:1 (*Book of Praise*).

Chapter XX

THE LOFTY WAVES OF ADVERSITY

WAS it really true what the congregation sang to the kneeling Beza and his bride?

There were weak believers who began to doubt it. They looked toward France and trembled; then toward Germany and uttered a cry of fear.

For German Protestantism was in danger. The signals of distress went up. And by the cowardice of one, the shortsightedness of another, and the treachery of Duke Maurice of Saxony, it was hurled from the acme of its power to the verge of the precipice.

Philippe Melanchthon

Calvin, who was deeply pained by the cruel fate of his compatriots, was again much affected by the adversities of his German co-religionists. He trembled for the life of his dear friends, Bucer and Melanchthon. And this man, by nature so bashful and timid, was, now that the German oak had been blown down by the storm, to become by God's will, the leader, upon whom the eyes of all the sad at heart were fixed.

Even before the war against the Schmal-Kaldic League burst out, Calvin had chosen the firm standpoint from which he regarded the German religious war. And his soul was full of bitterness at the false card which Maurice of Saxony intended to play.

140

"There is at present a rumour," he wrote, "at which I am not so much surprised as grieved, namely, that Maurice will co-operate with the Emperor, in order to ruin his nephew, John Frederick of Saxony, and his father-in-law, Philip of Hesse, and at last himself too, which is certainly not his intention. If that is true then the devil must already have got him entirely in his power. In the meantime I hope that our Antiochus, who at present makes us so afraid, will soon be put to such straits, that he will have no more time to think of the gout in his hands and feet. His accomplice, Sardanapalus, may God visit in the same way, for they have both equally deserved it at our hands!"

By Antiochus Calvin meant the German Emperor Charles V; by Sardanapalus, King Henry II of France, the son and bloodthirsty successor of Francis I.

It was as clear as day, that the warlike preparations of the German Antiochus were for the destruction of the Protestant Schmal-Kaldic League, but the Elector of Saxony could not see it. Moreover, the Elector was slow by nature; he was fond of procrastination, and kept hoping for a peaceful solution of the disputes.

At Mühlberg his army was attacked by the Imperialists. He was then in Mühlberg Church listening attentively to the sermon. His orderlies brought him the news that the Imperialists were crossing the river which protected his army, but he would not believe it, and remained in the church till the service was over. This dilatoriness cost him his army and his own liberty. His army was routed, and after a brave resistance he himself was taken prisoner.

For the Duke of Alva and the other Imperial generals, it was a source of inward joy to see the captive head of the German Protestants, and the warlike Bishop of Kildesheim, who in full armour had taken part in the battle, declared afterward, that he would not have missed the sight for hundreds of ducats.

Charles V made use of his triumph to set a terrifying example, and pronounced the unheard-of sentence that the Elector, John Frederick, should be beheaded for rebellion.

The Elector was playing chess when the death sentence was read to him. With admirable resignation he laid the fatal document down beside him, and looking at the Duke of Brunswick, who was playing with him, said calmly: "Cousin, pay attention to your game! You are in check!" The imperial flags were seen flying in all the Protestant districts; Wittenberg, the centre of German Protestantism, surrendered, and Charles V appeared with his forces at the grave of the great Reformer.

In reverent silence the Emperor stood at Luther's grave. But the grim Duke of Alva could not restrain his bitterness, and cried out in a mocking tone: "The bones of that arch-heretic should be dug up and burned to ashes."

From his lofty watch-tower Calvin viewed the disasters of his co-religionists. Like the old prophets of Israel, he could have covered his head with ashes and girded his loins with sackcloth. The fierce triumphant cries of the enemy cut like knives into his soul; he beat his breast and said: "It is on account of our many sins, and because we do not give God the honour due to Him, that Satan has such power over us. Therefore we must humble ourselves before God, and implore His grace." The hand of the Lord rested heavily on Calvin, and coupled with the general disasters there was sadness and suffering at home.

Idelette had spoken words of consolation to the noble Burgomaster, Ami Porral, when he lay at the point of death, and now she herself lay stretched on her death-bed.

Calvin had feared this. In the midst of his onerous duties, the anxious fear had more than once taken possession of him, that all was not well with his wife.

The premature confinement of the child, that she was allowed to keep only for a fortnight, had impaired Idelette's health. It is true, it seemed as if she would get better, but appearances were altogether deceptive. The sickness returned with greater strength, and in 1545 Idelette was on the verge of the grave.

Yet once more there seemed a ray of hope.

"My wife is improving," Calvin wrote to Viret; "but her cough is still bad."

Yes, that cough — that was the mischief! Consumption — that was the sword of Damocles that hung threateningly over the Geneva vicarage.

Idelette kept up bravely; she never spoke about her ailments; if her husband looked at her with the anxious eyes of love, she smiled at his unnecessary anxiety.

It would not do for him to know the truth, for that would destroy his domestic joy. But Calvin was not to be deceived, and when the busy housewife, exhausted and worn out, had no longer the strength to leave her bed, he knew that the end was near.

The faithful doctor redoubled his energy to save this precious life, but the oil was spent, the lamp went out, and Idelette went to the house where there are many mansions.

It was a beautiful spring day[26] when Idelette died; the birds were singing and the trees were clothed in soft, green verdure. Calvin remained in the sick chamber. His clerical brothers had been there and had offered up their prayers together.

She lay there, her faith in God never wavering. Not with the night boat, but in full sail, she was about to enter the eternal haven. She seemed already to have left this earth — her soul drank in the air of heaven.

Calvin sat there, crushed as it were, by the bedside of his wife, and those seven years of married life, which the deepest mutual love had made a pleasant oasis in the midst of the great sandy desert, passed like a vision before his mind's eye.

Now that this faithful helpmate was being taken from him, Calvin saw more clearly and distinctly than ever what a blow the Almighty was dealing him. And amidst these painful meditations, while his heart was filled with sadness, he heard Idelette's dying strains: "O glorious resurrection!" Lifting her kindly eyes upward, she murmured: "O God of Abraham and of all our fathers — never has one of the faithful, who trusted in Thee, been deceived."

At six o'clock Calvin had to leave her to attend to his duties.

He seemed to be an old man, walking through the streets. He saw nothing, he thought of nothing else than his dying wife.

At seven o'clock Idelette began to lose consciousness. And perceiving this, she said with astonishing presence of mind: "Let us pray — all pray for me."

---

[26] March 29, 1549.

Then Calvin came home again. He bent down over the beloved face; then he saw that she was near the heavenly Father's house. She could not speak, but he saw clearly that she still recognized him. He spoke to her of Christ, the great Conqueror of death, and of the hope of eternal life.

Then, however, his feeling overcame him, and he sought the quietest corner of the house, threw himself on his knees and called upon God for strength.

At eight o'clock the wife of the great Reformer breathed her last. It was not dying — it was a peaceful falling asleep; as of a child that falls asleep in the arms of its father.

"Is she dead or sleeping?" thought they who stood by, but Calvin knew, and with his face buried in his hands he sat down in sadness at the death-bed of his so dearly-beloved wife, who with him had borne the heat of the day and the cold of night.

The son and daughter of Idelette's first marriage were also there. Idelette had never spoken about their future when she should be taken away, so as not to trouble her husband. But three days before her death Calvin had referred to the subject, and to comfort her said that he would continue to be a father to the children.

"I have already commended them to God's care," was her reply.

"That does not prevent me from looking after them," said Calvin.

Great, striking, and affecting was the confidence that Idelette placed in her husband. This confidence was the reason why she had not spoken to him about her children. And when one of her neighbours, with the kindest intention, had urged her to do so, she had replied: "That they may live a good and holy life — that is the chief thing. I do not need to urge upon my husband the necessity of bringing them up in the true doctrine and in the fear of the Lord. If they are good, then I know that he of his own accord will be a father to them. And if they are not, then they are not worthy of my asking anything for them!"

When these simple and noble words were afterward reported to Calvin he exclaimed with sorrowful admiration: "This greatness of soul will have more effect upon me than hundreds of entreaties!"

Idelette dead! The sun of his day and the kindly star of his long nights set — O, it was like a heavy blow upon his heart!

Not till that lovely face was stamped with the image of death did he know how dearly he had loved her.

Many of the reformers married again. Bucer himself was a strong advocate for this. And Viret, that great child, once wrote

Peter Viret

with charming *naïveté*, "I am not very fond of widows, but as it is difficult to get all we want, we must not be too particular." And so Viret married. But Calvin never thought of marrying again; he himself was opposed to it, although he had married a widow.

The image of his wife was too deeply imprinted in his soul; a piece of his heart was borne away with it to the dark, gloomy pit of the Geneva cemetery, in which the earthly remains of his beloved wife were laid, and only the thought of an eternal reunion on the other side of the grave could comfort his deeply afflicted soul.

"The admirable providence of God separates us in this world to unite us again in His heavenly kingdom" — those were his own words.

Chapter XXI

THE GERMAN EMPEROR'S PRIDE BROUGHT DOWN

STRENGTHENED by God and knowing that His children are purified by suffering, Calvin set to work resolutely, without looking back. The more his brethren were persecuted, the more he longed for the unity of all the children of God. Through Melanchthon he hoped to unite the German Church with the Protestants in the South, to bring Geneva in close connection with Switzerland, and to unite the Protestants of France under one banner by the same creed. His ideal was one indivisible Protestant Church, divided neither by mountains nor seas, extending to England and Scotland, to Sweden and Poland. He first betook himself to Neuchâtel and Zurich to put an end to the suspicion prevailing there, to erase the distressing page of the Marburg Conference, where Luther's vehemence had prevented any compromise, and to explain as clearly as possible to the Swiss, that in the Sacraments the body and the blood of the Lord are really imparted to us in the spiritual and not in the bodily sense.

Calvin now had great and blessed influence on all Protestantism. While he had already shown before that he was not narrow-minded by signing the Augsburg Confession, he now drew the firm lines of unity. The sun at Geneva shone in unbroken splendour; it had become the greatest attraction of European Protestantism, and the greatest men of this eventful time stood in connection with Calvin. We mention Petrus Martyr, the son of Florence, whom Calvin, on account of his erudition, called the wonder of Italy; the theologian Bullinger, living in Zurich and having become a Zwingli the Second by his sincerity, activity, and zeal; John à Lasco, the bold, undaunted Pole; Renata of Ferrara, who glittered in the Italian sky like a bright star. In the heat of persecution the cry of "Close your ranks" had been heard in France. Many nobles had joined in a strong phalanx of Huguenots under the command of the heroic Jeanne d'Albret, the daughter of Margaret

Jeanne d'Albret

and the mother of him who has been called the greatest king of France (Henry IV). In the North new life began to stir, Sweden and Denmark gave the example; in Poland the sun was rising. In Germany there was some relief, and the Protestants had reason to exclaim in joy: "The Lord bends the hearts of kings like brooks." Strange things had happened. The Evangelicals had trembled before Maurice of Saxony, and lo! this powerful man, the grandfather of the Dutch Prince Maurice of Orange Nassau, became their deliverer. He laid siege to Magdeburg, but on entering the vanquished fortress he suddenly remembered that the inhabitants of Magdeburg were his brothers in the Faith. He addressed the burghers, who had gathered in the market-place, as their friend; he shook hands with the members of the Council and promised to treat them leniently. He did more. He formed a treaty with two Protestant princes, concentrated his army, and with his long, ruddy beard waving in the wind, he pushed on as swiftly as a mountain-stream, through the narrow passes, to surprise the Emperor.

Granvelle had once shrugged his shoulders at Maurice of Saxony; the Emperor had taken him only for an ordinary German prince, who was tipsy four times a week. However, Maurice had learned at the Imperial Court how to deceive the innocent; he had made dangerous progress in that hazardous school, and the pupil was finally to crush the great master, who deceived the whole world. The Emperor at Innsbruck was quite absorbed in the deliberations of the Council of Trent, and prepared to extirpate the Protestant religion with its ideas of political freedom, when the tidings reached him that Maurice was approaching in forced marches. He grew pale at the tidings, and he, who had dreamed of uniting the countries of Charlemagne under one sceptre, put on the worn-out apparel of an old woman to escape in this disguise. The road to Flanders, however, had been blocked when his army was defeated, and late in the evening of May 19, 1551, amidst showers and thunderstorms, the Emperor fled from Innsbruck to escape his former ally. He could not ride, as he was suffering from gout, and in a litter, as harassed as an outlaw, Charles V took the way to the East, while the torches of his attendants lighted the hardly passable path. Maurice of Saxony let him escape; he said that he had no cage fit for such a bird, and amused himself by starting him as one does wild game. Hardly had the Emperor left the town, when the shrewd Chancellor Granvelle informed the imprisoned Elector, John Frederick, that his captivity had come to an end by Imperial command, while he was only required to promise that he would follow the Imperial Court voluntarily until further orders. When the Elector opened the door the next morning, the Spanish guard had disappeared. He was at liberty. God had broken his chains.

Though the slowness of his military exploits had shown him to be an indifferent general, his constancy during imprisonment proved his excellence as a Christian. No efforts had been spared to induce him to sign the Interim, forming a proposal for the adjustment of religious peace! No threats could frighten him to sign a paper offensive to his Evangelical faith. The ignoble revenge of the Emperor did not hurt him either. His Court chaplain had been removed; Luther's writings and a costly Bible, printed on parchment and decorated with illustrations, had been taken away, but all these vexations had not disturbed his admirable peace of mind — he who had been vanquished at Mühlberg had retreated into an invincible fortress: in the entrenchments of a clear conscience.

Now he was free, but he kept his promise as a prince and a Christian. He hastened to follow the Emperor along untrodden paths, and the Emperor was deeply affected on meeting John Frederick again. He promised the Elector Imperial favour and mercy and then continued his flight as far as the centre of Carinthia. It was a weary, distressing flight; with the inexorable enemy at their heels the fugitives had to pull down the bridges behind them to delay their approach. All the splendour of the Imperial dignity was gone; within twenty-five days the glory of twenty-five years was demolished and nothing was left to Charles V of all his magnificence but the gout, from which he suffered more than ever. A Roman Catholic Council was held at Trent, but the members dispersed in great fright on hearing the trumpets of the Protestant army; the panic spread among the most faithful paladins of the Emperor, and left by all, he realized the frailty of all human power. The Protestants had seized Innsbruck, a meeting of German princes was held at Passau, and the famous treaty signed there secured the German Protestants religious liberty and equal rights with the Roman Catholics. For two generations this treaty effected religious peace; then the Thirty Years War broke out, by which Germany was devastated.

Chapter XXII

AN EVENTFUL CELEBRATION OF THE LORD'S SUPPER

CHARLES V aimed at a universal empire; Calvin's ideals were higher, he aimed at a Christian state: Christian in its divisions and its laws, considering itself responsible to God for the actions of all its subjects.

Laws are to be obeyed — that was the inexorable rule on which Calvin based everything. When applying laws he always took care, with great impartiality, that the rich did not come off scot-free, while the poor were punished. One of the first punished by the Government as a law-breaker was a councillor of Geneva; another was a burgher of high standing. An obstinate gambler got the confiscated cards hung around his neck, and was tied to the pillory for an hour in sight of the people. The organizer of a dissolute masquerade was obliged to implore forgiveness on his bare knees in St. Peter's; a perjurer was hoisted on a ladder with his right hand tied up, and put in the pillory for hours. On account of his having dressed somebody's hair indecently, a ladies' hairdresser was put in prison for two days; parents, who evaded the law of compulsory education and kept their children at home, were fined. Adultery was punished; adulterers were led through the streets like criminals. Afterward several punishments were made more severe; at a general meeting of the people it was resolved, that adultery required capital punishment. At the same time it was in the Geneva of the Reformation, that those men were living who had driven Calvin triumphantly out of the town, and who were to oppose him now the more violently, as the Evangelical leaven was doing its work more thoroughly. They were the Libertines. While Calvin had pitched his camp in Geneva as a centre for the great spiritual fight to be fought from the Apennines to the northern fjords and from the Atlantic Ocean to the Russian steppes, he was to be harassed most forcibly by his sworn enemies in this very camp, as he was before his banishment. The camp taken by him was over a volcano, and every day, every hour the eruption could take place, destroying himself and his congregation. In this critical fight earnest and pious men of severe morals and fixed national aspirations were on his side. They stood shoulder to shoulder, realising that their only strength was unity. And thus they defied the fierce attacks of their enemies, hoping in God. In 1546 the general strife broke out, when a manufacturer of playing-cards, who had sustained some loss, one night gave vent to his bitterness against Calvin. He called him a Protestant bishop worse than his predecessor; the councillors who supported him were traitors, and Calvin's religion simply deceit and tyranny. The Council condemned Ameaux, but Calvin thought he had been judged too leniently, and so the Council of Two Hundred condemned the manufacturer of playing-cards to implore forgiveness, torch in hand. In the camp of the Libertines this severe sentence roused much indignation; they disturbed the divine service when Calvin preached, and the authorities were compelled to have the gallows erected, in order to frighten them. The next year blood was shed. Gruet, formerly a canon and now one of the Libertine chiefs, threw off his mask and spoke words of great blasphemy against Christ. His house was searched and a number of blasphemous writings as well as a dangerous correspondence of high treason fell into the hands of the Government.

His guilt had been proved, Gruet had attacked religion and wanted to betray the town to the Duke of Savoy. His fate was not dubious, he paid for his crime with his life.

The case of Perrin, the Governor of Geneva, was still more painful to Calvin personally, for Perrin had been his faithful friend for a long time. Perrin's wife had been to a ball prohibited by the Council; the Church Council heard of it, and Calvin was not satisfied until the lady, though she belonged to the highest rank, was sentenced to some days' imprisonment. Perrin, who had also been to the ball, fled, but a letter written by Calvin caused him to be arrested. This was a letter full of touching tenderness, in which Calvin appealed to their old friendship, besought him to sacrifice his pride to the welfare of the Republic, and to submit to the decision of the authorities. This was too much for Perrin; he returned, willingly submitted to the decision of the authorities and underwent a slight punishment. Thus this thunderstorm passed by. They were reconciled. And Calvin thanked God. This was in May, 1546. In the month of June of the next year, Perrin got the very important commission of forming a treaty of commerce with the French Government. During his absence, his wife, with her venomous tongue, had again given rise to complaints, and on his return in the autumn, Perrin heard that she had been banished to Bern territory with her father, a man whose morals were very bad. Perrin flew into a passion. He brought back his wife, rushed into the council-room, and striking his fist on the table declared that he had rendered too many services to the town of Geneva to be insulted so grievously in his nearest relations. To Calvin this appeal to a high municipal position was intolerable. "If you will not submit to the yoke of Christ at all," he said, "go and build a town somewhere in which you can live at your pleasure; but as long as you are here, you shall not escape the laws; and though there were in your dwelling as many diadems as heads, God will surely know how to prevail." In all these disastrous quarrels this was his fixed rule. From the elevated, inviolable tower of his religious conviction he beheld the petty doings of mortals who tried to thwart him, the servant of the Almighty King. They were a troop of fools, not able to move without the will of their heavenly Father. This conviction turned the Reformer's blood into steel, and he wrote with a smile around his clearly-cut mouth: "The grievances undergone here are exaggerated abroad. In Lyons I was reported to have died in more than twenty ways. It is true that Satan here has means enough to ignite the fire, but the flame vanished like flax."

Meanwhile Perrin had played with fire. When he referred to his services rendered, the severe councillors wondered if these services were indeed so great. He had formed an advantageous treaty of commerce, but the most singular negotiations were reported to have been entered into on his own authority with a foreign power. No less a thing was alleged than garrisoning Geneva with a corps of French artillery. This was meant for a defence of the town, as Perrin asserted, but the Government maintained that in this way Geneva was entirely at the mercy of France It could not be proved that Perrin had committed treason; but, to say the least, he had acted with the greatest thoughtlessness, and the Council dismissed him from an office which he evidently was no longer able to fulfil properly. However, in the bosom of the Council itself opinion was divided on this point; there was a strong minority, protesting fiercely, and the waves of the people's passion arose in the streets and squares. The Council of Two Hundred degenerated into a Polish Council and wild cries of hatred for Calvin were uttered. Then Calvin, who was at a meeting with his colleagues, rose to throw himself amidst the wildly excited people, in spite of the most pressing warnings. He may have been slightly paler than usual, but he never hesitated. With folded arms he defied the rioters thirsting for his blood; then he passed the threshold of the town hall. The shouts and cries increased, daggers flew from their sheaths, while Calvin went to the centre of the hall resolutely and immovably. Then silence ensued, and amidst this ominous silence he called out: "If you desire my blood — here it is! If you want to banish me — I will go. And you may try once more to save the town without the Gospel!" Like hissing arrows these words left his lips; this man with his clearly cut face had become the conscience of Geneva. He was in their power. If they liked, he should not leave the hall alive. But there was nobody who laid hands on him, they dared not; his powerful eyes awed them. By respectfully making way for him, they acknowledged his superiority. Three days afterward Calvin reminded them of the approach of Christmas and that they should celebrate the Lord's Supper together. As for himself he bore no grudge and was willing to be reconciled to Perrin. At that moment he was sincere; many of his adherents may have been so too. For the moment there was peace again. But it was only apparent peace. The old hatred arose again, and Calvin was abused most shamefully. The Libertines would not let him walk about unmolested; they hissed him when he passed, changed his name into that of Cain and called their dogs Calvin to insult him. Hardly a year after peace had apparently been restored, Calvin was compelled to complain of Perrin and some other burghers, who purposely absented themselves from the communion service. Once more he earnestly tried to bring about a reconciliation, in order that the communion at Pentecost might not be desecrated by spite and enmity. The Council thanked him for his good intentions, but the Libertines secretly had intrigued so successfully that Perrin had been appointed first burgomaster a month afterward. Philibert Berthelier knew this. He was the son of the famous martyr who had died for his country in 1521, and used his advantageous position to abuse the Church

Council, which had summoned him, in the most disgraceful manner. Put under Church discipline on account of several shameful deeds, committed some days before the Communion service in September, Berthelier appealed to the Council. The sentence was annulled by the Council, where Berthelier's and Perrin's friends held the reins. They seized the opportunity to triumph over the Church, and declared that Berthelier was free to attend the communion, if in this he followed the dictates of his conscience. In this way the Council had shown its position definitely, but Calvin had also done so. He preferred death rather than allow Berthelier to attend the communion. Sunday came. The town was in a fearful suspense. The rumour was spread that the Council had secretly given Berthelier a hint to stay away from church, but that he had made up his mind to go with a number of friends. The bells were ringing. The people were already hastening to church. Gradually the large building, the arches of which were supported by twelve heavy pillars, was filling. The burgomasters, the Council, and twelve men of the armed body-guard now entered in the colours of the town, gray and black. They took their usual seats as on every Sunday. It was time — Calvin ascended the pulpit. His glance went over the crowd. The building was full; only some late comers pushed in hurriedly. There was the communion cup, and yonder, near a pillar, his eyes unashamed — among a defying troop of Libertines — Berthelier's shameless face. They had come to attend the communion service . . . Calvin was silent; the last drop of blood had left his face; immovable like a pillar stood the iron legislator of Geneva. Then his lips opened to deliver the usual short sermon; he read the liturgy and said amidst breathless silence, in a slow firm voice: "As long as God permits me to stay here, I shall show the constancy He has granted me, whatever may happen. And I shall follow the line of conduct, which my Master has made perfectly clear to me." He descended from the pulpit and blessed the bread and the wine. Then the Libertines rose, left their seats and approached the communion-table . . . It was a moment of suspense. There stood Calvin. He stretched his hands over the sacred symbols, his stature seemed to rise and his eyes flamed, when he exclaimed: "These hands you may cut off, these limbs crush, here is my blood — shed it. You shall never compel me to give what is holy to the godless!" The Libertines hesitated. Was it the awe-inspiring attitude of the servant of the Lord or the threatening murmur of the people that made them hesitate? They stopped; then they left the church. And never has a more exciting communion service been held at St. Peter's in Geneva. In the afternoon Calvin preached again. His sermon was a valedictory address to his beloved congregation, for every moment he expected the order of banishment. He had chosen as his text the farewell words of the apostle St. Paul to the Ephesians: "And now, brethren, I commend you to God and to the word of His grace."

The whole congregation was moved, there were tears in the preacher's voice; their hearts were touched. Leaving the church, Calvin went home to await the order of banishment. However, the order did not come; the Council dared not sign the warrant, and the people of Geneva were attached to Calvin more closely than ever. It was a matter of surprise that a small party, a fraction, had ventured to raise such tumult and revolt; in spite of the respected names borne by some of its members they did not at all represent the people of Geneva, and Calvin, whose seat had been endangered, was strengthened by the fierce fight. Calvin's victory meant Farel's triumph. Farel had come to Geneva, and alluding to their pantheistic ideas, he had called the Libertines atheists. When he returned to Neuchâtel, his place of abode, he was called to account by the Geneva Council, and refusing to be retained by the magistrates of Neuchâtel he returned to Geneva at once. He was recognized in the street by some turbulent Libertines, who surrounded him and cried: "Into the Rhone with the rascal!" The undaunted hero laughed at their threats, and, rescued by his brothers in the faith, Farel was led in triumph to Calvin's house. His cause had become their cause; they repaired to the town hall in great numbers, called Farel their father, and would not suffer him to be designated as a false minister. The Council let the matter drop; the people had taken the responsibility and the accusers stole away ashamed. The arrival of Farel, however, had been connected with a dismal and terrible event, which has been written about to this very day.

Chapter XXIII

THE GENEVA STAKE

NINETEEN years earlier, Calvin had been willing to risk his life to have a conversation with Michel Servet, and now — in 1553 — Servet came to the town of Calvin to end his life at the stake. He was a Spaniard, like Ignatius Loyola; a gloomy man with a strange adventurous mind, a student of geography and geometry, of medicine and theology, who revealed his learning in a flow of words, without ever having been able to get his degree. There was something intrepid in this man, but if his intrepidity became too dangerous for him, he did not mind getting out of difficulties by a series of untruths. His system was based on the pantheistic doctrine of the Anabaptists, and while he defended the right of astrology he attacked the doctrine of the Trinity with the same zeal. Twenty-three years earlier, people had already been excited by Servet's zealotry. Gentle Oecolampadius was alarmed at his doctrines, and Zwingli had advised Oecolampadius to do everything in his power to oppose this detestable blasphemy. It is true, that Servet dared speak words, which were intended as a shameless attack on Christianity, and that he wrote things which make us shudder. Well — in the confusion of his ideas and the unrestrained pride of his heart this man sadly imagined that the Reformers stopped halfway in their work, while he considered himself ordained to restore Christianity to its former splendour. However, in Calvin's eyes the denial of the Holy Trinity and his pantheistic ideas meant the disorganisation and destruction of Christianity, which Servet pretended to defend, and Calvin, in whose strong memory the attack on his own orthodoxy had made an indelible impression, felt the more need to adopt firm and rigorous measures against the dreams of the Spanish heretic. What spirit can have induced Servet to take the fatal road leading to the Geneva dungeon? He had just escaped from imprisonment at Vienna, where a Roman Catholic court had sat in judgment upon his heretical opinions, and the way to Italy lay open before him. He could have avoided Geneva. And when he entered the town, yet why did he stay a whole month? Probably he counted upon the help of the Libertines and the strong support of Perrin, who was still burgomaster; the rumour that Calvin's fall was expected will have reached him, and in his rashness, which characterised this man, he no doubt imagined himself to be the successor of the famous Reformer. Amidst the most violent disturbances, while the sword of Damocles was hanging over Calvin's head, Servet appeared in Geneva. Calvin was most distressed. Had he not enough to struggle with? He requested the Government to imprison Servet, and one of the magistrates gave the order. But according to the Geneva laws nobody could be imprisoned on a mere accusation, unless the accuser was also imprisoned. This was a law of the Medes and Persians, and Calvin would undoubtedly have been compelled to change the pulpit for the dungeon, had not his secretary offered himself as a substitute. Imprisonment, it is true, was nothing dishonourable in itself. In those days one was imprisoned as easily as one gets a warrant nowadays. On some days the prisons were like our waiting-rooms — so crowded were they. Hardly anybody escaped the dungeon, society ladies, members of the Council, men holding the highest posts, like Perrin, all had to enter it. In a ponderous deed of accusation of thirty-eight articles Calvin explained his objections to the doctrines of Michel Servet; the accused answered, defended himself, and boldly challenged Calvin to a public debate, relying on the good-will of some councillors. He would not speak, but he would let the Holy Scripture and the patriarchs speak. And they would destroy Calvin's doctrines.

Calvin wished for nothing better; his democratic blood made him rejoice at the prospect of fighting out the quarrel in church and in the presence of all the people. He made up his mind not to accept the decisions of a hostile majority — not he! However, the congregation would participate in the violent struggle, which their leader had to fight, to be edified and strengthened in the doctrine leading to godliness. Hard, fierce, and bitter was the struggle. Angels and devils fought for the soul of Geneva; the heights of heaven opened over the town and the depths of hell under it. And from this infernal abyss, where God is cursed and hated, arose the blasphemous words uttered by Servet, gnashing his teeth: "The Holy Trinity is a three-headed hell-hound."

The Council, afraid of possible disturbances, gave no permission for a public meeting; new sessions took place, while Servet, who had an ally in the jailer, beheld with eagle's eyes the violent religious political struggle in the bosom of the Geneva Republic. The written memoir required of him in the beginning of September was evidently drawn up under the impression of a considerable decrease of Calvin's power. Servet saw his papers increase in power in proportion as those of Calvin decreased; the accused began to be an accuser, and he collected the stones with which to crush Calvin.

He said in his memoir to the thirty-eight articles:

"Calvin is a liar, a blasphemer, and who dares assert that a murderer and a criminal accuser is a true minister of the Church? You, Calvin, do not know what you are saying; you are a villain, if you continue to judge of what you do not understand — do you intend to deafen the ears of the judges by your barking?"

Calvin appeared before the Court himself to dispute with Servet. He attacked the pantheistic doctrines of the Spaniard. "Suppose," he said to Servet, "that somebody stamped his foot on this stone floor and said that he was stamping on your God. Should not you be horrified to hear the majesty of God subjected to such blasphemy?"

No, Servet did not feel this horror. "I feel no doubt whatever," answered the man, "that this bench, this sideboard, and everything that exists forms the substance of God."

"According to you the devil himself is God!" cried Calvin.

And Servet answered with a laugh: "Do you doubt it?"

Here they were, the monstrous ideas which had struck the Reformer already eight years before in a correspondence with Servet, and which made him write to Viret as follows: "Servet proposes to come here, if I want him to. But I will not pledge my word, for, if he came, I should not suffer him to leave Geneva alive however little my influence might be." The authenticity of this letter has been doubted; afterward it was considered indisputable, in any case it clearly shows Calvin's point of view, which he never relinquished. He was most anxious that Servet should be punished; if the denier of the Holy Trinity should come off scot-free it meant for him the destruction of the work to which he had devoted his life. Now that he was alone, and the kind, comfort-speaking lips of

Idelette were closed for ever, there were moments in his life when his strong mind was on the point of sinking into the slough of despair; then he seized his pen to pour out his heart to Farel and Bullinger; in these moments of gloomy doubt he even thought of leaving the camp and ending his days in some remote place. Bullinger urged him not to give way to this dejection and complete the ruin of the town, trusted to him, by leaving it to its fate in a fit of despair. Farel came over himself to strengthen his beloved brother in his hard struggle. He declared he should deserve the most hideous death, if he caused anyone to forsake the most holy faith, and that Servet deserved the same punishment. It was the Roman Catholic idea which possessed Farel and Calvin and all the Reformers, none excepted. Servet was of the same opinion. On a letter to the Council he declared he was ready to die, were he unable to crush Calvin. However, he requested that Calvin might be arrested too and beheaded in his place if he had revealed Calvin's errors. Servet wondered why the magistrates were so long in pronouncing the sentence. He had said his last word — why should they defer the sentence? He called Calvin his only enemy, a sorcerer, who ought to be driven from Geneva, and claimed Calvin's fortune as compensation for the possessions he had lost through him. Three weeks more passed without Servet receiving an official answer. And then he understood that his prospects were dark. The arrogant tone of his sayings was no longer heard; he became meek and submissive, and his letters showed his distress. Meanwhile the decision had taken place, but outside Geneva. The Council had sent the papers of the lawsuit to Bern, Zurich, Basel, and Schaffhausen, and the answers came in on September 18. Each answer was double: one from the Council and one from the Church Council of the place, so there were eight answers. They were definite and unanimous; Servet must die! That was their harsh and inexorable demand. The Bern Council, whose advice was highly prized by Geneva, was not satisfied with capital punishment only, but demanded the stake, contrary to Calvin's wish to save Servet from the horrors of such a terrible death. Thus Protestant Switzerland had passed judgment, and the Geneva Council could only uphold this sentence. Acquittal would have been an insult to Church and State, whose opinion had been asked, and treason to the Reformation, the honour and safety of which were at stake.

Many members of the Council had hitherto considered the lawsuit only as one between a Spaniard, whose monstrous doctrines disturbed them, and a Frenchman, whom they hated. However, this Frenchman was supported by four powerful Protestant Churches, and it was no longer dubious which side the scales would turn. Then Perrin sprang to his feet to save Servet. He demanded acquittal, but the Council refused, for this acquittal would have caused Calvin's banishment. Then he requested the case to be brought before the Council of Two Hundred, less influenced by the advice of the four churches, and counting among its members many enemies of Calvin. This request was also refused; then Servet's doom was irrevocable, and in spite of the strong attempts of Calvin and his colleagues to save the unfortunate man from the terrible death by fire, Servet was condemned to the stake.

Farel was in his company on the morning of October 27 as his spiritual supporter, when the bailiff announced to Servet that this was his last day. He was left in ignorance about the stake, but the thought of having to die was sufficient to overwhelm him for a moment. Farel wished Calvin to meet the unfortunate man once more, and Calvin came with two councillors and friends.

Servet begged Calvin's forgiveness, and Calvin answered: "I hereby declare that I have never desired to take revenge on you for any personal insult."

When he had been led to the town hall, Servet heard that he was to die at the stake. It was a terrible moment. He pleaded that he might die by the sword, but it was in vain. And Farel accompanied him to the stake. Farel asked him if he did not wish to commend himself to the prayers of the spectators, and Servet answered in the affirmative.

However, Farel considered it his chief duty to convince the heretic of his errors even in his last moments.

At half an hour's distance from Geneva lies the Champel Hill. This hill is reached by a pleasant road, on the right two shady avenues, known under the name of the large and the small Philosopher's path from time immemorial. It is said that the Dutch theologian Arminius, who studied in Geneva, devised and completed his theological system here.

To this hill they repaired. From its summit could be had a magnificent view of the river Arve, streaming past in capricious curves, of the bright valley with its vineyards, the autumn foliage of which was glittering in the October sun, while the wide horizon seemed to be supported by the green tops of the Jura Mountains. Here Servet was to die. He knelt down to pray. Farel once more insisted upon Servet's renouncing his errors and so vehemently as to seem painful to us, but he refused so firmly that all the spectators were impressed.

"Invoke the eternal Son of God!" urged Farel.

But Servet exclaimed: "Jesus, Thou Son of the eternal God!"

It was only a change of words — that was all. Yet this change was the yawning gulf of their difference. Servet did not acknowledge the eternity of the Son of God. His writings were tied to his body; a wreath of straw and green leaves, sprinkled with sulphur, crowned his head. The fire was smouldering; the wood was wet; bitter and long was the death-struggle. And from the dense smoke came the voice of the dying man: "Jesus, Thou Son of the eternal God! Have mercy upon me!" Even now, after three and a half centuries, this stake has not yet been extinguished; the flames are bursting forth, and in the glow of these ruddy flames stands out the image of Calvin. However, this stake was not Calvin's wish; he had protested, and the Government erected the stake in order to show that it had the power of rejecting Calvin's request for mercy.

Yet Calvin desired Servet's death; all the blue water of Lake Leman cannot wash away this fact; the wings of this profound philosopher were tied by ideas, which we have learned to consider as errors. On the three hundred and fifty years' commemoration of the day on which Michel Servet ascended the stake, a number of ardent admirers of the great Reformer Calvin were gathered in Geneva to unveil a remarkable monument, consecrated to penance and remorse. The monument, made of a block of granite, bears two inscriptions. One is:

On the 27th of October 1553 died at the stake at Champel
MICHAEL SERVET
from Villeneuve, Arragon,
born on the 29th of September 1511.

And the other inscription is:

We, the respectful and thankful sons of Calvin, the Great Reformer, condemning an error, which was the error of the age in which Calvin lived, and valuing above all things Liberty of Conscience according to the true doctrines of the Reformation and the Gospel, erected this monument of penance on the 27th of October 1903.

It is strange — neither in Geneva nor in any other place in the wide world has there been an available spot for a statue in commemoration of Calvin, but to one of his most determined adversaries a monument has been erected. Its purpose is not the glorification of Servet, but at the same time he has been distinguished, which is hardly compatible with the anti-Christian and blasphemous ideas which he defended. And we feel entitled to ask if it is right to mention an error of Calvin's age without making mention of the errors of Michel Servet. Yet it is quite right that the error, which caused Servet to die at the stake, was an error of the age in which Calvin lived. The bearers of the most venerable names in the Protestant world rejoiced at the tidings of Servet's sentence of death. Beza was now satisfied, so were Haller, Sulzer, Musculus; gentle Melanchthon wrote: "The Government was right to put the blasphemer to death." It was the Roman Catholic leaven in the Protestant dough: in the Protestant as well as in the Roman Catholic circles it was the general idea that every heresy, spread among the people, should be punished by death. The Reformed churches had another special reason to adopt rigorous measures. It was a well-known fact that Anabaptists, Libertines, and Rationalists, all preachers of false doctrines like Servet, found and obtained followers in the Reformed circles. In this way the Protestants got a bad reputation; they were said to be tainted, infected with revolutionary ideas, and without the slightest doubt this opinion would have been confirmed, if Servet, who had been condemned to death by the Roman Catholic court of justice in Vienna, had got off scot-free in Geneva. It is true, he could not have been acquitted without violation of the principle which prevailed in the civil and religious world of Christianity: the principle that the public authorities ought to exterminate all idolatry and all heretics. This principle, exalted to a dogma, is centuries old. It is much older than Calvin and Calvinism, it existed even eleven centuries before Calvin; and the well-known church father Augustine was its creator. For fourteen centuries up till the days of the great French Revolution, this dogma swayed its inexorable sceptre and dominated the mind. It was said down in the Emperor Justinian's statute-book, brought forward again by the jurists of the fifteenth century, and adopted as a public right by all the European Christian countries in the sixteenth century. However, the cruelty of the Roman Catholic Inquisition is not to be found in Protestantism. while the Roman Catholic Church declared that all heretics deserved death, Calvin and the Protestant Churches wanted only those to be punished who made public propaganda for their heretical opinions. This does not alter the fact that the principle in question prevailed for fourteen centuries, and that the thirty-sixth article of the famous thirty-seven Articles of the Belgic Confession expressly mentions the extermination of all idolatry as the task of public authorities. In the different Protestant creeds this principle has been embodied. It is expressed in different ways; the tone is either milder or severer, but in reality there is no difference. The Second Helvetian Confession and the Westminster Confession, which go farthest, have spread most. As a matter of fact the question of the persecution of heretics in the Protestant world was not finally settled till the eighteenth century and in consequence of the Revolution. However, the abolition of this persecution was not the consequence of the revolutionary principle, for this rigid dogma had to give way to the idea of the Reformation, which has liberty of conscience for its motto, and does not suffer any man to have power over the conscience of another. Did not the Protestants of the seventeenth century fight for liberty of conscience? Who can deny this? They fought and suffered for this sacred principle, but while they respected liberty of conscience, they called liberty of worship into question. That was not all; they did not dare grant liberty of speech. This was the error, it was the error of the age, and Calvin, the father of the French Reformation, was the son of that age.

Chapter XXIV

STRUGGLE AND VICTORY

IN the autumn of the year 1553 Calvin had maintained his ground at St. Peter's in Geneva by his splendid courage at the celebration of the Lord's Supper; peace and quiet would have prevailed within the walls of Geneva if Philibert Berthelier and his followers had wished it. The Church Council requested him to acknowledge the serious and rightful grievances against him and, confessing himself guilty, to return to Christ. But Berthelier could not be induced to do this; his obdurate patrician mind objected to stooping to people whom he considered as intruders, and the weather-wise forecast a hurricane. Alas! It was so. It began with rows at inns, noisy, improper songs in the street, irregularities, and provoking violations of the regulations. Some ringleaders were arrested, but it was no good. Their friends visited them and turned the jail into a ballroom. The cause of the Libertines was brought before the people. They began to wonder how it was possible that Frenchmen, foreigners in Geneva, held the reins, and if it were not high time to stem the tide of foreigners. What was that Farel but a foreigner? And Calvin, who was at the head of the town, or at least imagined himself to be so, had not even been admitted as a citizen of the town (Calvin later became a citizen, in 1559). They complained that a lot of shabby people, the scum of Europe, crowded into the town, and that the famous Geneva of old would go to rack and ruin, if the national conscience of the children of Geneva did not sweep this miserable lot from the streets. This was, of course, malicious exaggeration. To be sure, there was chaff amongst the wheat. But more wheat than chaff, and Calvin did his utmost to free Geneva from impure elements. The noblest inhabitants of France flocked to it. Geneva was their place of refuge, their Pella, the cave of Adullam for all the oppressed. It even became their country, as their old country rejected them, and it may be questioned whether history shows another example of such a speedy and complete fusion of nationalities. They found no favour in the eyes of the Libertines, as they were allies of Calvin, whereas their praises would have been sung if they had assisted in unhorsing him. However, they refused to do so, for Calvin was their leader, their protector, their father — his name had been engraved on their minds, never to be erased. They knew Calvin as a child knows its father, and Calvin knew them; but the Libertines did not know them, as their hatred blinded their eyes. Without any emotion, quite insensible and unmoved, without a shade of pity or compassion, they passed these fugitives. That was not all. If the fugitives were poor, they were reproached with taking the bread out of the mouth of the poor in Geneva; if they tried to find work, the employers were set against them; if they came with money, they were scorned like traitors, who had come to Geneva to bribe its burghers. Sneers and jeers were lavished on these refugees, and this wrung Calvin's heart. "They shamefully despise the exiles of Christ!" he exclaimed in his bitter indignation. He seemed to have triumphed, but then the demon powers reappeared like a black tidal wave, threatening to wash away his life's work. He was accused, in consequence of his doctrines, of considering God as the author of sin. Castellio, the ambitious rebel, who had been banished from Geneva for calumny, harassed the Reformer from Basel with his fiercest Pelagian arrows, as Albert Pighius, the well-known Roman Catholic theologian and violent defender of free-will, had done in former times from Kampen in the Netherlands, while Bolsec, the former Carmelite monk, spread nonsensical ideas about the doctrine of Predestination. There were moments of great despair, in which Calvin cried out, like Elijah on Mount Horeb: "It is enough, receive my soul, that I may die!" The Reformer uttered such-like words, and, tortured by his enemies, vexed and teased like a horse by a swarm of hornets, he envied more than once his brethren who went to the stake calmly and triumphantly as if they were entering a banqueting hall. To be burnt by the Papists, that was only a short pain, and then the end. What could bind him to this life of sorrow? Idelette had been the star shining on his sombre life and making it bright by her loveliness. But Idelette was in her grave, and he had been left at his solitary post. It was a miracle that he did not lose his mind and had not to be locked up in a madhouse.

"One thing makes me persevere in my hard struggle," he wrote to an intimate friend, "that I shall soon be released by death."

If he appeared in the street he was hissed at. When he heard his name called out and looked around, people said: "We only mean our dog!" Calvin's name was given to dogs to make him despicable in the eyes of the public, and when he passed the Libertines, they said: "Cain! How are you, Cain?"

One day, fatigued with preaching, he came from the upper town; on the bridge he met three persons, who molested him and evidently wanted to knock him down. The day before, Perrin's wife had succeeded in running over another preacher, and this man nearly lost his life. This was the lot of Calvin who was called the King of Geneva, and who, when at work in the evening, was startled by knocks at the windows and the door, by shameful cries of derision. This was not all. Half drunken creatures held mock-processions with burning candles, through the town, bawling disgraceful parodies on the Psalms and quite laughing at the idea of being arrested. They caused riots, startled quiet burghers, and declared that the end of the Calvinistic tyranny had come. Perrin, who had once awakened such great expectations, seemed to be incited by the evil one. He proposed depriving the emigrants of all arms except their daggers, and this was acceded to. However, the next year he proposed taking away their daggers; a grievous insult, which Perrin made the more grievous by declaring that these foreigners had plotted to betray the town into the hands of the French king, Henry II. He pretended to have heard this on good authority. The king himself had said it in a letter, written to the Council of Bern. The fugitives were astounded at this monstrous accusation; but in the Council of Two Hundred, Burgomaster Lambert rose up full of indignation, as their defender and protector of their reputation. Lambert could venture to say more than the others, for his brother had perished as a hero at the stake of Chambéry. "Mr. Perrin!" he said, "don't you feel how absurd your accusation is? Are you such a fool as not to understand that the emigrants despise the man who murders their brethren and who will not spare them, if he lays hands on them? Besides, I greatly wonder why you should come with this accusation. You used to be less anxious about the safety of this town; seven years ago you did not mind helping to provide it with a French garrison!"

The burgomaster had more to say. He stated that the town had everything to gain and nothing to lose, if these true, honest burghers were admitted to the freedom of the town. They had admitted not more than fifty during the last five years; he strongly advised the Council to be more liberal on this point. The burgomaster's speech was successful; during the first months of 1555 sixty immigrants were admitted to the freedom of the town. At the same time the Council understood that the discipline, exerted by the Church, ought to remain in their hands. And they were convinced of this by a speech, made for them by Calvin, who, with the Holy Scriptures in his hand, clearly showed that public authorities had no more right to meddle with Church matters than the Church had to meddle with the rights of the State. The change of front in the Council acted like oil on the Libertine fire. It was especially the preachers whom they hated. The enemy did not understand what was the use of all this preaching and Bible-reading and catechism classes — what good came of them? Two preachers were more than enough for Geneva, and the others had better be dismissed. Some riots took place; rebellious fishermen and skippers armed themselves and appeared in the town hall to let the Council hear their threats — within four days three demonstrations took place before the town hall. This was the crisis; and Calvin wrote to Farel: "Remember this poor town in your prayers!"

One peaceful evening in May, the leaders of the Libertines put their heads together. Perrin and Berthelier were present at the meeting; they had a good glass of wine, and Perrin had the honour to be put at the head of the rebellion.

Berthelier was not so muddled as to be blind to the risk he ran if they should fail. He was not so sure of the victory, and would rather have gone home to bed. However, it was difficult to go back now; he had already gone too far. The cup was handed around once more, and then he firmly put himself at the head of a crowd of people, who were to save Geneva from the hands of the foreigners. "Away with the French!" was their motto. The burghers, sitting on the doorsteps under the sloping roofs, fled into their houses and bolted their doors, but the burgomaster, who was at the head of the watch that night, met the agitators calmly and warned them to go home. Go home — they had something else to do! Perrin snatched away the staff, the symbol of the official's authority; the watch was pushed aside and the cry of murder: "Kill them, kill them!" resounded in the streets. However, the bold enterprise came to a miserable end. The sons of Geneva, whose help had been called in, did not move, as they would have nothing to do with these ringleaders; the watch was reinforced, they scoured the streets and arrested whomever they could catch. The next morning the town had resumed its usual appearance, the rebellion had been nothing but a farce, and the shopkeeper laughed at it behind the counter when serving his customers. However, the Council did not laugh. For them it was painfully true, that they had to punish the rioters according to the strictest laws, and they wanted to show that the authorities, according to St. Paul, did not wear the sword in vain.

The sentence for Philibert Berthelier was as follows;

"We, burgomasters and councils of Geneva, make known, that on the 6th of June, 1555, the present sentence pronounced upon Philibert Berthelier and his accomplices has been publicly announced by sound of trumpets, and this on account of their detestable, shameful plot against the existing Church and against the town, as well as against the order and peace of the burghers. The above-mentioned Philibert Berthelier, one of the conspirators and an enemy of the town and its peace, has been condemned to be taken to Champel Hill and there beheaded. His body to be quartered and exhibited in four places in the vicinity of the town, as a warning to others who might commit a similar crime in the future.
"Thus signed by us."

Berthelier and Perrin, who were both condemned to death, had fled meanwhile, and Berthelier's brother, together with two other demagogues, had to pay the piper. They mounted the gloomy scaffold, the executioner's sword glittered, and their heads fell as sacrifices for the agitations of a party which had fought to the death against Calvin for eighteen years. Thus Calvin had gained the victory. Calvin the Reformer! Calvin the Victor! No, Calvin's ghost would arise from his grave, if we called him Victor. He never sought his own honour; his greatest honour was to serve; he had reached the zenith of his joy, when Geneva was the awe-inspiring scene of Christ the Victor.

And Calvin, who had compared himself with David without fear, in the introduction to his commentary on the Psalms, had now got rid of all his enemies.

Chapter XXV

THE TRIUMPH OF THE GOSPEL

REST? That was a word not to be found in Calvin's vocabulary. For forty years he wore the harness, and he was to die in it. For him rest only meant a change of battle-ground; if the centre was attacked less forcibly, he rushed to the threatened side-wings; and to France, which had driven him from its threshold like a leper, he particularly devoted his cares and prayers. Persecutions were again taking place in Protestant France; the smoke of the stake was rising to the blue sunny sky; the sufferings and death of the "five prisoners of Lyons," as they are called in the chronicles of the martyrs, filled the hearts of the Evangelicals with grief and melancholy joy. They were five youths, students at Lausanne, well known to Calvin, Beza, and Viret, who betook themselves to the south of France to sow the seed of the Gospel, followed by the prayers of the congregation. They were treacherously arrested in Lyons, brought before the judges and condemned. The sentence caused great dismay in Switzerland; the Government offered its mediation; Calvin did his utmost to save the five proclaimers of the word of the Lord. However, it was in vain; the sentence of death was signed, and Calvin, who could not save their lives, now, in his letters, gave them strength to face death. He wrote, with tears in his eyes: "Your fetters have become famous, the tidings of your death will resound far and wide, in spite of Satan, and to the glory of our Lord." In this way he wrote; firmly though deeply moved, constant in his courage and faith, himself prepared to sacrifice his body to God in the fire at the stake. In the lovely month of May, when everything breathes peace and quiet, the five martyrs, in ash-coloured clothes and bound with strong ropes, mounted the dungcart which was to convey them to the place of execution. It was a curious procession; the executioners with their rigid faces, the clangorous soldiers, the priests in their black garments, pointing to the condemned and calling out to the people: "That is right — firewood for hell!"

while the martyrs, not forsaken by the Saviour, resolutely sang
Psalm 9:

> *With all my heart I thank Thee, LORD,*
> *Thy wondrous deeds I will record.*
> *Thou art my joy, in Thee I'll glory.*
> *With psalms, Most High, I will adore Thee.* [27]

They mounted the stake full of courage; the youngest first,
while Martial Alba, the oldest, came last. He embraced his
comrades, one by one, saying: "Farewell, Brother!" And they
consoled each other by saying that their sufferings would soon be
over. The fire was lit, and from the flames their voices were heard
exclaiming: "Courage, brothers, courage!" Then the columns of
smoke rose up; the flames sparkled, and it was over. From his
dungeon in Rouen, Richard Le Fèvre wrote to Calvin: "I am writing
this to tell you that at Pentecost I hope to have entered the kingdom
of heaven, and to be seated at the banquet of the Son of God, if I
am not called before by our beloved Master." However, Le Fèvre
was mistaken. At Pentecost he was still on earth. It was not before
July 7, 1553, that the stake was prepared to convey the soul of this
holy martyr to heaven on the wings of the flames. While black
thunderstorms threatened to come down in France, the sky had
cleared on the other side of the Channel. Henry VIII had been
gathered to his fathers in Westminster Abbey in 1546, and with
him had sunk into the grave a religion which could only be confused
with the real work of the Reformation through bad faith or through
narrow-mindedness, Edward VI was only nine years of age when
the king died; the Duke of Somerset took up the reins of power as
regent, and issued a proclamation containing the application of the
true, pure Christian doctrines to the whole nation. England was
closely connected with Geneva in those days through Calvin, who
dedicated his exposition of the first Epistle to Timothy to the Duke.
In this serious crisis the Duke asked Calvin's advice, and Calvin
wrote the remarkable letter, in which he set forth his opinions as to
the course which the Reformation in England ought to adopt. It
was a far-reaching programme of action laid before the Duke by

---

[27] Psalm 9:1 (*Book of Praise*).

the Reformer; he proposed to turn England into a Geneva on a large scale, and he wished to see public authority used as a sword to gain the victory for the Gospel. It was this idea which had brought Servet to the stake and which suffered no heresy; which wondered if crimes committed against men should be punished and greater crimes against God should be left unpunished; it was the law of Justinian come into force again. The Regent agreed with the programme and would have had it made into a constitutional law without any delay, if political interests and religious hate had not caused him to fall into disgrace. It is true, the Duke's honour was restored, but he was to fall a victim to shameful intrigues a second time. Then the moment came when he had to work out another programme of Calvin's by resolutely climbing the steps of the scaffold. Without any hesitation he fulfilled this task, and dying as a martyr, he was mourned for by a young king, in whose name he was murdered. Edward VI had noble principles and a warm heart, and his excellent abilities gave rise to the greatest expectations. He had broad views; in every respect he had freed himself from the fatal ideas of justice which had prevailed for eleven centuries, and it was only after a long and persistent refusal that he had been induced to sign the death-warrant of a woman, who had denied the incarnation of the Son of God. The young king was burning with holy zeal for the Reformation, and his accession was quite a relief after the rule of a king, who had his wives beheaded in order to marry others, and who respected neither divine nor human laws in his kingdom, but only the law of his own will. Edward VI was fourteen when the Reformer of Geneva dedicated two of his works to him: the exposition of Isaiah and that of the Epistles. This dedication had nothing to do with flattery. Nothing was more repugnant to Calvin than slavish homage even to a crowned king. Calvin knew that these Commentaries were well adapted to the quick understanding and the shrewd intelligence of the king, and that they were suitable food for a prince who hungered after righteousness. Were not his tutors themselves astonished at the progress made by their royal pupil? Had not he a burning desire for knowledge? Did not he make a Reformation plan himself at that time — all unaided — in the form of a dialogue, showing his practical as well as his gifted genius? Des Gallars, a clergyman, handed the two dedications of Calvin to King Edward in London. They were accompanied by a letter, written by Calvin, in which he referred to what, in his opinion, ought to be done to complete the blessed work of the Reformation in England. The tone of this letter was simple — he spoke to a king by the grace of God, but between the lines one could read the tenderness of a friend, of a spiritual father, and Edward received this letter as a respectful greeting from a spiritual king.

As a token of his veneration Edward sent Calvin a costly present, and Calvin, in whose thoughts England was uppermost, answered with a short exposition of the eighty-seventh Psalm. His homage to the king consisted in a warning not to forget the kingdom of heaven, his love in a reminder, that a true Christian is above a crowned king. Then combining king and Christian he continued: "Sire! It is an invaluable blessing that God has called you to be a Christian king!"

Not only with the king, but also with him who was the king's right-hand — Archbishop Cranmer — Calvin kept up an earnest and far-reaching correspondence. The hand of the tyrant, called Henry VIII, had rested likc lead on the shoulders of Cranmer, but the hope of seeing the English people one day refreshed by the living waters of the true Reformation had never left him. With this young, energetic king by his side he dreamt, in his enthusiasm, of a mighty union combining all the Protestant Churches. "Close your ranks," was the watchword heard from Rome, and Cranmer wondered if the time had not come for the Protestants to do the same. The Roman Catholics had their Council of Trent — why were no means devised to hold a Protestant Council as a stronghold against the other?

With the vehemence of a Protestant of the sixteenth century he wrote about this ideal to Calvin. And charmed with the grandeur of this plan, with which he entirely agreed, Calvin replied that he should not mind crossing ten oceans, if need be, to attend such a glorious Protestant meeting. Edward VI! Calvin's heart began to beat when he heard his name. Never did he find a king more eager to build the walls of Zion and pull down the kingdom of Satan. But what Calvin experienced a hundred, no a thousand times, happened again — his hope was nipped in the bud. When the young king ascended the throne he was already doomed to an early death, phthisis undermined his precious life, and he was not yet sixteen years old when he entered the kingdom of heaven, about which Calvin had written to him with so much eloquence. "This is the end of Protestantism!" said the Roman Catholics in England in exultation, and Bloody Mary, who succeeded her half-brother,[28] did everything in her power to realise this prophecy. Queen Mary's childhood had been without any joy. Educated in the strict ceremonies of the Roman Catholic faith by her mother, she had from infancy hated the Protestant heresies, and her father, Henry VIII, who had driven her mother from the throne so unjustly. Thirsting for revenge she ascended the throne. It is true she had promised not to make any change in religious matters; but no sooner did she hold the reins of power than this promise was forgotten. She prohibited the vernacular in divine service; she dismissed all married priests and left them to their fate with wife and children, bereft of everything.

Cranmer was thrown into a damp dungeon, and so great was his fear of the queen, that he denied his faith to save his life. But though he forsook his Saviour — Christ did not forsake him. With a bleeding heart he bewailed his fall; he recanted, and, led to the stake, he held his right hand in the flame first, because this hand had signed the abjuration. A long cry of anguish arose, England was plunged into sorrow, and the heart of the English people was greatly embittered. Yet the queen was inexorable, she had sworn that she would destroy Protestantism root and branch, and in her zeal she was so indomitable, that even the Pope and Charles V were alarmed at her ardour. The tables were turned. Edward VI had prepared in his country a hospitable Pella for the French brothers in the faith, driven from their country by the Roman Catholic fury, now England was turned into a shambles, and a number of English fugitives betook themselves to Geneva, there to find shelter till the storm was over.

---

[28] The author omits that the seventeen-year-old Lady Jane Grey was Queen for nine days between Edward VI & Bloody Mary. Her moving story is told in one of the best historical novels ever written: *Coronation of Glory* by Deborah Meroff. The second edition is available from Inheritance Publications. —Editor.

In this way the bond between England and the town of Geneva became stronger and closer than ever. The name of the great Reformer sanctioned it, the Church of England got its Calvinistic stamp, and with Queen Elizabeth, who succeeded Bloody Mary, the persecutions came to an end. To this queen Calvin dedicated his exposition of the prophet Isaiah, but the queen never accepted the dedication. Had the Reformer vexed her? Was she annoyed at what he had once said: "Women-rulers are less desirable"? Indeed, she was, and Queen Elizabeth never forgot these words. How splendidly did she refute them in her long, magnificent reign! When her mother, Anne Boleyn, showed her when a baby to Henry VIII, he angrily stamped his foot on the ground and cried with a scornful laugh: "A daughter! What is a daughter to me!" Yet his daughter was worth ten sons, and this queen became the founder of England's greatness. What Calvin had said about women-rulers, John Knox repeated in his sharp way and thus incurred the hatred of two queens. One has already been mentioned, the other was Mary Queen of Scots. It is said of this Scottish queen, that nobody could behold her without admiration or love, and that nobody could read the history of her life and death without grief and sorrow. She, the daughter of the rough mountains of the North, grew up at the wanton Court of France and was educated in the strict Roman Catholic faith. She was as frivolous as she was charming, noble-hearted, but at the same time capricious and hot-tempered.

John Knox was her powerful opponent. He had proclaimed the word of the Lord at St. Andrews, when this fortress was surrendered to the French. He was sent to the gallows and sighed in slavery for two years; then he regained his liberty. Knox was the spiritual son of Calvin, and the living link between Scotland and Geneva. He was already fifty when he made Calvin's acquaintance and came under his influence. He went farther than Calvin; he made heroes, not martyrs, of the Church, and traversed Scotland like a Protestant crusader, Bible in hand and sword girded on. The queen trembled before this powerful man. He told her frankly that Christians have a right to rebel, if they are hindered in their religious ceremonies. This was a thesis never defended, but always refuted by Calvin, but Queen Mary did not know the Bible as well as Calvin, and she had to give way to the Scottish Reformer, who compared persecutors to madmen requiring a strait-waistcoat, that they might not trouble anyone. He wished that she might one day become the Deborah of Scotland, but this was a figure of speech she did not understand, and bitter tears of vexation streamed from her eyes, as all her threats fell powerless before his granite forehead. Knox was a man of steel; hard, inexorable, the harnessed "beggar" among the warlike Scots. More than once he went to Geneva; there he saw the triumph of the Gospel after the fall of the Libertines, and exclaimed in exultation: "Since the days of the Apostles the earth has not beheld such scenes!" It was an amazing fate that brought the daughter of wealth and cultivation face to face with this Elijah of the Reformation. She had been hospitably received by the stubborn Scots, though they were averse to her faith, and they would have remained faithful to her, if her frivolity and the wanton dancing at her Court had not roused the indignation of the Puritans. Knox made the churches resound with his severe sermons, and he inserted in the prayers of the service these words: "Enlighten, O Lord, the heart of the Queen — if it pleases Thee!" Knox did not spare anybody; he was an iconoclast, an opponent of the nobility, hard, rough, and upright in his virtues as well as in his faults a giant, kneeling before God but rising like an eagle before man. On his tombstone has been rightly written: "Here lies the man who never bowed to the face of man." Ardent preachers from the south of France brought Calvinism to the Netherlands — we have been taught so — history books tell us so. However, a famous historian (Dr. F.L. Rutgers) has discovered that these ardent preachers only existed in the imagination of historians, and that, on the contrary, there would be something to say for the supposition, that Dutch preachers went to preach Calvinism in some places of France. The Dutch had an aversion to France, and this national trait also appeared among the Dutch Protestants. France was their sworn enemy, with whom their people had fought so many a hard fight, and though Condé and De Coligny wished to annex their country in order to secure them liberty of conscience, they flatly refused to accept this proposal. This suspicion of everything coming from France was so deep-rooted that Franciscus Junius, a clergyman in Antwerp, who had come from France, was strongly suspected, in spite of his excellent gifts and noble character, as the congregation in their teacher only saw the Frenchman, and it took them a long time to forget his nationality. That Calvin took a great interest in the religious movement in the Netherlands need not be mentioned, and that he made the acquaintance of a great many Netherlanders is without doubt. He must have met Petrus Dathenus, when this remarkable man was preaching in Frankfort; Marnix of St. Aldegonde and his brother attended Calvin's lectures in Geneva, a great many Anabaptists and Libertines, who lived in great numbers in the Netherlands for a long time, became acquainted with Calvin's doctrines. The Reformer did not speak Dutch, but neither did the German Emperor, Charles V, understand German. Charles could not understand his own subjects and had to call in the aid of his Chancellor, Cardinal Granvelle, to translate the German correspondence into French. French was heard far beyond the French frontiers; it was Calvin's native tongue, while he had a perfect command of Latin, the universal language of scholars and educated burghers. Farel did not like the Southern Netherlanders, he called them unsteady and unreliable, but Calvin knew them better, and in his work, *On Vexations*, he highly praised the courageous contempt of death shown by the martyrs of Flanders and Artois. No French preachers, but Calvin himself, influenced the Dutch people. This influence was not sought for by Calvin; his work had soon got known here.

What by the grace of God distinguished him particularly: the absolute acknowledgment of the Sovereignty of God, the implicit obedience to the Holy Scriptures, the profundity of faith, the clearness of his doctrines and their unlimited application to life — all this appealed especially to the Dutch. The characteristic quality of the Dutch Reformation, as far as this can be mentioned, is not the religious superficiality of Humanism, not the sober intellectuality of Zwinglianism, not the inertia of Church conservatism, neither the licentiousness of Anabaptism or Libertinism, but, above all, the doctrine embodied in Calvinism, in the profound comprehensive sense of the word. In various ways and by various means, God at the same time brought together and united His Church in the Netherlands and His servant in Geneva.

Chapter XXVI

FROM THE THRONE TO THE MONK'S CELL

DOUBTLESS Calvin's attention was drawn to the Netherlands and to Brussels in October of the year 1555. In the lively capital of Brabant, the States General of the seventeen Provinces had assembled; the Emperor Charles V was there, so was his son, Philip II, the sombre king with his sickly face, whose name is written with bloody letters in Dutch history. It was a brilliant meeting in the Palace at Brussels. There were the chief magistrates in their robes and chains of office; the knights of the Golden Fleece in their glittering armoury, the flower of Dutch nobility. The Emperor had visibly aged, the peace of Passau had turned his light hair into snowy white. He had to lean on a wooden crutch for support; his hands, ankles, and knees were stiff with gout; this man of fifty-five looked like an old, decrepit man — only from his dark blue eyes there flashed at times both pride and majesty. The royal personages: the Emperor, his sister, the Governess Mary, and Philip II, were seated under the canopy. Then the Emperor rose slowly, leaning on the shoulder of a young man, who afterward got the name of William the Silent. Leaning on the shoulder of William of Nassau, the Prince of Orange, Charles V gave a short survey of the thirty-eight years of his reign. He described his campaigns, nine in Germany, six in Spain, seven in Italy, four in France, ten in the Netherlands, two in England, and two in Africa. He mentioned eleven sea-voyages, his victories and peace negotiations, and tried to convince his audience of his arduous endeavours to promote the welfare of his subjects and the defence of the Roman Catholic faith. The Netherlanders had experienced that he had defended the Roman Catholic faith. Most severely had he treated the Reformation in these provinces. He had intended to exterminate the heresies by his sharp placards, he had threatened to behead the men, to bury the women alive, if they did not return to the pale of the mother-church. Luther's and Calvin's writings were forbidden on pain of death, and the placards became more and more severe. But had this availed? Had not the sacred fire, purging the hearts of the martyrs, proved stronger than the fire consuming their bodies? Psalms had ascended from the flames, and the blood of the martyrs had become the seed of the Church. Charles V had instituted the Inquisition; the martyr, Jan de Bakker, was the first of the long series of martyrs, estimated at 50,000 in these provinces. However, Charles V was not what Philip II became, a bloodthirsty zealot. His politics influenced his religion. Among his regiments some were Protestant; they had their own preachers, who followed the Imperial Standard to the Netherlands, and, unpunished, spread a faith which, if believed in by the Netherlanders, threatened them with death. The Emperor was more opposed to Calvinism with its ideal of liberty than to the Protestantism of the German princes; and he had a number of stakes erected in the Netherlands at the same time that the German religious liberty was secured by the peace of Passau. The Roman Catholics in the Netherlands greatly wondered at his inexplicable resignation to this peace, and they could not make out the man, who, if he had been an ardent supporter of the Pope, would have risked his last soldier to annul the peace of Passau. As has been stated before, he was not a zealot, and his stadtholdership influenced his religion. Indeed, he had not forgotten that his army had once plundered Rome, and that he had even ventured to attack the Pope. Therefore, his hatred of Calvinism was as much political as religious; he considered Calvinists as people, in whose blood ran the desire for political liberty, and he had tried to crush both heresies at one blow. But was Charles V then like Philip II? Did he take a cruel delight in torturing subjects, whose way of serving God was different from his! Let us be impartial and not forget that the Emperor lived in a time when religious liberty was considered a monstrous folly, and that he had sworn to defend the Roman Catholic religion. He had not only promised to do this, but sworn it. Besides he was reminded not only by the clergy, but also by many nobles, that an Emperor by the grace of God was bound to keep the oath sworn to defend the Church of God. He was also aware of the terrible scenes resulting from the sinful degeneration of the Reformation. At the Imperial Court the errors of the Anabaptists were well known. The Anabaptists, as numerous as mushrooms in the Netherlands, were turbulent and restless by nature; the revolutionary blood ran through their veins, and they frightened the quiet burgher, while they put the Reformation in a most unfavourable light. The notorious Jan Beukelszoon, of Leyden, maintained that he could do more than cutting, which he had learned as tailor. He called himself King of Zion, and became one of the ringleaders of the sect, who considered themselves as the chosen people of the Lord, who were to bring the millennium on earth. They betook themselves to Munster to give loose reins to their passions and carnal appetites, till the town was taken by storm, a terrible judgment passed, and Jan of Leyden was pinched to death with red-hot tongs. These facts, however, did not prevent Charles V from treating the Protestants in the Netherlands most mercilessly. Chivalrousness was unknown to this chevalier; mercy was ignored by this Christian Emperor. He was a mean, untrustworthy, cunning man; he deceived his enemies by taking advantage of their trust in his promises; he had the unfortunate Elector, John Frederick of Saxony, led about like a bear with a chain, and there were but a few moments in his life in which his human feelings prevailed. He was bent on extending his territory and spent millions on increasing the splendour of his realm.

However, in small things he was most thrifty; the soldier who brought him the sword and the iron gloves of Francis I, was sent off with a hundred crowns, while a sum of ten thousand crowns would not, indeed, have been too great for such a capture. The three soldiers who swam across the Elbe with a sword between their teeth to procure him the boats for the victory of Mühlberg, were rewarded with a jacket and four crowns — that was all. No, not all — they each got a pair of stockings besides. At that price Charles V bought a whole electorate, and he smiled with pleasure like a merchant driving a good bargain. This battle of Mühlberg was not a thing to be smiled at by the Dutch Calvinists. Like Calvin, they turned away with disgust from Maurice of Saxony, who betrayed the cause of Protestantism by taking the side of the Emperor. They were not reconciled to him before he had made another change of front, humiliated the Emperor and saved German Protestantism. It was even prohibited to mention the peace of Passau in the Netherlands, where it was looked upon as high treason. It is the more to be wondered at, that the Emperor met with so much affection and sympathy in these provinces. On the other hand, it must be remembered that he had a special gift of making himself agreeable. He who went to Africa, because Europe was too small for his ambition, also rode to the ring with the Flemish nobles, shot at the popinjay with the cross-bow at Antwerp, drank beer with the Flemish peasants, and amused them with Flemish jokes. These things the States General remembered, when he abdicated. Besides they were moved by his helplessness, and the Emperor himself, affected by this sad and solemn moment, spoke in an unusually touching way.

Then he turned to his son. He pointed out to the young prince that the brilliant realm, over which he was to sway his sceptre, would abundantly pay the debt of gratitude, if his reign should be distinguished by a wise and loving care of his subjects. Prosperity would approve of his abdication, if his son proved himself worthy of his goodness, and this would happen, if he kept the laws and defended the Roman Catholic faith. Finally, he addressed the States General. He admonished them to be loyal to their new monarch and to maintain their union; he besought them to forgive all his errors and offences, assuring them that he would remember their obedience and affection in every prayer to the Supreme Being, to Whom he was going to devote the rest of his life. Never had the Emperor spoken in such a touching way. He was weeping, all were deeply moved, from all corners of the large hall sobs were heard. At this solemn moment the Netherlanders forgave their monarch his crimes; the broken privileges, the placards, the strangling poles, and the fires of the martyrs — all were forgiven. Had not he killed their bodies to save their souls? At this last supreme moment they thought that they heard the beating of a father's heart in his voice. Philip threw himself at the Emperor's feet; the Emperor wept, so did his son. These tears were real, they were the last ever shed by Philip. While Charles, the persecutor, departed to bury himself within the sombre walls of a Spanish cloister, Philip, the executor, came forward to burn out in the Netherlands the Calvinistic heresies as a wasp's nest is burnt out. The threatening thunderclouds gathered on the horizon; the reports which reached Cannon Street at Geneva became most ominous, and the first flashes of lightning announced like flaming heralds, the terrible Eighty Years' War.

Chapter XXVII

THE GREAT MASTER

WHAT are we, when we think of Calvin's work and energy? He was very weak, spat blood, and suffered from unbearable headaches. He suffered more than most people; fevers undermined his strength; a harsh letter, a bitter word, could shock his very soul. In spite of this he surpassed all his contemporaries in working-power; he turned the night into day to finish his gigantic tasks; he dragged himself to the pulpit, even though excruciating rheumatic pains racked his body; and sinking down in a chair, exhausted and dead-tired, he still complained of laziness and indolence. A gigantic task was resting on his shoulders in Geneva. He was a preacher, a teacher, and a pastor, as well as the attorney-general of the Protestants; his house was an information-office; it was the great centre of attraction for foreigners, who were con-sidered as guests. He was unsalaried Minister of the Interior, while the very hand, which wrote to kings and electors, directed words of consolation to a humble labourer, persecuted for his faith, and the powerful author of the *Institution* managed to find time, in spite of his endless troubles, to procure good posts for God-fearing servants and to help young

Calvin's chair in the pulpit of the St. Peter's Church

people in getting married. Everybody depended on him; he was everybody's adviser; the Marquis of Vice, who lived in St. Peter's Square, knew everything about it.

Galeas Caraccioli, Marquis of Vice — everybody in Geneva knew him. Foreigners, fugitives, wanderers coming from the South, asked for him, and they were told: "Oh, the Marquis of Vice, the Reformed Elder of the Italian colony — he lives there!" He was a Reformed Elder, and his uncle was Pope in Rome — similar relations occurred more than once, in a time when the Reformation inexorably separated the son from his father, the husband from his wife. In the gloomy dungeons, on the instruments of torture, on the scaffolds, much was suffered, but this breaking up of families severing the tenderest ties of love was worse. It was exceedingly deplorable; from the sixteenth century, the century of the Reformation, a sharp cry of pain resounds through all ages. The Marquis of Vice, the celebrated man, belonging to a family counting twelve principalities in its two branches, drank the bitter cup to the last drop. Like a long, glorious summer's day, life lay before the marquis when he married an enormously rich duke's daughter, at the age of twenty. He seemed to be fortune's favourite; the Emperor Charles V appointed him Chancellor; honour, respect, fame greeted him everywhere, his wife and children were the glory of his marriage, and many a one envied the knight, as brave as he was amiable. Then one day a Spaniard came sowing the first seeds of discord in this happy household, to proclaim frankly with the resoluteness of a Luther and the ingeniousness of a Calvin, the doctrine of vindication through faith only. Ochino, the Capuchin, followed, while Petrus Martyr, the great theologian, developed the same ideas in his lectures. Before the marquis had been married five years, the seed of the Gospel took root in his soul. On a journey to Germany afterward his conversion was completed, and he returned to Italy to say for ever farewell to his family, who refused to renounce the Roman Catholic faith, in which they had been brought up. He staggered as if intoxicated under the heavy burden, which his weak shoulders had to bear. That he would have to leave his sunny country, his posts of honour, his palace, a glorious future, was hard; but, what was the lack of all this compared with the loss of an old father, whose pride he was, to the loss of a wife, whose

soul was united with his by strong, fervent love, to the loss of the
nine children, who were as dear to him as the apples of his eyes!

His wife met him with the baby in her arms. His heart seemed
to fail him, but he departed. The marquis came to Geneva on a
summer's day. The Reformation had inexorably got hold of him,
and there he was — a poor, wretched man, who had left his joy in
life behind in the sunny South . . . Did the reformers receive him
with sympathy and compassion? Did they offer the lonely man the
cup of brotherly consolation? The answer may be read in the dry
returns of the Geneva Town Council. It says in the registers that
the marquis was admitted on condition that he would behave in
submission to the others, and that they would keep an eye on his
movements. No consolation awaited him but suspicion, they were
not quite sure that he was not a spy, and so the former Chancellor
of Charles V was put under supervision of the police. Where could
the wretched man pour out his heart? Where else than in the cave
of Adullam opening into Cannon Street! So the marquis came to
Calvin, and here he found consolation. Calvin was his friend, his
protector, and did not think it beneath him to declare that his own
faith had been strengthened by the striking example of this Italian.
Meanwhile the departure of the marquis from Naples had roused
great agitation in his native town. His father immediately sent after
him, and a member of the family found the lost man in Geneva and
sent word to Naples that the marquis was living in a lowly, simple
dwelling. Everything that this messenger, a cousin of the marquis,
could do to make him return he did. With tears in his eyes he
described the state of despair, into which the marquis had plunged
his family: the grief of his old father and the despair of his wife.
The fugitive was deeply moved, but he persevered in his decision
to live in liberty of conscience, and his cousin had to go back without
having effected his purpose. Then his father summoned him to
Mantua, informing him that he had found for him a place of refuge
on Venetian territory, where he could freely profess his faith. The
marquis hesitated; but the consideration, that the proposal was a
favour from the Roman Catholic Church, induced him to decline.
Then his wife requested to see him, and the marquis came to Vico
to embrace those who were dearest to him on earth, after a seven
years' absence. They saw each other to say farewell for ever; this

they knew, for his wife was as firmly resolved to remain faithful to the Roman Catholic Church as he was to cling to his Evangelical faith. The hands of this husband and wife were clasped, they looked into each other's eyes full of woe and love, and yet they were separated by a terrible abyss. To take leave of his old father was hard, but to take leave of his wife and children was harder. They would not let him go, they followed him into the hall, and his wife implored him to have pity on her for love's sake. All were weeping: the cousin who had seen him in Geneva, and the marquis himself. A pretty girl of twelve clasped his knees and sobbed: "Father — do stay with us!" All the little hands kept him back, it was a scene to melt stones into tears. Yet the marquis departed without looking back, his heart torn with the bitterest grief. When he had returned to Geneva, he made up his mind to be divorced from his wife. Then both would be free — he and his wife.

It was Calvin again who had to give advice, and Calvin sat down to write to the marchioness. He shrank from advising a divorce, and tried to find a way to secure liberty of conscience for the marquis and at the same time the happiness of domestic peace. This way he found by proposing to the marchioness to come and live in a free and neutral place, where they could each serve the Lord according to their conscience. Thus the matter would be solved in the most satisfactory manner. It seemed a little like the proposal which the marquis had declined, but this was not really the case, for now he would claim as a right what was formerly allowed him as a favour. However, the confessors of the marchioness were harder hearted than Calvin; under their strong influence she declined, and a divorce was the mournful solution. The marquis married again. Michel Cop conducted the wedding service at St. Peter's. The marquis set up his household according to his modest means; his clothes were plain and simple. Yet he was constantly visited in his lowly dwelling by the most substantial citizens, not as an indigent man, but as a prince in the audience-hall of his palace. He no longer bore the title of marquis, yet he was saluted with the respect due to his former rank, and the people of Geneva called him the marquis. Never was a more faithful Reformed Elder. He not only strengthened Calvin in his belief, but the whole congregation in theirs; he was a true overseer; he constantly paid pastoral visitations. He visited the poor and saved a little of his small income to relieve their needs; he was to be found at their beds, when they were ill or dying. Through his amiability and sincerity he overcame the suspicion of the Council, and the same Council which had put him under supervision of the police, offered him the freedom of the town. The case of the Marquis of Vice was not singular in its kind. It was repeated over and over again in this terrible time, when the children of the Reformation had to sacrifice their earthly happiness with a bleeding heart in order to gain heavenly bliss. A stream of fugitives left Italy; at their head the eloquent Ochino, who had ventured to ask: "He who created you without your aid — cannot He re-create you without your aid?" and therefore he was considered among the dangerous heretics and the first against whom a summons was issued. A great number of fugitives followed him: men belonging to the old nobility, former priests of high rank, rich merchants, and highly cultivated women. They had to leave everything behind in order to retain their freedom; along secret paths they tried to reach the snow-bound passes of the Alps and the Swiss frontiers, ever in danger of being betrayed into the hands of fierce persecutors. He who remained behind, inexorably went to the dungeon, the rack, the scaffold, or the stake. In Venice the condemned fugitives were rowed to the sea in a boat at midnight. A splash was heard — a low shriek of farewell, woefully resounding over the dreamy sea — and all was over.

Geneva had its full share of the fugitives, and Calvin received and consoled them, taking care of them like a shepherd of his flock. He was their protector, and when wisdom made prudence necessary, he was compassionate. When everyone suspected the marquis, the Chancellor of the hostile Emperor, Calvin opened his door to him and welcomed him most heartily. This welcome given by Calvin was the beginning of his rehabilitation, and this was completed when the Reformer dedicated to the marquis his exposition of the first Epistle to the Corinthians.

What an imposing series of detailed elaborate Bible commentaries by Calvin appeared in these turbulent years of Geneva! In 1546 and 1547 the two Epistles to the Corinthians appeared; in 1548 six commentaries; in 1549 two; in 1550 three.

Thus Calvin expounded thirteen books of the Bible in a period of five years, while he was overwhelmed with other work, without mentioning the numerous writings done in the same period of time. Each commentary was an important event, an historical fact in the Protestant world.

"They mark," says Bungener, "a revolution in the study of the Bible, and in this respect they not only take the first place in the history of theology, but also in the history of the human mind. Common sense dethrones book-learning; it is truth that is sought for in every verse and word, in the broadest and shortest way. Many passages have undoubtedly been improved, but only by following Calvin's very method. In a word, biblical knowledge owes him what every branch of knowledge owes a man, who transfers it to the range of facts and bases it on observation and experience. He may make mistakes, but he will have paved the way for all further progress of knowledge, and in this sense he will have a right to consider as his what will afterward improve some part or other of his work. Besides, with regard to Calvin one should not suppose too soon that one has understood better or seen better than he. Modern exegesis has often felt surprised at the discovery that what it considered as new was already to be found in Calvin's writings; frequently his elucidations, formerly rejected, are now considered the best. Even in those things finally, which he could not know, and on which travelling, archaeology, and other branches of knowledge did not throw light till after his time, his astute mind was often competent to see the truth in spite of all the errors and ignorance of his age. The different schools in the Middle Ages had only studied the Bible as a subject for exercises or book-learning. The field of the Holy Scriptures was dug for the sake of the digging, not the finding, it was dug again and again without bearing any fruit. The Reformer, however, never used his spade in vain, he would not open even the smallest furrow, if it could not bear fruit, if it could not produce an idea inspired by God. Though without any fervour, Calvin's commentaries are full of life, and owing to their characteristic truthfulness, their lack of fervour is a new element of power and authority. The reader realises that the author is a man, who says only what he can prove unobjectionably. Hence the result, which surprises at first, when the reader remembers that the author is Calvin, the strict Calvin. This may be explained, because he feels at ease with the author, who conducts him through the field of the Bible, relating what he has seen himself, showing the flowers for a moment only, the fruit for a long time, and offering those fruits most willingly, which seem the soundest and most nourishing. Yet he is more than a guide; he consults you in some measure, making use of your experience and kindly urging you to increase your knowledge. It is as if the reader also holds the pen in his hand, feeling the author's superiority only through the pleasure of hearing him say clearly and ingeniously, what he has thought himself or at least wished to have thought."

Yet the charm of Calvin's writings is greatly surpassed by the charm of his personality, and one does not do justice to Calvin if one judges him only from his writings. On the contrary — one gets a wrong idea of his life, if one does not penetrate into his soul, his heart, the impulses of his inner self. There was a severe trait in his character — a matter of course in a man who was called upon to be a Reformer. He was also quick-tempered and irritable, while his irritability, a serious fault, acknowledged and repented of by Calvin himself, was increased by his violent bodily sufferings and an opposition often fierce and frequently diabolic. As the sun breaks through the clouds, so his inborn amiability broke through his fits of ill-humour. When the showers were over the sun shone in the famous Cannon Street in Geneva, where any child knew the bright house of John Calvin, surrounded by a shady garden. It was like going on a pilgrimage; from all corners of the earth foreigners came here to enrich their minds, but more so to find consolation for their hearts. He was called the Pope of Geneva. This was going too far. He was the Father of Geneva, nobody can deprive him of that title of honour. Bossuet designated Calvin as a gloomy genius, which shows that the pious Bossuet looked at things from a gloomy point of view when he used this expression. Calvin had a cheerful mind, he liked to laugh and joke with his friends. When old Bonivard was going to be married for the fourth time Calvin roared with laughter. It is true — he did not often laugh. At that time there was not much to laugh about; it was a time when the children of God were thrown into dark dungeons and persecuted like wild beasts, when the martyrs gave up their souls to Christ at the stake. Calvin had powerful influence through his works, but this influence was increased by his irresistible charm. There is a Calvin, come down to us through tradition, with a parchment face, with ink instead of blood in his veins, and with a heart of granite. This Calvin, this gloomy genius, stands in the ruddy glow of Servet's stake, with a harsh grin on his cruel, heartless face, and those who have hated this Calvin and his doctrine have exclaimed for more than three centuries: "This is Calvin!" But is this true? Is not this a falsehood? Is not this vile calumny? The real Calvin was a man of flesh and blood, a sincere friend, who gratefully acknowledged the slightest kindness. He spread warmth around him, his friends liked to be in his company, the Cops, the Cordiers, and so many others found no rest before they breathed the air of the town which has been called the town of Calvin. He has been called stingy, he has been called a hypocrite; a Roman Catholic author has called him a child of Sodom. And all this he had to bear; his memory has been mocked and derided, because he burned with zeal for his faith, and the following words were wrung from his soul: "Even a dog barks when his master is attacked, should not I raise my voice when the majesty of God is attacked?" Stingy — was he stingy? A notarial document records what he left behind; we have his last will, the famous testament, which the Reformer made shortly before his death, and which contains the following: "As for the few earthly goods which God gave me to dispose of, I appoint as my sole heir, Anthony Calvin, my beloved brother, but only for honour's sake. I bequeath to him the silver beaker presented to me by Mr. Varennes, requesting him to be satisfied with this, as he will be, I am sure, as he knows that I do it for no other reason than to leave the little I have to his children. Further, I bequeath ten crowns to the University and as much to the poor foreigners' fund. Further, the sum of ten crowns to Johanna, daughter of Charles Costan, and his half-sister on his father's side. Further, forty crowns each to Samuel and John, sons of the above-mentioned brother, my nephews. Further, thirty crowns each to my nieces, Anne, Susan, and Dorothy. As to their brother David I give him only twenty-five crowns, as a punishment, because he is frivolous and unsteady. As far as I know, this is all that God has bestowed upon me in the form of means, books, furniture, household matters, and everything else." Adding these sums together we get two hundred and twenty-five crowns! And to realise this amount, everything, the library, the manuscripts, and the furniture had to be first turned into money. But all his goods did not even bring in that amount, but only two hundred crowns — that was all; it is Beza who records it. When we consider Calvin's character, we cannot help wondering. When he himself or his family are concerned, money seems to have lost its value; but if others are concerned, Calvin turns a practical merchant, thinking of every penny. Is not it remarkable? Calvin refused to marry an immensely rich lady of noble birth. "What is money to me?" he said. "A dowry of purity and virtue is sufficient for me!" Yet when one of his friends wished to marry, he thought money very important. He knew the young girls of the town, the surroundings even of Neuchâtel. In this amazing brain of his, that noticed and retained everything, was recorded how they were educated, what their character was like, what virtues and what faults they had, besides the extent of their dowries. The very unselfishness which made him despise money for himself urged him to value it for others. If a young man of his community came to Calvin to be advised about his intended marriage, Calvin would leave his most profound studies to tell him that a household means money, and that a man must calculate the cost before he begins to build the tower. How Calvin worried to get a wife for Viret! And how many did he help by word and deed in this respect! But his care went much farther. With what fatherly tenderness did he watch over the interests of his friends' children; he took interest in all of them; his shoulders, which, like an Atlas, bore the cares of a Protestant world, also bore the cares of all his friends. Calvin was interested in the smallest details of everyday life, especially when others were concerned. He possessed in an unwonted degree the gift of all great demagogues, of paying attention to details, to trifles. For him there were no trifles, everything was important, and this explains the intensity of his actions. Now we begin to understand why the house in Cannon Street attracted such numbers of people. There not only the brain of European Protestantism was at work, but also the heart. Here flowed in a stream of letters from England, France, Poland, Russia — Calvin's house was the international post office of Protestantism. Each foreign letter was a matter of great importance, at a time when letters took the place of newspapers. The news that a letter had arrived was spread like wild-fire, and its importance was increased by the bearer, who was almost considered as an ambassador. In Calvin's house gathered people bearing the most respected names that were known in Geneva. Other points of view were shown by these letters; old plans were put aside and new plans of campaign were formed. Under Calvin's roof gathered the general staff of Protestantism; there the chances were calculated; from here the missionaries of the Gospel were sent into the wide world without purse or scrip. They did not hesitate. They united the stoical courage of the Russian anarchist with a burning love of Christ and humanity; wherever in any part of Europe a hard furrow had to be sprinkled with blood, that the seed of the Gospel might grow in it, there these heroes were ready to shed theirs; wherever the fire of the stakes required fresh fuel, they offered their bodies. They were the sons of Calvin; on the firm rock of predestination their house was built, and while they were singing their immortal Psalms their souls triumphantly rose to heaven. In Geneva Calvin had a hard fight and a bitter struggle. The Libertines had to be converted into Calvinists; the stubborn pride of the free burgher had to be bridled by discipline; men full of the pleasures and enjoyments of life had to be put to the yoke of strict morals. Merry, dancing, wanton Geneva, which had surpassed all other towns in unbridled pleasures for centuries, was then called upon to surpass the others in strict morals, purity, and earnestness of life. Geneva was to become the Jerusalem of Evangelical Christianity. A Christian state, a Christian town, a Christian household. A Christian! — that was Calvin's ideal! And does not a Christian's life form a chapter of the *Institutes*? Geneva found itself in a singular time and in extra-ordinary circumstances.

Like a horse surrounded by hornets the town was surrounded by grim enemies, longing for the moment when they could divide it among them. It was like a lost post, projecting and solitary; like a weak camp amidst hostile lines of battle, like a ship with burning sails trying to reach the harbour.

Michelet, the famous French historian, in a moment of inspiration gave his impression of this amazing spectacle in the following famous words: "At the moment of the death of King

Francis I, one hundred and fifty families fled to Geneva; soon there were fourteen hundred families, consisting of at least five thousand souls. This French élite founded with an Italian élite the real Geneva, that wonderful place of refuge, situated among three peoples and existing only through its moral power. Over against the immense and terrible trap, into which Europe fell by the desertion of France, nothing less than this heroic training-school was necessary. Now the struggle begins. Loyola is undermining the ground; above the ground, Spanish gold allures and the sword of the Guises murders. And in this narrow, closely surrounded corner, this garden of God, the bloody roses in honour of the freedom of the soul are budding under the hand of Calvin — Reformer!"

Geneva was the spiritual centre of Protestantism. And the spiritual centre of Geneva was Calvin. He had become so through the astuteness of his learning, the resoluteness of his character and his zeal for God, the flames of which were only extinguished by the dark waters of the Jordan of death. Most striking was the simplicity of his life; profound and sincere was his contempt of the world and all its shining glitter; a wonderful influence had his strict puritan way of living had on the life and character of people and nations. It entered into their brain, their soul, and their blood — it strengthened humanity's nerve. From where did the prostrate Huguenots get their valour which still excites our profoundest admiration? What inspired the Dutch to attack the Spanish tyrant in his own waters? Who taught the Scottish Covenanters to struggle and to die? Calvinism has retained its force, as purifying leaven, for centuries; it has influenced the lives of the noblest spirits in England, and are not the fathers of the powerful American Republic children of Calvinism?

"You are condemned by God, Calvin!" exclaimed his antagonists, "for you sink into the grave without descendants!"

"I have thousands of them," was Calvin's reply. Calvin was mistaken — there were millions of them. And now — after four centuries — his memory is being blessed in five parts of the world.

However, this excellent instrument in the hand of the Lord was not a faultless instrument. We have already mentioned his temper; he could be most vehement. In his debate with the despicable Caroli, who accused him of heterodox opinions respecting the doctrine of the Holy Trinity, he flew into a passion, which alarmed his enemies and startled his friends. Calvin had two mortal enemies: they were Rome and his temper. But let us be fair and not forget that body and soul are closely connected. During the last twenty years of his life Calvin suffered a great deal from most painful diseases. He was seldom without pain, and during the intervals between the attacks of the gravel and stomach-ache he had to endure the fierce and often vicious attacks of his embittered enemies. This made him frequently lose his temper, it made his words harsh and his pen biting. However, in the Bible which he has expounded, was a description of Moses, who had to struggle against the same sinful irritability, and by the grace of God became a leader of the people, surpassing all in gentleness. Calvin stared at this picture, and in spite of many stumblings he obtained much self-control which took root in his Christian humility.

A Spanish nobleman was once greatly astonished at the house of Admiral Michael de Ruyter,[29] and the same sensation was once experienced by Cardinal Sadolet, when he knocked at the door of John Calvin. With unfeigned astonishment he looked at its windows and its front, at the small, humble dwelling, and his astonishment knew no bounds when a simple man, dressed in black, opened the door. This man was the great Reformer himself. We know what this house contained: furniture lent to Calvin by the town. The inventory had been written in duplicate, one signed by Calvin, the other by the secretary of the town, mentioning the following pieces of furniture: two walnut bedsteads, another bedstead of carved maple, a walnut square table, a maple bench for it, a walnut sideboard, two walnut trunks, a walnut carved cathedra, a desk, four long tables of pine-wood, two walnut tables, a dozen wooden chairs. Besides, Calvin possessed some pieces of furniture bought by himself. In his study there was a table and a bench for it, another bench for visitors, and a big bookcase and steps — that was all! Not a chair, not even a sofa. And in this simple bare workroom were forged the swords of real Damascene steel, which inflicted

---

[29] Michael de Ruyter is generally considered the greatest sailor of the 17th century and one of the most important heroes in the history of Protestantism. A popular account of his life is *Salt in His Blood* by William R. Rang, also published by Inheritance Publications. The same publisher is planning to reprint *The Life of Admiral de Ruyter* by P.J. Blok which was translated into English and original published in 1933 in London by Ernest Benn Ltd. —Editor.

such deep, bloody wounds. The front of the house was to the north, from where the cold winds blow, the back to the south, toward the warm rays of the sun. There was the garden Calvin used to walk in with his friends: Farel, Viret, his brother Anthony, and his Geneva friends; from this garden Idelette, no doubt, got her vegetables. The windows still command the same view as they did four centuries ago. On the left rise the Jura Mountains, with their lofty summit; on the right the majestic Alps; in the middle lies the blue lake glistening in the sunlight. Calvin must often have enjoyed this magnificent prospect, for, although the Alpine Club was unknown then, Calvin had an eye for the beauties of nature. He admired nature, he enjoyed it; and he who described the stars in his sermons in such enthusiastic, eloquent words, must have observed them glittering in the sky over Geneva at night. He delivered his sermons, his lectures, even some of his essays without manuscript. In those days there were but two sources which he could consult: the Bible and the church fathers. The Bible Calvin studied incessantly and persistently; the church fathers he studied in the night, when time did not permit him to do so by day. Among the sixteen hundred million people living on earth,[30] there are probably not a hundred who by practice have obtained such an excellent memory as Calvin possessed. It has been called incomparable; it struck people at a meeting in Lausanne, where he quoted long passages from the church fathers — by heart — as accurately as a phonograph. In that wonderful brain, ideas were piled up as in a big, well-provided warehouse; they formed a well-rounded, complete system. Calvin had all the treasures of his knowledge at his disposal to enlighten the congregation and to resist the enemy. He looked after the religion and morals of his fellow citizens without neglecting their hygienic and social interests. In this town dissoluteness had been associated with dirt and neglect, but with the strictness of the Calvinistic ideas the hospitals and the schools were improved. Calvin liked fresh air; he had the windows opened, as vitiated air would cause infection, and while he prayed in the pulpit for the aversion of the plague, of the black death, he said at the same time that man is not an inanimate object, but that he has got a mind in order to use the means conducive to his health. Geneva owed its good

---

[30] Please remember that the author wrote this book in the first decade of the 20th century. —Editor.

hygienic rules in the sixteenth century to nobody else but Calvin. His many-sided genius seemed to have a knowledge of everything. He gave Robert Etienne valuable hints about the art of printing, and Etienne owed the greater part of his reputation as a printer to this advice. If an inventor applied to the Council, Calvin was called and had to inspect the new invention, the new branch of industry, the complicated instrument — if he lived in Germany now, the Emperor William would probably have asked his opinion on Zeppelin's airship. Neither surgeon nor dentist could get a licence for carrying on their useful occupations, till he had been subjected to the penetrating looks of Calvin. If he nodded assent and said, "It is right!" it was right, nobody doubted it.

A le

Sully, the powerful minister of King Henry IV, was highly praised for what he did in the interest of French industry. This praise he deserved, yet Sully had a predecessor long before in Calvin, who made the industry of Geneva, which had become dull, flourish again, and provided the town with new sources of welfare by his advice to erect cloth and velvet-weaving mills. In this way he benefited the town, where he had come as a stranger. However, he never forgot the country to which Noyon belonged. He loved France, he wrote a great many of his works in the French language, and while he dedicated his principal work to the King of France, his heart was turned to his beloved French people. The national aspirations had not a greater influence, because his look ranged over all Europe. And from the lofty Nebo, which he had climbed, the national boundaries had to fade and the national colours to pale, for the grand task of winning the world for the Reformation.

John Huss! Martin Luther! John Calvin! Huss appealed to the Slavonian race; Luther to the Germanic race; Calvin raised all barriers to appeal to the world. Huss has been called the awakening genius of the Reformation; Luther sang its triumph in songs, which make the German mountains re-echo; Calvin was the unwearying worker, completing the task of both by embodying the Reformation in a system, which commands the admiration of Christianity to this very day by clearness of ideas, acuteness of expression, and inexorable, never-shrinking consistency. He agreed with Huss in the doctrine of predestination, with Luther in the doctrine of vindication, but he did not stop here — he resolutely continued his remarkable expedition along abysses, in the company of angels and

lvin

devils, and when he had reached the utmost extremity of human thought, he clasped his hands to exclaim in adoration: "Oh, the depth of the riches both of the wisdom and knowledge of God! How unsearchable are His judgments, and His ways past finding out!"

Chapter XXVIII

DAYS OF JOY AND SORROW

CALVIN'S name had obtained European fame, and his works, bearing a universal international stamp, had found their way to the confines of European Christianity. He dedicated several writings to princes and kings with the purpose of making them strong supporters of the Reformation. He had cast his eye on Gustavus Vasa, the cautious and valorous King of Sweden, on King Christian of Denmark, and on King Radziwill of Poland.

In a moment of inspired self-consciousness Calvin wrote to the Polish King:

> *I, who am the messenger of the King of Kings and His herald, have to proclaim His Gospel — I summon you in the name of this King to promote the extension of the Kingdom of God before all things. All, the great and the small, the high and the low, must be roused from their dangerous slumber. It is especially the duty of kings and princes to support this good work with all their power.*
>
> *God has granted them their high rank only that they may enlighten and improve others by their faith and example!*

Four such letters he wrote in one day, which proves what an extensive correspondence he had with princes! However, while his looks were cast on Poland, he heard the cheers in the streets of Paris welcoming Henry II and his consort, the sly Catherine de Medici, and these cries were blended with the shrill cry of anguish of the suffering Evangelicals. This period was momentous on account of the heat of persecution, but no less momentous on account of the victories of the faith. A blood-witness from Geneva, who ended his life in the flames, showed such constancy, that the hands which had to do the executioner's work began to tremble.

The executioner himself confessed the faith, for which he had tied the martyr to the strangling-pole, and he went to Geneva to be strengthened in his belief by Calvin. Anthony Laborie, thrown into the damp dungeon, complained of not being allowed to suffer more for his Lord. He left a wife and children behind, consoling them with most touching letters. He gloried in being oppressed, and deploring his weakness and worldliness, he conquered the world. When he had set foot on the scaffold, he thanked the executioner that he had come to deliver him from the close cell of his body. Many of the spectators shed tears, and in religious enthusiasm, while the flames were rising, he exclaimed: "I see Heaven open!" He said these words with such force and such conviction, that the crowd involuntarily looked up and stared at the clouds. And Heaven received the soul of this Stephen of the Reformation. The harder the wolves pressed, the closer the sheep of Christ kept together, and in spite of the unheard-of persecutions, small congregations were formed. One dark night, the servants of the Inquisition discovered a small light in a remote part of one of the streets in Paris. They heard besides the soft tones of a solemn Psalm — it was the Song of Simeon. Then there was silence — there was praying. The priests had little difficulty in instigating the people, for the people were already restless, turbulent, and excited by the defeat of St. Quentin, the Northern Pavia, where Coligny's valour had not been a match for the better discipline of the Spanish-Dutch Army, under Lamoraal of Egmond. In a moment the people were ready to take vengeance on the Protestants for the national calamity. It was a little past midnight. Twenty-one Reformers were condemned to the stake. Among them was a young woman. She dressed all in white and went to the scaffold, as if she were going to a wedding-party. None of them hesitated; youths went to the stake with the submission of graybeards, for whom the world has no charm, and the graybeards with the fire of youths, who see the glory of the future.

Calvin, Farel, and Beza did everything that was in their power to come to the aid of their distressed brothers in the faith. "Thirty of our brethren," thus Calvin complained to a German prince, "are still pining in a horrible dungeon at this moment. The Waldenses are persecuted anew. One of their preachers is undergoing a terrible imprisonment. In Dauphiné especially, people are raging at everybody who is a Protestant. Cardinals themselves undertake to lead the investigations of the Inquisition which has been established. The King of France tries to deceive the German princes by making them believe that he only wishes to disturb the Sacramentarians in his realm, but I swear before God and the angels that not to believe in the Mass is a sufficient reason to be persecuted to death in France." However, the palm tree was growing in spite of oppression. Though in the reign of King Francis I and King Henry II more than fifty thousand Huguenots are said to have lost their lives, and the Inquisition, working in the Spanish way, made most strict investigations, Protestantism was spreading steadily.

Amidst the hostile fire the organisation of the Churches was being effected, and under the influence of Calvin, who always had the unity of the Church in view, the first national Synod was held in Paris. The Synod made a very poor impression; it lacked all outward splendour. And how badly attended it was — the meeting consisted only of the representatives of eleven Churches, including the community of Paris, by which they had been summoned. Yet it was an impressive gathering. They were heroes who had gathered here. They risked their lives, for they might be caught by the hirelings of Rome every moment and be led to the scaffold. Yet they did not hesitate for a second, and angels must have guarded the doors of this Synod, which laid the foundation of an organisation, for which the materials had been collected during a whole generation. The Reformed Church of France increased rapidly now that the communities had been united into one body. Every day the army increased, which had woven the crucified Christ on its banner, and before long there were two thousand communities, the members of which consisted of water-carriers and wood-cutters as well as the highest aristocracy of France. The Prince of Condé, Admiral de Coligny, and the King of Navarre belonged to them. And with what spirit these nobles were animated may be heard from Jeanne d'Albret, who exclaimed with never-shrinking resoluteness: "I would rather cast my dearly-beloved son together with my crown into the sea where it is deepest, than go once to the Mass!" Jeanne d'Albret was Queen of Navarre. And her son afterward became Henry IV, called the Great. De Coligny was Admiral of France and

Lord of Châtillon. Calvin's first letter reached him during his imprisonment in the Netherlands; it was an admonition to bless the solitude into which the hand of the Lord had led him and to listen attentively to His voice. The next year De Coligny was liberated from the Spanish prison. Well might he gratefully look back to the gloomy dungeon, brightened by the light of the Gospel; as one newborn he returned to France to prepare, in quiet retirement at his country-seat, for the high distinction of falling as the noblest victim to the terrible St. Bartholomew's night. Calvin strengthened his faith, roused his zeal. Calvin had become the spiritual adviser of all Protestant France.

However, the day broke when the Reformer had to put down his pen and, like the common burghers, take up arms, for the storm which was then raging in Protestant France, next turned to Geneva. Without doubt, Geneva was the hotbed of heresy; if it could be extirpated this would be the end of vindication through faith. Then the connection between faith and liberty became evident. While France was gathering its forces to plant the papal flag on Protestant Rome, the town was put into feverish haste to build and fortify its bulwarks. While printing-machines groaned and laboured to print the writings, which Calvin had published as a defence and attack, this remarkable man was already busy surrounding the Gospel with bulwarks. He worked himself in the entrenchments — the author of the *Institutes* had become a warrior. The words burgher and Protestant began to be synonymous at Lake Leman; the Geneva citizen was under military and spiritual regulations; in the camps strict notice was taken, whether the arms were sharp and the doctrines pure. The storm passed; only in the distance the flags of France had been waving, and more closely than ever Calvin kept his eye on the Church under the Cross in France, as he called the Protestant communities there.

During the times of anxiety which he went through, there were some bright moments in which he beheld the blue sunny sky, and in those moments he glowed with enthusiasm, so rare in his life. Indeed, it is remarkable what he wrote then — it is the triumphal shout of the general, feeling the approach of victory.

"It can hardly be believed," he wrote, "with how much zeal our friends devote themselves to the propagation of the Gospel! As desirous as some are to ask benefits of the Pope, so eager are these to request that they may be allowed to serve the Churches under the Cross. They besiege my door in order to get a part of the field to cultivate — never had the King more zealous servants than mine are. They contend with each other for the posts, as if the Kingdom of Jesus Christ were already firmly established in France. I try to keep them back sometimes. I show them the detestable edict, commanding the destruction of every house where our divine services are held. I remind them of the fact, that in more than twenty towns the believers have been killed by the people, but nothing can arrest them in their course." Calvin felt happy, when he realized that he was considered as spiritual leader by these heroic martyrs; he was proud of it — not for himself, but for the sacred cause which he defended.

However, a cup of bitterness was put to his lips, and Farel wrote: "So it pleases the Lord to try this His servant, our beloved brother Calvin, that he may not pride himself on the greatness of His revelations."

How was it possible? While the Reformer had cleansed the Augean stable in Geneva with an iron broom, had improved the morals and prevented licentiousness, his own dwelling had become a house of adultery. Shame covered his face when the matter became known, and secret enemies whispered: "There is the brother-in-law of an adulteress!" A violent rage and a more violent grief tore his heart asunder. All Geneva was astounded; the community mourned, as if the ark had fallen into the hands of the Philistines, and people wondered sorrowfully how in the world it was possible that Calvin had been deceived with his eyes open. How things happen! Calvin had no suspicion; he trusted his servant, who had robbed his master for at least two years without the latter's noticing it in the least, and at last the scoundrel committed adultery with his master's sister-in-law. What a sombre spectacle it was when Calvin, with his brother Anthony, had to repair to the Church Council. Anthony stated at this gathering, in a faltering voice, that his wife, Anne le Fert, who had been let off seven years before through lack of evidence, had been caught in the act of committing adultery with his brother's servant. The case progressed slowly. The adulteress persistently denied her guilt, and Calvin seemed broken down by the shame which had been brought on his family. "This domestic sorrow almost overwhelms me," he sighed; "the judges find no reason to set my brother free, and I see in this blindness a righteous punishment for our blindness, for during two whole years I was plundered by the thief and did not see anything!" At last the judges pronounced the divorce, and Anne le Fert was banished from the town forever, covered with shame. Five years later a new shame tore Calvin's heart asunder. First his sister-in-law — then his stepdaughter, the child whose mother had been Idelette de Bure. This cut him to the quick, for the memory of his dearly-beloved wife was sacred to him. Judith was her name. It was again the same disgusting story — adultery! And this woman had been praised so highly by Farel at her marriage! "A model of a chaste virgin; an example of piety rich in Christian virtues." Thus Farel had denominated her, and behold! her marriage ended in adultery . . .

This time Calvin did not remain in the town; the scorn and shame were too great; he fled to the country, that he might not be seen by anyone.

Hark! the knells are tolling! Man is going to his last home. "Seventy years," says the Psalmist, "or, if we are very strong, eighty years." Then all is over. Then the dream is dreamt, beginning with a cry and ending with a sob. The famous Melanchthon experienced this. Alive and well and dead within a week! The accurate chronicler made the following note: "Magister Philippus Melanchthon reached 63 years and 63 days, and died." On the Thursday before Easter Melanchthon had already heard the gentle knock of the messenger of death. Though unwell he had gone to church, in order to attend the Lord's Supper with the community. The day after — on Good Friday — he had even delivered a sermon on Isaiah 53. He slept calmly that night, and on awaking he felt as if he had become young again, the sunny days of his youth seemed to have come back, and it was as if he were a boy in church listening to the words, "I have greatly desired to eat this Passover with you before I die." He was seen in the street on that Saturday, going to the printer — it was the last time that the beloved Magister was seen in the streets of

Wittenberg. When he came home, Melanchthon felt exhausted, and on Easter Sunday the churchgoers told each other with dejected faces, that Magister Philippus Melanchthon was seriously ill. This meant death; Melanchthon was sure it did. And while a secret yearning for home moved the silver cords, he said to a friend on Easter Monday: "I long for my deliverance and to be with Christ." In his study a bed had been placed; there he lay down, and this was to be his death-bed. All the professors were present. They surrounded the couch with sad and gloomy thoughts. And among these professors Melanchthon's dying eye discerned a girl weeping. "I have loved you very much, dear niece!" he said. "Be always obedient to your parents and the joy of their lives as much as you can! Trust God — He will not forsake you. I will pray Him to protect and bless you!" All knelt down near the bed; a crowd of people had assembled outside, waiting in fearful suspense; all Wittenberg was moved. A passage of the Holy Scriptures was read to the dying man, who repeated these words in a whisper: "That they all may be one, as Thou Father art in Me and I in Thee!" "Do you desire anything else?" he was asked. And he answered with the yearning eagerness of a stranger, who sees his native mountains gleaming on the horizon: "I only desire to go to Heaven." The sun set, the day declined; it was over, and there was great distress in Wittenberg. Calvin felt grievously deserted when the sad tidings reached him.

"Oh, Philip Melanchthon," he exclaimed, "you who now live with God and our Lord Jesus Christ — you shall await me there until death shall have united us in the blessed enjoyment of eternal peace!"

Melanchthon dead! His sister-in-law an adulteress! He himself ravaged by increasing bodily suffering, verily Calvin experienced that this world is a vale of tears for God's children!

Surprise is felt on hearing that Calvin suffered from malarial fever in mountainous Geneva; but we must add that Geneva of the sixteenth century, from a hygienic point of view, could hardly be put on a level with Geneva of the twentieth century.

It was surrounded by marshy moats which polluted the air, and in this respect it was no exception to the other towns and districts, which, until the seventeenth century, were hotbeds of infection just as low tropical countries are now.

Calvin had, besides, a tendency to rheumatism; he was gouty and his lungs were not sound. He was consumptive; but his consumption confined itself to violent vomitings of blood or oppressive bronchitis, while he probably died of gravel.

This rheumatic tendency was the source of many complaints which made his life one long succession of sufferings; but to give truth its due, we must add, that this man, who inspected hospitals to ensure good medical treatment and who gave Geneva those excellent hygienic prescriptions, on the other hand did everything to foster his own tendency to disease. Forcibly and impressively he held forth on the sixth Commandment, but in complaining of his inborn slothfulness and sluggishness he was in danger of being his own murderer through excessive work. And this exhausting labour, combined with a sedentary life and endless cares for his reformatory task, sapped his vitality.

A physician of our time would have closed his books before his very eyes, would have taken him by the arm and said: "Come, Professor! To the mountains! To the Alps! Everything else will come right!"

But at that time they also knew that rest and mountain air were good for one; Calvin knew this too, and yet he took no rest.

His cares were too many; his zeal too great; and in the fire of this zeal the fragile thread of his life was consumed.

Had this zeal been less — he would have suffered less and lived longer. But, on the other hand, he would not have produced the excellent work for which his followers venerate and love him, and the son of the cooper of Noyon would never have become the most prolific of Reformers.

Chapter XXIX

A TORCH OF SCIENCE

CALVIN, the man of Predestination, saw in everything unity, firmness, regularity, and order; in the fixed and unshakable decree of the Supreme Being he perceived the foundation of the laws of Nature as well as of the spiritual and moral laws; and it was this conviction which was such a powerful motive and incitement to tread the broad field of science with a firm step.

He was not the man to avoid but to rejoice in that which God has given to the world, and instead of neglecting the temporal he wanted to make it subservient to the glory of God and the salvation of mankind.

The Roman Catholic Cardinal Borromeo had once during a destructive plague epidemic ministered to the sick and consoled the dying with the heroic courage of a Christian; but Calvin, who also was prepared to risk his life, did more by adopting excellent hygienic measures.

So the man of Predestination was at the same time the man of science, and from 1541 he always rose and went to bed with this thought uppermost in his mind: "How can we give Geneva a University?"

The unrest of the times prevented the realisation of this great plan, but in 1558 a favourable wind swelled the sails. Calvin had opened a national subscription, which realized ten thousand guilders — for that time a considerable amount — while some excellent teachers, in every way fit for the work at a university, had gone to Geneva, driven to this by a dispute with the hard-handed Government of Bern. So the general conviction gained ground that God was smoothing the way for the founding of a University, and the Council no longer hesitated to put their hand to the plough.

For this purpose Calvin had already selected a large garden planted with vines and which was the property of the town. On March 25, 1558, a committee of experts, conducted by Calvin, surveyed the site; three days afterward they already brought out an extensive report.

It was a favourable report. The healthy site was commended; the building would offer an unrestricted view of the lake, while at the north side sufficient space would be left for a promenade.

The Council approved and they immediately set to work.

Calvin was full of enthusiasm; he forgot the fever which heated his blood, and seemed ten years younger. He was frequently seen on the construction-ground inciting the masons and carpenters to speed; it was extremely irksome to a man of his activity when the builders had no bricks to build a wall, or were short of roof-tiles; but in spite of adversity it was possible to open the college, which was to form the nucleus of this famous University, on July 5, 1559

Geneva was that day in festive guise; all work was suspended; the church-bells rang out merrily in the warm summer air, and a select company streamed to the large and spacious Church of St. Peter.

The Government came strongly to the fore on this day on purpose, for there was a political side to this ceremony. Formerly a University had been offered Geneva on condition that they accepted the Duke of Savoy as their protector. That they had thought too high a price — so they refused. And now — two centuries later — Geneva, as a sovereign power, founded this University, independent of Savoy, as a lasting monument of her independence.

Roman Catholic Europe was dumbfounded at this audacious act. No one could understand this. In the sixteenth century a Pope, an Emperor, or a King was required to found a University, and this small insignificant town said: "I will do this alone, with God's aid."

And behold, it was done! Everyone whose heart was in the right place helped, and the poor five-pence offered by a simple Genevan baker's wife sounded through the centuries with a brighter jingle than the gold-pieces which that sombre heretic-hater, Philip II, spent on the founding of the University of Douai — with the intention of frustrating the Genevan attempt.

The University was small as yet, but it would grow. Calvin had not asked for more than was reasonable: five professors, of whom he was one. The subjects of Greek, Hebrew, and philosophy had one professor each assigned to them, while the vacancies of medicine and law would later on be filled.

The Government had issued a proclamation:

"It is by the great mercy and grace of God that it has been given to this town to become at once the foster-mother of piety and science. And we shall find cause to appreciate this glorious blessing yet more highly when we remember the time in which this plan ripened. We all remember the storms which for many years ravaged our republic; the conspiracies of criminal citizens, the instigations from without, the efforts of Satan to destroy this stronghold of piety, which day by day threatens and diminishes his rule. Owing to this, the execution of our plan was long thwarted, but at length perseverance and trust in God won the day. There will doubtless yet be many who censure this undertaking as too rash, but whosoever pays attention to the guidance of God and is accustomed to direct his affairs, not according to human wisdom, but according to his trust in His immeasurable power, will judge otherwise, and impressed by the grandeur and the blessing of this work will hope for the best.

Every citizen who read this proclamation understood whose perseverance and trust in God were especially meant, and more than ever, every eye, dim with tears, was turned on this man of God, who, with a pale emaciated face, but with a quiet enthusiasm in his soul, sat there among the councillors.

Amid profound silence the Reformer rose. In a short speech he communicated to them the resolution of the Council to found a University within the walls of Geneva, and then in a fervent prayer invoked the blessing of the Supreme Being on this new institution. He stood on Mount Nebo; in his mind's eye he saw the lustre which this torch of science would spread throughout Europe.

Then the Town Secretary came forward to read the confession of faith and the statutes, which were to be binding on teachers and students alike, while Beza, who had been appointed rector, conjured them in a touching speech to remain faithful to their vocation.

The University was the fruit of prayer, and like dew and sunshine that prayer rested on it.

The success of the new institution was almost unequalled from the very beginning. No less than nine hundred young men from all parts of Europe were enrolled as students during the first year; an almost equal number, mostly French and English refugees, were formed into evangelists and teachers by attending Calvin's theological lectures.

And the Reformation in these countries would scarcely have prospered so well, had not this stream been fed at the limpid source which bubbled up to the surface on the shore of Lake Leman. But Calvin was not easily satisfied. He was for ever on the look-out for defects and shortcomings, and he was ceaselessly engaged in trying to obtain the best teachers for his University.

He tried to make them understand that the small salary paid at Geneva was more than compensated for by the honour of the post; he assured them that the flower of Italy were eager to obtain a chair, and that the students of Geneva marched victoriously throughout the length and breadth of France, spreading the Gospel as they went — like a merchant praising his wares, so did Calvin praise the University to obtain the most excellent teachers.

What an enormous flight did this institution of Calvin's take! From its foundation until the latter half of the eighteenth century it was the great University for the literary and theological education of Protestant Europe.

LODEWYCK, GRAAF
VAN NASSOU.

"Send the wood to us," so they said at Geneva, "and we will send you the arrows cut from it in exchange!" And this was done. Such an arrow was Lodewyk of Nassau, brother to the great William the Silent; Marnix of St. Aldegonde, the poet of the immortal *Wilhelmus song*, was another arrow; Francis Junius, preacher under the cross, afterward the famous professor at the newly-founded University of Leyden, was a third arrow.

The town itself plucked the richest fruit from its institution. Next to the Church, nothing contributed so much to bring about that wonderful change from an unknown and insignificant town into a world-famous school of new creative thought. The Genevan people themselves were seized by a passion for knowledge. Everyone was anxious to be taught; it became a general competition; and thus was born a cultured and literary Geneva.

There was now an extensive choice of candidates for the Council; from now on they were drawn from every class; and in the midst of those anxious times which the republic had to pass through, a strong and self-conscious nation was formed. Owing to the extension of education, the town was spared the poverty of the proletariat, and the only aristocracy known was the aristocracy of piety and culture, of morality, talent, and patriotism.

The citizens mutually trusted each other, they formed a living wall to protect the fortress against the attacks of the enemy, and in the hour of danger they showed what a small republic, by trusting in God and keeping its gunpowder dry, is capable of.

It was the Gospel that had leavened the mass, and which in Calvin's hands had wrought a wonder such as is scarcely to be equalled in Christendom.

Geneva had been morally regenerated. It was necessary, for how else could it have become the light-giving torch, the training-school and refuge of the nations?

The town had denied itself, destroyed itself, all places of amusement were demolished, its dancing-rooms were closed, and it became the school of heroes and martyrs, of the chosen among the elect, who passed through the flaming gates of the stake to reach the life eternal.

And at this sight, which became a spectacle for angels and devils, a cry of joy escaped from the breast of the stern law-giver of Geneva: "The old has passed away, behold everything has become like new!"

The famous college where Calvin lectured has changed but little in the course of centuries. A humble porch formed of massive columns gives admission to the building. The granite of the pillars is weather-beaten; no wonder! they have stood there so long.

And in the arched roof of this porch there are three inscriptions which indicate the character of the instruction given there. The first inscription, in Hebrew, runs as follows: "The fear of the Lord is the beginning of wisdom;" the second is in Greek: "Christ has become to us the wisdom of God;" while the third is in Latin and repeats the saying of the apostle James: "The wisdom which comes from above is pure, peaceful, and full of mercy."

When a stranger asks to be conducted to the house of Calvin, a certain writer says: "Then do not take him to the house in Cannon Street, but to the tiny college which Calvin founded and the threshold of which he crossed so often. Show the stranger the arms of Geneva; show him those three inscriptions which testify to the Latin, Hebrew, and Greek, which is taught there and say to him: 'Those arms, those texts, this old building, this monument of our history which years have not changed: this is the house of Calvin.' "

Chapter XXX

IN GREAT OPPRESSION

WHILE Geneva was nearing the harbour, the ship of French Protestantism drifted on the high seas with torn sails. The antithesis of the Reformation held France breathless, and the dates 1559 and 1560 are written with blood in the annals of the Huguenots.

They were traced to their most secret conferences; they were treacherously surprised; like sheep they were led to the slaughter.

A word of disapproval about the celebration of Mass might cost a life; the reading of the Scriptures, the singing of a Psalm was punished by death.

To a former Augustine monk a free pardon was offered if he would agree to call the woman to whom he was married a concubine. He willingly went to the stake to maintain his wife's honour; he died for the sake of her reputation, and thus he fulfilled the law of Christ.

It is pathetic and touching in the extreme to hear how delighted those martyrs were, when on the last day of their life they were permitted to indite a letter to Calvin. They did not wish to leave this world without expressing their earnest thanks to this man for his Gospel words, the embracing of which sent them to their death, and it is impossible to read those epistles without shedding tears.

What must have been Calvin's feelings on receiving those last avowals of friendship? Through him they had become martyrs; he was so truly one with them that the flames of their stakes scorched his throat and their wounds rent his heart.

But he was not allowed to reveal his feelings, for he was the general who had to forget himself in order to win this great and furious battle. Again and again the agonies of his fellow-believers fell on his heart like blows, but he fought against his anguish like a hero and repressed his sorrow, to secure new victories to the realm of Christ.

The stakes and strangling-poles were at the height of their glory; the suffering was terrible, while the streets resounded with the anguished cries of parents, who were dragged out of their houses by a mad mob and sacrificed to the fury of the populace. Their children, left orphans, wandered weeping through the streets, poor, neglected, and hungry. They were accursed because their parents were accursed, and human pity turned away from them because capital punishment was the price paid for assisting heretics or their relatives.

The Parisian dungeons in which the Protestants were confined were dark, damp holes; in one of those holes the air was so foul that a candle could not be kept burning there. The poet Marot had become acquainted with those prisons and he compared them to hell. The worst of those dungeons was a deep cellar, which received neither light nor air from the outside; it was impossible to stand erect there or to sleep, while the back part was full of water. This cellar had no stairs and was reached by means of a trap-door; the prisoner was lowered into those black depths attached to a rope which passed over a pulley. At the end of a fortnight the wretched prisoner was either dead or mad . . .

King Henry II, that bloody persecutor, who, acting on the advice of a cardinal and a concubine, had resolved to extirpate Protestantism from his dominions, root and branch, one day expressed a desire to meet one of those heretics, just for the fun of the thing. The cardinal gratified this whim and sent for a tailor who was known to be rather foolish. But through this simple son of the people was fulfilled the saying: "Thou should be dragged before kings and governors for the sake of My name; and this shall happen to you as a testimony. Resolve then in thy heart not to think beforehand of what thou should reply, for I will give thee speech and wisdom."

The King's shameless mistress was present. She wished to find out all about this, but she found this tailor to be more than a match for her.

"Be satisfied that you have polluted France, Madam!" he said, with inexorable sternness; "but do not attempt to mix your poison and filth with such a holy and hallowed thing as the true religion and the truth of our Lord Jesus Christ." The King rose from his seat, furious; he ordered the trial of the tailor to be hastened, assuring him at the same time that he himself would be present at his execution. And the King kept his promise. The King was seen standing before the window of a large mansion, his face turned to the stake on which the martyr was to be burnt.

The crowd saw the King; even the martyr saw him. And the look of that man amid the flames was so awe-inspiring, that the King turned his face away and swore never again to be present at a scene like this, as the pleasure of seeing heretics being burnt was too dearly bought in that way.

Calvin heard of this. Then this Elijah's prayer escaped in holy wrath from his lips: "May the Lord in His omnipotence punish such horrible cruelty. Amen!"

And this prayer was heard.

The persecutions continued. There was no justice left in France; the last flood-gates that might have turned this tide of human blood were opened when the high tribunal met.

All the judges were present, and the deliberations had been going on for about two hours when the King entered, his face sombre, with a silent gesture.

Anne du Bourg, the brilliant lawyer, was speaking in a tone of burning indignation; he denied the right to persecute. He was risking his head — that he knew full well, but without an instant's hesitation he went on.

Then the King rose. His eyes flashed ominously.

He whispered to Montgomery, the officer on guard, to at once place du Bourg behind the horrible gratings of the Bastille. And while seated at dinner he ordered six others to be taken into custody.

It was thus this terrible King understood the free administration of justice.

Du Bourg's imprisonment took place amid those brilliant festivities which Paris at that time witnessed, and the groaning of the victims was lost in the shouts of rejoicing with which the streets rang.

It was certainly worth while. Two royal marriages were impending; the Duke of Saxony was to espouse the King's sister, and Philip II of Spain the King's daughter. In honour of these royal couples a princely tournament was held in the neighbourhood of the gloomy Bastille, where Du Bourg chanted his mournful Psalm.

Out of the depths of sadness,
O Lord, *I cried to Thee;*
Thou who canst fill with gladness,
Lend now Thy ear to me.

At this tournament the French Court shone in all its lustre; the King, in a brilliant many-coloured coat of mail, was the hero of it all.

The flower of the French nobility was present; Duke Alva, with his merciless face, was seen, and Alphonse, the eldest son of the Duchess Renata, had come to Ferrara for this occasion.

Du Bourg heard the shouts of joy; the air was filled with the bright sound of trumpets, and the cries of "Long live the King!" were heard above it all.

But all at once the shouts of joy were silenced; cries of horror reached the ears of the prisoner; then all was silent, silent as death. What had happened?

The King had held sham-fights with three of his knights, when he hit on the idea of inviting Montgomery to a fourth. And with his own hands he handed him the weapon which was to cost him his life. A thrust of the lance pierced his right eye; the wound grew worse, and this same King who, forgetting a former oath, had sworn that his eyes would delight in the sight of Du Bourg's flaming stakes, was to appear before the judgment-seat of the Supreme Being before his victim had drawn his last breath, while the officer who had laid hands on Du Bourg had been destined to become the instrument of this horrible end.

And in the fatal issue of this brilliant tournament many Protestants saw the finger of God.

And it was whispered from mouth to mouth that the royal corpse had been placed in front of hangings, into which these significant words were woven: "Saul, Saul, why dost thou persecute me?"

The King was dead. And the light-hearted Parisians shouted: "Long live the King!"

Thus did Francis II, the son of Henry II, ascend the throne. He was a mere boy, fifteen years of age, weak in body and mind, entirely unfit to take in hand the reins of government, on which the Guise faction and Catherine de Medici cast covetous eyes. The mother of the young prince was forty years of age. She was distinguished by learning and ingenuity; faithful to the traditions of her race, she encouraged the attempts of artists and scholars, which however did not prevent her from satisfying her ambition by means of shameless intrigues. She was extremely cunning; a human life counted for little in her eyes, as St. Bartholomew's night proved. But she knew how to control her hatred when necessary for the furtherance of her political interests, and assumed the mark of friendship to mislead her enemies.

She coveted the crown, but being a foreigner there were many obstacles in her path; and while sharing the government with Duke Francis of Guise and the Cardinal of Lorraine, she hoped for a time when the monarchy would be hers.

But there were still others, who, by reason of their descent, might claim the crown; the three brothers Bourbon, the eldest of whom became King of Navarre through his marriage with Jeanne d'Albret. He had embraced the Reformed faith, but not with all his heart. Irresolute and wavering, he was ruled by his favourites. More than one sharp arrow was directed at his heart by Calvin, without curing him of his half-heartedness, and this King, of whom the Protestants expected so much, turned his back on them at the critical moment.

The second brother bore the title of General, and had not brains sufficient for a corporal, while the youngest brother, Prince Louis of Condé, was a man of undeniable courage and bravery, a capable general, earnestly devoted to the Huguenot cause; he was, however, inconstant, without perseverance, and no match for the cunning diplomacy of his enemies.

In the summer of 1560 King Henry II died; December 23 of the same year witnessed Du Bourg's death.

In the chapel at eleven o'clock in the morning of that day the sentence was read to him, in which he was condemned, as an obstinate and implacable sacramentarian heretic, to be hanged and hoisted on a gallows, to be placed in *Place de Grève* in front of the town hall: a fit spot — beneath which a fire was to be lit, and the afore-mentioned Du Bourg to be thrown into it and burnt to ashes.

At three o'clock on this short day of December the hangman appeared, the prisoner was placed in a red cart, with a priest beside him. Then the gloomy vehicle moved forward, surrounded by four hundred foot-soldiers and two hundred horse-soldiers, all of them with Swords drawn, to prevent the danger of a riot. For Anne du Bourg was a celebrated and beloved man, the nephew of a French Chancellor and a generally respected lawyer.

The streets were crowded, one could have walked on the heads; and the cart which was conveying the martyr to the scaffold could scarcely proceed through the dense mass of people.

Du Bourg seemed absorbed in reflection; his thoughts had already passed the threshold of eternity; his lips were moving, he was singing Psalms in a low voice. And Calvin relates that his face was illuminated with joy when the scaffold was reached.

Arrived at the place of execution, he took off his mantle and coat — with the tranquillity of a tired child that undresses before going to sleep — safe in its mother's care.

The hangman put the rope around his neck, on which Du Bourg, looking at him in surprise, exclaimed: "Is not that unnecessary, since I am to be slowly burnt?" The hangman replied, that in consideration of his high station in life the sentence contained a secret clause, according to which he was to be strangled first and then burnt, to diminish his suffering.

Then Du Bourg cast a last look at that Babel which shed the blood of God's beloved children like water, knelt down on the scaffold, and exclaimed: "Oh Lord, my God, do not desert me, that I may not desert Thee!"

A few moments later his body swung high in the air, on the gallows, while the crowd, awestruck, exclaimed: "Jesus! Maria!" Then the executioners lit the fire and the body was cast into the flames to be burnt to ashes.

Calvin was full of anxiety; the persecutions went on, and it was to be feared that the bow which was too tightly drawn would some day snap.

He walked to and fro full of care, surveying the French battlefield from his high watchtower.

He foresaw the possibility of the Protestants forming a political party, and that not the cross, but a waving banner would become their symbol. That was the cause of his anxiety. The most effective victories which could elevate the Church of Christ in his eyes, were the victories gained on the scaffold and at the stake, while the triumphs gained in a bloody war only got a shrug of his shoulders. Have his predictions concerning France turned out false?

And had the Reformation, like a spiritual Nile-stream, been allowed to fertilize the fields with its blood for another ten years, might not France have become an impregnable fortress of Protestantism?

There was the "Amboise Conspiracy." That was the beginning; there the fatal knot was tied which bound French Protestantism to politics.

The conspiracy was set on foot by a nobleman, La Renaudie, who organized a meeting at Nantes, to which he invited the most violent opponents of the Guises, both Protestants and Roman Catholics, in order to put a stop to the growing power of the Guises, which threatened to become a danger to the State. In glowing language he described the critical state of their country; he appealed to those present to assist him in breaking down the tyranny of these ambitious men by imprisoning them and having them sentenced at a sitting of the States General.

The meeting, at which the most embittered enemies of the Guises were present, agreed to this resolution on condition that nothing was to be undertaken against the King or the Government, while Renaudie told them that at the right moment Condé would place himself at the head of the movement.

The conspiracy was betrayed, the Court was removed to safe Amboise, and the Guises took a bloody revenge, while Condé, who swore to his innocence, was taken into custody.

Calvin alluded to this fatal conspiracy in a letter to De Coligny. It was necessary, as it was rumoured that Calvin had given his full approbation to this conspiracy.

Where did people get such talk from? Calvin was altogether opposed to it; with the utmost decision he rejected the aid of carnal weapons in a fight where God's Word is the sword of Gideon, with which great deeds are done. His feelings were diametrically opposed to the aspirations of those men, who, with gloomy eyes and compressed lips, awaited the signal to avenge the blood of the martyrs on the cruel Church of Rome. Calvin thought such a deed a crime, which the Church, under the Cross, would one day repent of.

But the reins slipped from Calvin's hands.

And at this unusual sight of rebellion and mutiny in his own ranks, the Reformer uttered this mournful complaint: "Alas! Alas! I never thought to see the day when we should have lost all trust in those that call themselves the faithful; must then the Church of Geneva be thus scorned by her children?"

The Church of Geneva — that was Calvin. He was the heart of that Church. And identifying himself with that Church, he was its interpreter in calling the use of carnal weapons an abuse.

For a moment we are surprised and confused by this new principle put forward by Calvin. But it is no new principle; Calvin remains consistent; and he draws a sharp line between possession and conquest. Let Christianity march forth to conquest; all knees must bend to the name of Jesus Christ, the Lord of all. But in this march of conquest the weapons to be taken must not be guns or swords; the only weapons must be faith, an inward resolution, good works, and the patience of the saints. It is a spiritual strife. And when souls have been won for the cause of the great King, then the Government should form a magistracy corresponding to this condition.

The Church under the Cross, that was Calvin's ideal of the suffering and struggling community of Christ in France. And amid the clash of arms he stood on his spiritual watch-tower, and undaunted he flung his powerful protestation against war into the face of the fighters.

He had no rest; his two letters written to his brothers in France in June and November, 1559, were full of touching earnestness. He did not address himself to one small community, but to all the Churches; to the two thousand Protestant communities, to the Huguenots, who, sword in hand and singing their powerful martial hymns, were preparing to fill the world with their immortal fame.

Suffering — nothing but suffering — that was the task which Calvin commended. He assured them that the dark clouds would disperse and that God would send His light to make their hearts rejoice. He would console them better than a mother. He would take pity on his poor persecuted sheep and would pull out the fangs of the bloodthirsty wolves or change them into lambs. Thus spoke Calvin. But the persecutions were continued with undiminished violence, and the latent hope, that the death of Henry II would bring a change, had vanished into smoke.

"During the reign of Francis II," so Beza says, "the fury of Satan was unrestrained, so that we may say of his rule, which only lasted seventeen months, what Jesus says in the Gospel of St. Matthew that, had those days not been shortened, no one would have been spared; but they were shortened for the sake of the elect."

New edicts for the destruction of the heretics were issued; in every Parliament a special committee was charged with condemning everyone suspected of being an adherent of the Evangelical truth, to be burnt to death. Paris and Toulouse, Dijon and Bordeaux, Lyons, Poitiers, and many other towns were zealously employed in extirpating all Protestant heresies; it was a general competition as to who could set aflame the largest number of stakes. But amid this rage De Coligny came forward from the solitude of his country-seat, and unconcerned for the consequences, publicly placed a petition for freedom of conscience and public worship at the foot of the throne on the opening of the meeting of notables.

Calvin's stern face lit up when he heard of this courageous act, and, full of admiration and restrained enthusiasm, he wrote to the Admiral: "We have every cause to praise God for the rare courage which has been given you, to proclaim His glory and to further the extension of the realm of Christ. Even if everyone were blind or ungrateful, even if all your labour should seem lost — be satisfied, in the conviction that God and the angels approve your deed!"

Again a King died who had not been a King, the child Francis II. Gloomy clouds of death seemed to drift over the French throne. Two kings within two years! Henry II died in 1559; Francis II in 1560.

And the people again cried: "The King is dead — long live the King!"

It was Charles IX, then a boy of ten, who, twelve years after, amused himself with firing on his defenceless Protestant subjects from the window of the royal palace.

The royal mother soon dried her tears, and sharp-witted as she was, she gave Condé a post of honour instead of sending him to the scaffold.

She wished to win over the Bourbons by favours without estranging the Guises, and she gave the Chancellor l'Hôpital the command to convene the States General within the walls of Orléans. The relief thus afforded the Huguenots was great; Psalms of speedy delivery were sung; it was whispered from mouth to mouth that l'Hôpital, this Roman Catholic statesman, had a heart and not a stone in his bosom.

Much more could be said of this excellent statesman.

He was a noble and upright man; he had an open eye for the miseries of a country rent by fierce internal dissension; at the opening of the States General he spoke words of peace and reconciliation.

He had discovered that Christianity preaches love, not bitter disputes, that it was high time to be led by gentleness, and abolishing the mutual nicknames, to retain only the honourable name of Christian.

So the programme faintly outlined by l'Hôpital aimed at the true salvation of his country; but alas! his oars were too short to row against the stream. The States General adjourned without having done anything, and the Bill, consisting of 150 clauses drawn up by the Chancellor to improve at any rate the most crying abuses in Church and State, could not be carried, owing to the scornful opposition of the clergy, the officials, and part of the aristocracy. Yet there were unmistakable signs of the wind veering. The Queen-Regent and the whole Court were present at the sermon preached by the Bishop of Valence, who was known to be in favour of the new doctrine; many noble families held Protestant services in their castles; the Reformation even penetrated into the apartments of the Royal Palace.

Here and there a Roman Catholic Church was used for Protestant worship, and a flood of refugees, who returned from Geneva, repeated with French enthusiasm the strong fervent expressions of faith they had caught from Calvin's lips. The Chancellor kept up his courage. Now that the Reformation was taking such an enormous flight, he foresaw that a bloody civil war would be inevitable if the reconciliation were not on a sound basis. It was just these terrible dangers which would promote a reconciliation, and with the consent of the Queen Regent he convened the famous meeting of Poissy, in order to bring about an arrangement between Roman Catholicism and Protestantism.

On August 23, Beza arrived at Poissy. He had already been staying in France for several months; the previous winter he had held one of his famous hedge-sermons outside the walls of Paris in a heavy shower of rain, attracting six thousand hearers, and two months afterward, this number, during an afternoon sermon, had risen to twenty-five thousand.

The Court looked forward to meeting this man whose name was so famous in the Protestant world, in a state of intense expectation, and Beza afterward communicated his impressions to Calvin.

"When I had exchanged a few words with Admiral de Coligny," he relates, "I was greeted by the King of Navarre and Condé with the utmost cordiality."

Beza was one of Calvin's most excellent pupils. He had a gentle character; kindness was written on his face; Geneva, which would not give Calvin leave, could not have sent a better substitute.

The 9th of September was the auspicious day of the opening of the conference. A throne had been erected in the large hall of the convent, and on this throne Charles IX, the child of twelve, seated himself.

On his left sat Catherine de Medici, on his right his brother, the Duke of Orléans and the King of Navarre, and behind him the highest nobility had taken their seats. It was a most impressive gathering; thirty-six bishops and archbishops, besides a great number of graduates and clergymen of various ranks, were present.

Silence was commanded, the noise ceased, and the child sitting on the throne spoke a few words, learnt by heart, which opened the meeting.

Then l'Hôpital rose to explain again the state of affairs in an earnest speech; he predicted the fall of the State if party-disputes did not cease, and proposed as a fair demand that the Protestants should be heard in their own defence.

Duke Francis of Guise, the grim enemy of the Reformation, then approached to usher in the Protestant preachers.

There were eleven of them, as the twelfth, Peter Martyr, had not arrived. And every preacher brought two representatives elected by the communities, so that altogether the embassy consisted of thirty-three members.

There was a general movement to see those notorious heretics; all eyes were turned to those simple men, soberly attired in their black gowns, who, with heads bared, walked toward the balustrade which separated them from the throne.

Beza was the foremost. It was whispered that this man was Calvin's shield-bearer, and it had to be acknowledged that he was worthy to bear the shield of the David of Protestantism. In this historical arena where the children of the Reformation had to confess their faith, Beza moved as freely as if at home in his study.

Free and unrestrained in his manners, well formed, with noble, regular features, born from head to foot an aristocrat, in the full vigour of his manly strength, this man could not but create a deep impression.

It had become very quiet; the fall of a pin might have been heard; and amid this solemn silence, Beza said in a firm, respectful tone: "If we wish this meeting to be crowned with success, O King, we must, first of all, implore the blessing of God on it." Then he knelt down without waiting for a reply; all the Protestants knelt down with him.

It was an affecting moment; the sheep of Christ, sheltering under the wings of their invisible Protector, in the midst of the wolves . . .

Then the Protestants rose: "May the Lord," said Beza, "guide this meeting to the glory of His Name, the confirmation of France's happiness, and the salvation of the whole of Christianity!" The glory of God's name, the happiness of France, and the salvation of Christianity — such was his programme.

He then held his famous speech. But when in the fire of his speech he used the expression: "Christ's body is as far removed from the sacred bread as heaven is from earth," the gathering burst into fierce cries of indignation.

"He blasphemes God," they cried. "Why should we stay here any longer?"

It would have been more prudent of Beza not to have used this strong expression, for which he offered his excuses to the Queen-Regent the following day. It had been his intention to bring out the spiritual meaning of the bread and wine at the Holy Communion, and in his anxiety to be faithful to his convictions he had used an expression which might just as well have been omitted.

But Calvin thought differently. He was a man who liked exactness in all things, and he declared that God had guided Beza's mind and tongue when he uttered those offence-giving words. So the different opinions about the Holy Supper were to be the wedge which would irrevocably split Christendom asunder.

Or was it yet possible to bridge the gulf which yawned between Protestantism and Roman Catholicism? And could a formula be found to satisfy both sides?

Among the Roman Catholics there were many hearts which bled because of the schism, and they prayed to God for deliverance. And deliverance actually seemed at hand; in a conference between two Roman Catholic priests and two Protestant ministers, of whom Beza was one, the happy formula was found which could be signed by all.

It ran as follows: "We believe that when partaking of the Supper, Christ truly imparts to us His body and His blood through the power of the Holy Spirit, and that in a spiritual sense we eat the body of Christ and drink His blood through our belief in that sacrament, in order that we may be flesh of His flesh and bone of His bone. In this sense we accept the presence of the blood and the body of Christ in the Supper." There was great rejoicing over this beginning of a reconciliation; the Cardinal of Lorraine declared that such had always been his opinion concerning this point; and Calvin, driven to his bed by a violent attack of rheumatism, felt his heart rejuvenated, while he wrote to Beza: "The Lord be praised! He will exalt us, even to the clouds, that we may embrace the feet of Christ and look down on His and our enemies with triumphant eyes."

But Calvin had been carried away by his enthusiasm; the conference adjourned without having come up to the expectations, and the famous formula signed by Protestants and Roman Catholics, was rejected as heretical at the great meeting of Poissy.

Nevertheless the edict of January, 1562, may be termed a consequence of the conference of Poissy.

The freedom of worship, for which the Protestants had long asked in vain, was now granted them, on the understanding that they should hold their services by day and outside the towns.

Calvin was satisfied. "If only we are allowed to keep this freedom," he argued, "then popery must inevitably totter to its fall."

The Huguenots had no less cause to rejoice, while Beza, full of fervent gratitude, wrote: "He who never permits His sheep to be tried above their strength has had mercy on His new-born lambs and the shepherds who had begun to graze them." Beza remained in Paris for the time being. Catherine de Medici desired this; and Calvin also desired it. But their motives were different. Calvin thought of the future of French Protestantism, the Queen-Regent of the future of her rule. Her soul was filled with distrust of the great power of the Guises in which she saw a menace to her authority, and she asked De Coligny how many Huguenot communities there were and how many soldiers they could raise.

The reply must have gratified her. The Protestants were five million in number; there were 2150 communities, and this number was always on the increase.

Theodore Beza

But Beza did not like to hear this talk of soldiers; he wished to keep the Reformation apart from politics, and tried to prevent the fatal alliance at the same moment that the French Reformation was already afloat on the political waters with all sails set.

The suction had been too strong. In a cleverly drawn-up manifesto Catherine de Medici appealed to the Huguenots to aid her in maintaining her authority against a faction that, with a false Roman Catholic device on their lips, aimed at overthrowing her government. Instead of being mutineers and firebrands, the Huguenots were all at once changed into faithful subjects; to be a Protestant was to be a true Royalist; and the common enemy was the Duke of Guise, who plotted to obtain the throne, and who was at the same time the most furious heretic-hunter.

Beza was in Paris. He preached daily. And the Psalms of the Huguenots sounded bolder than ever. For they knew the Queen-Regent had become their friend. They had been oppressed long enough — now there was an end of it. They had been led to slaughter like sheep, but everything had its appointed time, and they would now use their fists, should the enemy dare to come. They no longer tolerated the interruption of their religious services; the police had been warned by the authorities to help them if they had well-founded complaints, and one evening the streets of Paris witnessed the strange spectacle of a Protestant mob conducting thirty-six Roman Catholic priests to prison.

It was at this time that Calvin dedicated his splendid exposition of the Prophet Daniel to all true believers in France.

Even then his enthusiasm had already left him; like a prophetic perspective, gloomy visions passed before his mind's eye, and full of sad reflections he wrote in his dedication: "You will have to fight long and fiercely — I foresee a bloodier and more stubborn struggle than you may possibly believe."

Twelve months after, he finished his lectures on the Prophet Jeremiah and was about to commence the Lamentations.

The Lamentations — it frightened him. And he anxiously asked himself whether this might not prove to be a bad omen. It had dawned in the East; but the red streak on the horizon had not been the splendour of the sun, but the reflection of blood, the warm gushing blood which would stain the lovely hills and valleys of France.

Chapter XXXI

THE MASSACRE OF VASSY AND ITS CONSEQUENCES

AMID the intoxication of their rapidly increasing power, the Huguenots were thunderstruck at the news that King Antony of Navarre had gone over to the Roman Catholic camp and the standard of the Guises.

They called it an incredible piece of news, and its truth was questioned when the first shock was over. But it was all in vain; the truth could no longer be denied, and the man who had been proud of being called the head of the Huguenots, went over to the enemy bag and baggage.

"Sire," the Spanish Ambassador had said to him, "if you return to the old faith, my high commander, Philip II, will restore to you your kingdom of Navarre or else Sardinia as a compensation. "Sire," the Spanish Ambassador had added, "Charles IX is mortal and his brother also. Well, then, what is to prevent you from ascending the French throne when you have cast off your Huguenot guise?"

The King of Navarre had heard enough. Beza tried his utmost to keep him for the Huguenot cause, Calvin wrote long urgent letters; Jeanne d'Albret shed bitter tears — it was all in vain. "The pity I feel for your fears," Calvin wrote to her, "show me their depth and bitterness. But however that may be — it is much better to be sorrowful for such a cause than to be indifferent to your spiritual interests."

Maltreated by her husband, overcome with grief and sorrow, she proceeded to her states of Bearn. She left her son behind, begging him with a troubled heart to remain faithful to his mother's creed. He did not. Nevertheless he always had an affection for the Church his mother clung to with such heroic faith; and although not a member of that Church — he always remained its protector.

So King Antony of Navarre had become the ally of the Guises; France never saw more unnatural alliances than in those days.

On one side stood the Guises, King Antony, the former head of the Huguenots, and Montmorency, a relation of De Coligny. On the other side stood Condé, King Antony's brother, De Coligny and his numerous Huguenot adherents, and Catherine de Medici, who, in her heart of hearts, abhorred the Huguenots.

But the unnaturalness of these alliances was only surpassed by the hatred of the factions, by the religious bitterness raging in their hearts. One spark was sufficient to set France aflame, and the massacre of Vassy was not a spark, but a flame which reached the gunpowder stores.

Was the Duke of Guise guilty of the massacre of Vassy?

Between the Guises and Vassy there existed an old feud ever since the first-named had obtained the rights to the first fruits of the town.

Nevertheless the inhabitants of Vassy were of a vigorous, independent spirit; the majority of them earned their living in various trades and industries, and they held a lively spiritual communication with the democratic citizens of the large town of Troyes.

After the conference of Poissy a Protestant Church was founded at Vassy; the authorities warned them that this took place within the jurisdiction of the Guises, the bitterest enemies of the Reformation. The preacher took no notice of this warning; the services commenced with a meeting of a hundred and twenty persons at the house of a linen-weaver, the next day there were six hundred.

Six hundred hearers out of a population of only three thousand; that was a record! Vassy was converted; it had been won for the Reformation, and under the blue vault of heaven the famous hedge-sermons were held. Guise was warned; he sent some soldiers to assist the officer of justice in suppressing the small church, but with no result. Then the Bishop of Châlons appeared, together with a famous monk, armed to the teeth with scholastic wisdom, who was to explain the true state of affairs to the inhabitants of Vassy. The Bishop invited the most important inhabitants of the town to come and hear this man, but they replied that not for all the treasures of the world would they consent to listen to a false prophet, and they went to their own preacher.

The Roman Catholics were indignant; with the Bishop, the officer of justice and other authorities at their head, they marched to the meeting-place of the Protestants.

The preacher was in the pulpit; the Bishop wished to speak, but the preacher cried out that he was no bishop, no true shepherd. "You do not preach," the preacher said, "you do not feed your flock with the Word of the Lord, and your appointment is not ratified by the people."

The Bishop departed amid loud cries from the people; obscene words were shouted after him, and this scene, which put one more in mind of a revolution than of the Reformation, made things worse.

The Bishop departed full of bitter rage; Guise stamped his foot with fury, but he controlled himself and bided his time. He wished to teach Paris a lesson — Paris, which for five months had thought the Guises dead, by suddenly dealing a heavy blow to break the enemy's power, which would show them that he was still living. But his courage was more than matched by his cunning. He raised a troop of soldiers which made one think of war, but at the same time he took with him his brother, the Cardinal, his son, who was yet a child, and his wife, who was expecting a second child, when he set out on his expedition. Thus he was afterward able to declare, with his hand on his heart: "It took place accidentally, else I should not have dreamed of taking my wife!"

In reality the Duchess did not witness the horrible spectacle; she was in the neighbourhood, outside the walls of the town.

The Duke might have supposed that the inhabitants of Vassy, in the face of a menacing Roman Catholic force, would give in and surrender a few heretical ringleaders to be strangled. But this did not happen. And when the Duke heard the church-bells ringing in the distance and it was reported to him that the Huguenots were going to their meeting-place, he cried out: "Let us be present at it!" This command was greeted with joyful exclamations. Vassy was a small but flourishing town; it would be worth plundering . . .

Near the gates of the town they met a citizen dressed in black. This black dress was enough to excite the suspicions of the soldiers; they stopped him and shouted: "Are you a Huguenot preacher? Speak up — where did you study?"

The man could prove that he was a bootmaker; his hands showed it. Besides, he had never studied at Geneva. So he escaped with the fright.

Arrived at the monastery, the Duke dismounted. He dined there, and afterward walked up and down the long corridor with the prior and the officer of justice, and seemed very excited.

The Roman Catholics who had gone to mass, were told not to leave the church on any account; then the Duke gave his soldiers a sign to advance to the shed where the Protestants were gathered together. And the Duke followed them.

At a distance of twenty-five paces two musket-shots were fired at the window of the shed. And, overturning some people who were trying to lock the doors, the soldiers rushed into the wooden building, raising the terrible cry: "Slay them! Slay them!"

The gathering consisted of about 1260 persons, most of them of the trading-class. There were among them five linen-weavers, a butcher, a wine-merchant, a bailiff, and a schoolmaster. The most important citizen among them was an alderman of Vassy. The Roman Catholics assert that the Protestants commenced hostilities by throwing stones, an assertion which sounds extremely improbable, when we bear in mind that the Protestants were confronted by enemies who were armed to the teeth.

When the Duke arrived, three Huguenots had already been killed, and his presence was a further incitement to proceed with the massacre. It was easy work; the Protestants were unarmed, defenceless they served as targets for the soldiers; they were dispatched like sheep — one of the Duke's lackeys afterward boasted of having murdered six Huguenots. Surrounded inside and outside by the hostile hordes, some of the Huguenots tried to escape through the thatched roof, and mad with fear they jumped into the town moat to save their lives. Some of them feared to take the dangerous leap, while the Duke shouted from above: "Down with you, rascals!"

The cries of the dying resounded far and wide, and reached the ears of the Duchess, who, impelled by human compassion, begged her spouse at least to spare the pregnant women. And from then on pregnant women were spared.

The Huguenot preacher, who had only recently come from Geneva and who had remained in the pulpit, managed to escape amid the general confusion, and had almost reached the door when he stumbled over a corpse and was seized, and, heavily wounded, taken before the Duke.

The Duke rudely asked him what had moved him to lead the people to rebellion? Whereupon he still had strength to reply: "My Lord, I am not a rebel — I have only preached the Gospel."

Guise contemptuously turned his back on him, and left him to his lackeys who treated him cruelly.

His end was touching. With his dying lips he stammered the Psalm of praise:

> *Into Thy hands I give my spirit;*
> *I'm ransomed by Thy favour,*
> *Lord, God of truth, my Saviour!*[31]

The young Cardinal leaned exhausted against the wall of the cemetery, his eyes fixed on the horrible spectacle. The Duke showed him the volume which had been found in the pulpit; the Cardinal opened it and said: "It is the Holy Bible!"

Sixty of those peaceful church-goers, whose only crime had been that they had served God according to their conscience, were dispatched on that fatal Sunday of the 1st of March; the number of the wounded was simply innumerable.

A cry of anger and horror rose from the Protestant camp when the massacre of Vassy became known, and with the rapidity of a prairie fire the fatal news spread throughout the length and breadth of France. Drawings were made of the scene of the murder, the art of illustration was born, and the pamphlets inscribed by the drawing-pencil made a deeper impression on the people than those inscribed by the pen had ever made.

Guise felt lonely and deserted. Even his wife and his brother, the Cardinal, could not justify his conduct. But his fox-like cunning did not desert him. He went to Nauteuil, where he defied the outburst of public indignation with his dreaded and illustrious name,

---

[31] Psalm 31:3b (*Book of Praise*).

and invited the old Marshal of France, Montmorency, to pay him a visit.

Montmorency did so; he had no objection to crossing the threshold of this French Achan.

Then the Duke was saved. And so sure was he of his triumph that when the Queen-Mother invited him to Saint-Germain, he replied that he had prepared a feast for some friends at Nauteuil.

The Marshal conducted the Duke of Guise to Paris with an impressive retinue of armed noblemen. Condé was still in Paris, but his forces were small in number, and he had not much support from his brother, the Cardinal of Bourbon, for this man, who bore the title of lieutenant-general to the King, was not quite responsible for his actions. He ordered both Condé and Guise to depart. Condé went, but Guise did not. And Montmorency, who had become his advocate, told the Parliament that the venerated voice of the people had induced the Duke to remain in the capital. Was this true?

Guise had, on his entry into the town, been very coolly received by a large part of the populace. At the corners of the streets in the squares, there had been people who, notwithstanding the brilliant military array which escorted the Duke, had clenched their fists and shouted imprecations after him.

The Duke acted his part masterly. He declared with affected grief, that at Vassy he had done nothing but protect his honour, his wife, and his child, that he knew very well they aimed at his life, and thirty assassins had been sent to Paris after him. He begged them to look into this matter, and the truth would be confirmed. He had never abused his power, and now he no longer had any power, because he had handed it over to the King, into the hands of his Marshal. He asked for nothing but justice; he would voluntarily go to prison if the Government wished it, and where he had committed an error he was willing to submit to the consequences.

Thus spoke the murderer stained with the innocent blood of Vassy, who, in reality, by means of his forces, held the town and Parliament under his control, and who ordered the child, called Charles IX and King of France, to follow him, the king of murderers and of the civil war, to Paris.

From this fateful day the French Protestants assumed the white sash, while Guise and his adherents followed the red banner. For red was the colour of Spain, of King Philip II, and of the massacre of Vassy . . .

So the Duke was the victor, before the civil war had begun; he called himself the true defender of the Roman Catholic Church, and accepted with complacency the homage of a people excited to frenzy, and seized the reins of government.

The King of Navarre was an easy tool in his hands; and this tool went to Fontainebleau to fetch Charles IX and the Queen-Mother, a woman who had only just given the Protestants permission to take up arms.

On April 6 the King was already in Paris, and six days afterward a fresh murder was committed at Sens. Sixty killed at Vassy, a hundred at Sens — the thirst for blood was on the increase. The signal for wholesale murder had been given; the Seine and Loire were red with blood; in long rows the unburied corpses floated down the stream toward the sea. In vain did Beza hasten to the Queen-Mother to demand satisfaction for this violation of an edict issued by the Government itself. He received no satisfaction, and the King of Navarre, forgetting duty and honour, had the insolence to remind him with a mocking smile, that it was the vocation of God's Church to be beaten without making resistance. But Beza could find the right word at the right time.

Looking into the eyes of the traitor King with proud dignity, he said with cutting severity: "Sire, it is certainly true that the Church must receive blows without giving blows in exchange, but remember it is an anvil which has worn out many hammers!"

The Protestants were not unaware of the seriousness of the moment. They examined their conscience and turned over the leaves of their Bible, looking for texts which would justify armed resistance. Their hand yet wavered; for they lacked a French Knox who dared to preach from the pulpit the Holy War of the Lord and the Crusade of fire and steel against false prophets.

They applied to Geneva for advice. Calvin admonished and warned them; he spoke of the left cheek which has to be turned to the enemy when the right cheek is smitten. His letters were like hammers to impress them with the truth, that only a spiritual strife is permitted, and that the death of the body is of small consequence if only the soul is saved.

The Huguenots had done so — up to the important year 1562. With untiring patience they had endured the most cruel persecutions; with sublime disregard of death and with a song of triumph on their lips, they had gone forth to die, and in the last agonies of death still strengthened and comforted by the tender words of consolation which Calvin sent them in his letters.

They were yet willing to deny and forsake themselves, but their wives, their children? Were their families to be defencelessly butchered? They had to obey the authorities, but who were they? Was it not high time to overthrow the power of the Guises, who guarded the young King and his mother like prisoners? The Huguenots took to arms, although they had received no summons. They formed into bands and without order or discipline, without a leader or guide, they marched in the direction of Paris.

Condé, a prince of royal blood, was their natural commander, now that the King of Navarre, his brother, had deserted them.

But Condé, who was as thoughtless as he was devoted, waited for De Coligny. For this great patriot possessed the cool judgment, the clear head and the firm will which Condé so sadly lacked.

De Coligny kept them waiting. Courier after courier stormed his castle to beg him to buckle on his armour in the face of this threatening danger, but his eye saw farther into the future than the eye of the near-sighted prince. He shrank back at the thought of a civil war. He knew that the Huguenots were in the minority, and that this minority would be still further diminished by the chances of an unfortunate war. He knew that only a month previously, Condé had asked the Protestants of Paris for ten thousand dollars, and that he had obtained no more than sixteen hundred, and at Paris Condé's condition had been so precarious that, according to a certain sharp-witted man, the servants of the Parisian priests could have hunted him out of the town.

The worst thing was that this weak Protestant party was not united, but was divided into two factions; the Protestants, pure and simple, who were prepared to risk everything for the faith, and a fickle crowd who, through different circumstances, chance, a grudge against prevailing abuses, had drifted into the Protestant camp.

That was the party which De Coligny had to lead, to command, to save in spite of itself; opposed by three-fourths of France and a Spanish King.

In every civil war women appear on the scene — Kenau Hasselaars, who, wishing to believe the impossible, make it attainable by the turbulent passion of their souls. There was Madeleine de Roye, sister to the Admiral, who had preceded her brothers on the path of the Reformation; her daughter Eleanore, recently married to the Prince of Condé; Claude de Rieu, the wife of Dandelot, who with touching conjugal fidelity had shared his gloomy prison at Milan; Queen Jeanne d'Albret, who made good her husband's desertion by redoubling her devotion to the cause; Charlotte of Laval, the woman who was worthy of being the wife of France's greatest hero. Tortured by gloomy forebodings, De Coligny sat in his castle while his ear caught the cries of distress of his persecuted fellow-believers. His wife, Charlotte of Laval, shed hot tears. She complained that her husband, otherwise one of the most faithful, had now betrayed the Church and surrendered his brothers in the faith unprotected to the Guises. But she was mistaken. It was a woman's passion which spoke in her, while he, a great statesman and general, calculated the consequences.

"Charlotte," said he, "put your hand on your heart! Examine your conscience! Speak. Are you capable of bearing the scorn, the reproaches of a people which judges according to success? Are you capable of bearing flight, poverty, hunger — the hunger of your children, Charlotte? Death at the hands of the hangman? Your husband dragged to a dungeon? Think it over — I give you three weeks!"

"Three weeks!" she cried passionately; "do not heap on your head the victims of three weeks!" That word decided him. From his sense the wife had appealed to his heart, and he thought he heard the voice of the Lord in it. Now thought and deliberation were at an end, he no longer inquired about the number of his friends or of his foes, and jumped into the saddle: he and his heroic brother Dandelot, to fight in the holy wars of the Lord.

The first error of the French Protestants had been to choose the weak King of Navarre for their head; the second was that they accepted Condé as a substitute for the unfaithful King.

For not Condé, but De Coligny was the man who could have brought the fight to a successful issue; and the difference of opinion, the gulf between their ways of thinking, their aspirations, their inclinations, darkened the Admiral's eye when seated at the same supper-table with the Prince.

Already on the day after that Sunday it came to a violent altercation, as Condé and the nobility wished to apply for foreign assistance, while De Coligny opposed it with might and main. He was one of the true national party, and called it tempting God to beg for assistance from abroad, as the Guises had done. The die had been cast meanwhile — the passionate French blood knew no other way out. Condé galloped to the south with a brilliant troop of noblemen, amid shouts of joy and applause. And the blithe and joyous Protestants entered the gates of Orléans with him.

De Coligny followed at the head of the burly, stern Calvinists. He planted the Protestant standard in Orléans; he put the trumpet of war to his lips, to call spiritual Israel to arms, and he wrote on his banner: "The Glory of God and freedom to King and Country!"

Beza was also present. The vigorous advocate of the Reformation at Poissy became the military chaplain of the armed Huguenots, and appointed a solemn day of prayer and repentance to invoke God's blessing on their arms.

The whole kingdom seemed all at once changed into one huge armourer's workshop. The Huguenots needed no incitement to arm themselves. The death-agonies at Vassy had startled them, and the cries of distress at Sens had decided them. They seized their swords to defend their lives and the lives of those most precious to them; and they got into a state of over-exertion and over-excitement in which they would have been capable of committing a murder merely to prevent another murder.

At the same time the plague was raging in the towns. In Orléans ten thousand people, in Paris eighty thousand were carried to their graves, while those that survived were preparing to tear each other to pieces. Within six weeks the French Calvinists were under arms.

The Duke did not feel at ease; he was disagreeably surprised; the Spaniards that Philip II had promised would not arrive till August, and now it was April. In his anxiety Guise wrote to the Roman Catholic cantons of Switzerland to hurry on with their auxiliary troops, and by promising a large amount of money he tried to raise mercenary troops in Germany.

The clergy of his church provided him with the money. Forced to it by his need, he put the knife to their throats, and their terror was the key with which he opened the Roman Catholic money-box.

He had still another weapon: that weapon was intrigue, the secret game of diplomacy, for which his fingers seemed to have a special aptitude.

He used the name of the young King, and the crafty stage-tricks of the Queen-Mother, together with the splendour of the royal court, to obtain the victory. She had seduced the King of Navarre; she was capable of seducing Condé. To keep up the show, he left the Chancellor l'Hôpital with her; the noble-minded Roman Catholic, who had to cover the base practices of Francis of Guise with the cloak of his virtue.

The Protestant reaction on the massacre of Vassy was deplorable. Roman Catholic shops were plundered, monks were maltreated; priests were murdered. But to acknowledge the truth, these were isolated cases, and Protestant revenge confined itself on the whole almost exclusively to the images of convents and Roman Catholic places of worship. The saints were torn from their pedestals and destroyed; the famous relics, of which so many miracles were related, were summoned to perform another miracle to prolong their existence. It was a wholesale destruction of images! A rude dissipation! A horrible deed.

Calvin never approved of such deeds; his soul abhorred violence; he was a man of order and discipline.

But was the destruction, the damage, irreparable, as it was said? Was not rather the massacre which destroyed the lives of so many Protestants irreparable? Much has been said concerning the anger of the Roman Catholics when the misdeeds committed by the Protestants in their revenge became known. What had the Protestants done in Picardy, in Champagne? Nearly everywhere they were persecuted to death for the wrong which had not been done by them, but to them. The old mother of the Guises completed her revenge on the unhappy town of Vassy by dismantling its fortifications and demolishing the walls, while savage soldiers were quartered on the inhabitants. It was the prelude to the future dragonades, and the grave-diggers at Vassy were busily employed. Then the Spaniards that Guise had asked for to assist him, arrived from across the Pyrenees. Their barbaric cruelty exceeded the highest expectations. The hard-hearted Gascon Montluc, a man of blood, who boasted of having adorned every tree on his road with corpses, relates that those black devils, whom he had supplied with two hundred women to do with as they liked, had preferred cutting open their bellies, even of the pregnant women, in order to destroy the little Protestants. Is it then surprising that the Protestants who had been called to arms, longed to be at home to defend their families? Or that De Coligny was compelled to call in foreign aid, which the enemy had been doing for the last two years? Dandelot travelled to Germany, another ambassador went to England.

It was a civil war which would decide the fate of the Guises and the Bourbons, but this war was at the same time a war of religion which would settle the dispute between the Roman Catholic and the Protestant faith. Thus the leaders understood the case. That was why Guise had applied to Spain; why Condé applied to Queen Elizabeth, while Calvin ordered the churches to raise the pay for the mercenaries.

With the liveliest interest and a heart full of cares Calvin watched the foaming tide of the civil war. He had a keen eye for the great difficulties which the Reformation had to pass through, because in its course it crossed the tortuous paths of politics, but he was of opinion that the war had been pressed on them, and he followed the campaign with bated breath.

The brave Dandelot had a difficult task at the German courts. The difficulty was to open the eyes of the Germans to the real state of France, and to clear away the mountain of lies and slanders which blocked up their view. He was surrounded by swarms of spies of the Guises who penetrated into the cabinets of the German princes and stole the Protestant letters from their tables. It was only by means of infinite patience and inexhaustible perseverance that Dandelot succeeded in obtaining a partial success, and returned to France at the head of six thousand German soldiers to assist the Protestants in their need. De Coligny was in Orléans with a select body of brave men, while the rest of the Protestant army had degenerated into guerilla-bands, which overran the country, stealing and plundering, and who had taken as their war-cry, "an eye for an eye and a tooth for a tooth."

Those bands made terrible havoc. Their passions had been let loose. But their barbarity was far excelled by the storm of Roman Catholic fury which changed beautiful Provence into a desert.

Never has war been waged more horribly. Listen to an account of how religious hatred raged in Provence!

"Sommeroire and his followers now had the whole of Provence in their power, and the plan to eradicate the Protestant religion was carried out with inhuman cruelty. Its followers were shot, cut down, hanged, thrown from bridges, from windows, from high walls on to the pikes of the soldiers. Many were buried or burnt alive, others were beaten to death, stoned, killed by opening their veins. Living persons had their entrails, their eyes put out, their limbs cut off one by one. The corpses were thrown to the dogs — hewn-off heads were used at games of ball . . ."

Chapter XXXII

A REFORMED FEMALE JUDGE

WHEN we see a kind human face, after having witnessed so many inhuman horrors, our souls feel refreshed, as if we had met an angel.

Look up, and you will see such a kind human face!

Do not be afraid — today we are quite safe here on the high road connecting Orléans and Paris.

Tomorrow the troops of Guise will march past, the snorting of their horses, the clatter of their swords against the cuisses, and the rattling of the gun-carriages will fill the air.

But today we are safe. Do you see the woman on the pinnacle of yonder castle turret? Your eyes are keen — do you not recognise that woman? Consult your memory! Your face tells me you do not recognise her. No wonder — thirty years change a human being. Especially in the sixteenth century.

Oh, she has changed much, this young charming Duchess Renata of Ferrara! Her hair has grown gray; deep wrinkles have furrowed her face; she has grown old.

Amid troubles and difficulties has her ship of life sailed over the high seas. When Calvin left Ferrara, an exile without hearth or home, to seek a quiet place of refuge in the North, he did not forget this spiritual child of his. He was sore afraid that she would not be able to take the last decisive step, but would halt at the cross-way, where Margaret of Valois had remained, disheartened, with the sad complaint on her pale lips: "The wind is so piercing and my heart so cold! And I am so hungry, so thirsty and so benumbed!"

Like Margaret of Valois she could not tear herself from the Unity of the Church; she was one of the moderate party, which wasted its strength in the hopeless attempt to keep together what could not be united, and which was completely defeated at the Council of Trent.

But Ignatius Loyola and the persecutions which broke out in Italy helped her, when arrived at the cross-way, to take the path of the Reformation. Her attitude became more and more decided. The Jesuits were surprised at her neglecting the fast-days, and no longer going to mass or confession. The Jesuit spies also discovered the strange fact of her secret correspondence with that arch-heretic Calvin, and from that moment they left no stone unturned to persuade the Duke to have her tried before the spiritual tribunal of the Inquisition.

But it had to be done with the necessary circumspection, as Renata was the daughter of a King, and sister-in-law to Francis I. Any insult to the Duchess he would certainly have taken very ill, and the Pope's policy at the moment did not make it desirable to take vigorous measures. The longed-for hour to recall this unfaithful daughter of the Church to a sense of her duty had struck when Francis I died, and Henry II was trying to wash away his sins in the blood of the martyrs.

The grand-inquisitor was sent to Ferrara to bring her back to the fold of the Church. Those were anxious days for the Duchess. She stood there alone and deserted. The Duke did not understand her, neither did her children; Margaret had already passed beyond all earthly strife; her old friends were excommunicated, banished, or languished in dungeons, while Geneva was unattainable. But Calvin, her spiritual father, did not forget her.

He prayed for her and wrote: "When you are in great anxiety, be assured that I feel my share of it. May the Lord keep you in His Holy care, and guide you, through the Holy Spirit, that you may glorify Him more and more!"

He did more . . . he sent the young, courageous minister, Francis de Morel, to console and strengthen her in her anxious circumstances. De Morel, a born nobleman, who shrank from nothing, managed to meet her in spite of almost insurmountable difficulties; she regained her constancy of mind, and bore herself like a heroine in replying to the speeches of the grand-inquisitor. But with this her fate was also decided. In the middle of the night a closed carriage drove to the door, she was ordered to get in, and at a smart pace the carriage was driven to the state-prison, which had been got ready for her.

Then unbelief overmastered her; her strength was broken and nothing was left but a poor weak woman, who, after a week's imprisonment, sent for the grand-inquisitor. The face of the Jesuit beamed with satisfaction; he had triumphed; the Duchess was prepared to confess her sins, and at his hands she received the host. She regained her liberty, her children. Once again she took up her abode in the palace, and the Duke praised her because she had behaved like a sensible woman.

But the Duke's joy was surpassed by the sorrow and dismay in Protestant circles. Nobody felt the blow which had been struck at Protestantism more deeply than Calvin; her fall was worse than a lost battle; on that gloomy evening when she received the host at the hands of the grand-inquisitor, the last bulwark of the Reformation on Italian ground had been lost.

Nevertheless the heart of the Reformer was filled with tender compassion; his great knowledge of human nature enabled him to understand how great her anguish must be, and instead of threatening with the fire of God's holy wrath, he consoled her with promises of the Lord's infinite mercy.

How Calvin managed to send her those letters puzzles us. The Jesuits were cruel and crafty spies, it was almost impossible to slip through the meshes of their nets. And yet it took place repeatedly; cunning was matched by cunning, and again and again the Jesuits were outwitted.

For six long years, life for the Duchess passed in sad monotony. Then the Duke was stretched on his death-bed. She was his faithful nurse; she attended to the least of his desires, and promised the dying man to fulfil his last wish, and to break off her correspondence with Calvin.

This resolution caused the Reformer bitter pain; he had not expected this, and his reply was full of restrained anger when he wrote: "In promising this you have sinned, and offended God; yet this promise is not binding. You know, Madam, that Herod was not only praised for keeping the oath, which he had sworn lightly and unthinkingly, too well, but that he was also doubly damned for it . . . I do not say this, to press you to write to me, but in order that you may feel no stings of conscience where God leaves you free. I have done my share, Madam, in informing you of this."

That ought to have been sufficient for the Duchess.

Renata's eldest son now became the reigning Duke. One thing this young man knew: he was dependent on the Pope, his liege lord, and this liege lord still suspected his mother of heretical feelings.

It was a case of bending or breaking; she would either have to devote herself exclusively to the Roman Catholic Church or to leave the country; that was the alternative; there was no other way for the young Duke.

Then Renata chose the latter.

Calvin warned her; he was afraid that her wavering attitude would be pernicious to her in France, and that the stifling atmosphere of the French Court would complete her ruin.

Yet she persevered. And it was a sensible resolution. In the midst of the raging passions and slaughter which succeeded the conspiracy of Amboise, she entered the gates of Orléans. She was frightened at the state of things; she saw her beloved country on the verge of ruin. And Francis of Guise, the grim and triumphant enemy of the Protestants, was her son-in-law . . .

He greeted her with courtesy; it flattered his pride that the Duchess Renata was the mother of his wife Anna of Est, and the daughter of a famous French King. Surely it was with his consent that Anna travelled several days in advance to meet her mother, and his eye rested with approval on the family group when the grandmother nursed his little boy on her knees.

How fortunate that God had hidden the future from her sight! Had the bloody vision of that future appeared before her mind's eye she would have been crushed by sorrow, and have fled from this child, who now looked up at his grandmother with a sweet smile, in unutterable horror; for this child, flesh of her flesh, and bone of her bone, would in the St. Bartholomew's night become the assassin of her noble friend De Coligny.

From the pinnacles of this castle Renata could see on the far horizon, rising above the trees, the proud towers of Châtillon, the hereditary possession of the Colignys.

And with a certain preference did she select this castle and the town of Montargis belonging to it, as her abode in order to be in the neighbourhood of this excellent man. Her father's warlike spirit seemed to come over her when she entered the castle.

It was a gloomy castle with small windows, dark passages, and narrow stairs — a rude contrast to the graceful and charming country-seats in Ferrara. It had besides long been untenanted; the courtyard was overgrown with grass and weeds, while the twenty-yards-high walls, which rose perpendicular from the river, were in a ruinous condition.

But nothing could shake her resolution. Here she had a fixed point where she ruled absolutely; and amid the waves of the civil war which beat tempestuously over France, it was of the greatest importance to fortify that point.

Many alterations were necessary, but in the first place the fortifications had to be repaired. The Duchess recruited a small select band to man the castle; guns were placed on the walls; the walls were strengthened; the gates were made heavier, the trap-doors examined, and the embrasures and loopholes were cleared of the encroaching weeds. Then she resolutely set to work to clear out other more noxious weeds in her estate: the bitter religious hatred which existed between Roman Catholics and Protestants in her dominions.

The Roman Catholics were in the majority and were annoyed when the Duchess declared herself to be in favour of the Protestant religion. They fell upon a Protestant congregation and murdered a great many of them. The Protestants attacked some Roman Catholic churches in revenge, knocked the images to pieces, and committed many other misdeeds which made the papists furious.

The Duchess would not tolerate such things. She ordered the Roman Catholics who had murdered Protestants, and the Protestants who had attacked Roman Catholic churches, to be severely punished. She had her private chapel adapted for Protestant worship, but she would not suffer the preaching to degenerate into reviling, and she gave the ministers strict orders to eschew all improper and offensive expressions. Hot-blooded Protestants did not understand her, and the Genevan Reformer was besieged with complaints about her strange conduct. To eyes clouded with passion, her wise policy seemed half-heartedness, and her reserve, fear of man.

Calvin was reminded that her wavering had always been the cause of her misfortune, and that a man like De Morel, who once before at Ferrara had visited her at the right time, might become the strong oak to which the weak ivy could cling.

But those zealots were mistaken. The Duchess was no longer the weak ivy; her character had been refined in the fire of suffering, and proud and self-conscious, as beseems a daughter of kings, she went the path she had chosen. Young De Morel came; the Duchess herself had urgently requested this. But he was not able to change her point of view. His youthful impetuosity was dashed to pieces on the rock of her ripe experience; she rebuked his severe and rigorous spirit, which would prevent the celebration of mass within her dominions, and took on herself the defence of a Roman Catholic Church which was threatened by the Protestants.

For this passionate De Morel it was something unheard of, something above his comprehension; and he was surprised at this woman, who was three centuries in advance of her time. He was out of temper, embittered, annoyed; he doubted whether she were a true-hearted Protestant, and in his letters to Calvin he gave him to understand this unequivocally. But, on the other hand, this woman confused him completely, for she opened wide the gates of Montargis for all persecuted fellow-believers in the neighbourhood; more than once he was struck dumb at the large sums of money she handed him for the suffering Protestants, while with warm devotion she offered them her private chapel for the celebration of the Lord's Supper, for baptism, and the solemnisation of Protestant marriages.

The earnest striving of the Duchess could not long remain hidden to De Morel's honest mind; his coolness disappeared, and he began to write letters to Calvin which testify to a cordial appreciation. It was not necessary. The eagle's eye of the master had seen farther than his disciple. He had already recommenced corresponding with her, and in January, 1561, he sent her one of those encouraging and consoling letters of which he seemed to possess the secret. He reminded the Duchess that, in order to tread the right path, we must break with all earthly ties. Many difficulties yet awaited her, but if only she continued to fix her hope on Him, who would complete the good work begun in her, all would be well. She was not to cease supporting the poor followers of Christ, for in doing this, she was a fellow-worker in God — a title, desirable above all others. The traveller hastens on his road when evening begins to fall. Therefore he admonished her to use her increasing years as an incitement to leave behind her a good testimony in this world.

"If you remain strong and persevering, I hope that God will make your generosity and fidelity so productive of good that all the faithful will bless your return to France and confess that God has truly had mercy on them through you, and that He held out His saving hand when He brought you back to your country in your old age."

All distrust was gone; they had been mistaken. And many a Huguenot's eye grew moist when he heard that she, the mother-in-law of Francis of Guise, had set out for the meeting at Poissy together with Beza and De Morel.

Chapter XXXIII

THE SWORD OF THE HUGUENOTS

ONCE again traversing the gloomy road from Poissy to the civil war, we are dismayed. For forty long years, more than the average length of human life, the Protestants had not thought of resistance or opposition; like sheep they had been led to the slaughter without uttering a cry. They had suffered themselves to be tortured, strangled, burnt, buried alive. But the constant influx of new members, especially of the warlike nobility, had caused a turn of the tide which now demanded a quick and bloody decision.

The Duchess was at Montargis when the storm burst, and hers was the task to dress the wounds which had been inflicted by her hard-handed son-in-law. It was feared that the Roman Catholics, who formed the greater part of her subjects, might attack the Protestants; so she resolutely ordered the gates to be closed, the drawbridges to be raised, and the guards to be doubled.

Montargis became the great place of refuge for the Protestants who fled from the sword of the Guises, but the gates which had been unlocked for the Protestants, once again opened to admit the Roman Catholic peasants, who dared not await the arrival of Guise's pillaging troops. The people streamed into the castle; within a short time its walls harboured many hundreds of fugitives: young men, old men, women, and children, who lamented and stretched out their hands to the Duchess.

Renata helped and consoled; her pity performed wonders of mercy; she stood godmother to the children that came into the world amid this misery. And amid this sea of distress which streamed in through the lofty castle gates, she did not forget Orléans, but sent large sums of money to those two heroic women who practised the works of Christian charity in the hospitals overcrowded with plague-stricken patients.

Calvin's heart was moved when the tidings from Montargis reached him.

"Speaking according to the world," he wrote to the Duchess, full of gratitude, "a princess must feel insulted at her castle being turned into a hospital, but I think that no more honourable title can be given it, after all the mercy you have shown to God's children, who find a place of refuge with you. I sometimes think that God has left you this opportunity in your old age, to enable you to pay your former debt to Him, caused by your timorousness in days gone by. Naturally I only express myself according to the ordinary way of speaking, for even if you had done a hundred or a thousand times more, you would never be able to discharge the debt you owe Him for the good He daily showers on you. But I mean this, that He honours you greatly by using you for such a task, by making you bear His name in order to glorify Himself through you, by revealing His Word to you, that inexhaustible source of blessings, and by making your house a place of refuge for the followers of His Son. So rejoice, for with many reasons for sorrow, you have also reason to rejoice now that God reveals His approbation by choosing you, in order to be glorified through you!" But her care and anxiety increased; the Guises were ever gaining ground; the basin of the Loire fell into their hands, and with Bourges the last bulwark of the Huguenots in central France succumbed. Renata might now expect the triumvirate; Anna of Est, who had travelled in advance of the victorious army, brought her the tidings. It was a sweet consolation to the Duchess that Anna was the messenger, for Anna was very fond of her mother; from her mother she had inherited a warm heart for those that were unhappy and oppressed, and in her filial love she tried everything to soothe the Duchess. There was no need for the Duchess to be anxious; it was not a religious war; no one would have to suffer for his religion; they only aimed at subjecting the rebels who were a danger to the State, but Renata sadly shook her head; she warned the preachers on her estates to depart at once, and brought the fugitives inside her strong castle. One thing gladdened her heart: the arrival of Charles IX. And the pleasure seemed mutual when the young King paid his respects to his grand-aunt.

But her fervent prayer to be allowed to speak to him privately in order to explain the true state of affairs to him was not heard. Her son-in-law frustrated her plan; the King's visit was made so short that it was impossible for her to exchange a confidential word with him. And she had to consider herself fortunate when, on her pressing, a royal command was issued which prohibited pillage and arson within the territory of Montargis on pain of death.

The troops of Guise were surprised; such a mode of warfare was not at all to their liking. But the discontented officers became a little more reconciled to this limitation when they were told that one of them was to be appointed commander of the town, and that the Protestant services in the private chapel were to be held only for the Duchess and her retinue.

In this manner did the Duchess and her son-in-law part. And when she met him again, the grim enemy of the Reformation lay stretched on his deathbed.

Francis of Guise hesitated which way to take, Orléans or Rouen; then a council of war was held and the army marched up to the walls of the populous town of Rouen. The inhabitants perceived the red banner of the Guises with fear and trembling; the King of Navarre, who formerly had been the head of the Huguenots, was commander-in-chief of the forces which were to besiege the town.

It was stoutly defended, but the Guise army proved too powerful for the Huguenots. The town was stormed, and through the breach which they had made, the flood of furious soldiers streamed into the town.

During eight days the wretched town was left to the unbridled passions of the undisciplined soldiers; then the judicial murders followed; the preacher Marlorat, a gentle, amiable man, highly esteemed by Protestants and Roman Catholics alike, who had been present at the conference of Poissy, here confirmed his faith with his blood.

But even the days of the King of Navarre, the victor of Rouen, were numbered. During the siege a musket-shot was fired from the walls, and the King was carried to his tent with a serious wound in his left shoulder. This ball put an end to his short dream of glory and splendour; on October 15 he was wounded, and he died a month after, on November 17. On his death-bed he saw the terrible mistake of his life: with eyes full of tears he confessed his sin, and confessed Christ, in whose name his soldiers had murdered the noblest citizens of Rouen.

Condé had meanwhile received his German mercenaries, and now no longer delayed marching to the capital at the head of an impressive force. A panic seized the Parisians when the rumour spread: "The Huguenots are approaching!"

The fright was general; one of the magistrates almost died of fear; three thousand Spaniards were expected, and instead ten thousand armed Protestants appeared at the gates . . .

But the gates of Paris were impregnable, for they were defended by the Queen-Mother. Near a windmill she had a meeting with Condé; she approached him with her most charming smile, and three precious days were wasted.

We are surprised, and ask how on earth it was possible for Condé to talk and waste his time while France, in her last extremity, was looking up to him as her saviour.

What was he thinking of?

What had happened to the iron Calvinist?

What fatal net held him ensnared?

For three days the Queen-Mother and the beautiful Delilah of her Court held Condé captive; then they turned their back on him for the Spaniards were approaching. So the Huguenots had their leader back again, but he did not lead them; he was led, for the German mercenaries wanted their pay and marched to the coast to receive the money Queen Elizabeth had promised. The principal force of the Guises marched parallel with them; close to Dreux the Roman Catholics offered to give battle to the Huguenots, and Condé considered it a point of honour due to his princely blood to accept the challenge. It was in the middle of winter. The Protestants numbered twelve thousand, the Roman Catholics seventeen thousand men. But even had the number on both sides been increased tenfold, the importance of the battle would not have been greater, for this first battle between the Roman Catholics and Huguenots of France decided the fate of French Protestantism. When Calvin met his colleagues on the memorable morning of this battle, he said that during the night he had heard a loud noise as of trumpets sounding. The noise had been so distinct that it could not have been imagination, and he begged his colleagues to join him in a prayer to God as something important would surely take place on that day. It was piercing cold that Saturday; a cutting north wind whistled over the fellow fields when the soldiers left their watch-fires.

Beza delivered a powerful speech, which excited the Huguenots to the greatest enthusiasm; then De Coligny drew his sword, brandished it over his head, and rushed into the hostile ranks at the head of his cavalry.

The Huguenots had five thousand, the Roman Catholics only two thousand horse-soldiers, but the Roman Catholic infantry numbered fifteen thousand men, while the Protestants could not muster more than seven thousand.

Guise, matchless in cunning tricks, did not now belie his true character. He always acted according to fixed well-considered rules, which enabled him to justify himself should be become involved in a lawsuit, and this prudence now cautioned him not to fight without the sanction of a King and a Queen-Mother, over whom he ruled.

The Queen-Mother burst out laughing when this question was put to her.

Just then the King's old nurse entered the apartment, and she asked her: "Well, Nurse, what do you think of it?"

"Well, Madam," replied the woman, "since those Huguenots are never satisfied, it is time to bring them to reason."

At the commencement of the fight Guise went to the Spanish soldiers, who had made a wall of carts to break the shock of the hostile cavalry, and from this fortified encampment they saw De Coligny attack Marshal Montmorency, disperse his soldiers, and take the wounded Marshal prisoner.

Condé attacked the Swiss, and swept over them like a hurricane. But those men remembered that their fathers had beaten the Protestants at Cappeln thirty years ago, and they rose again between the hoofs of the horses, and fought with their usual death-despising courage.

Guise had looked on coolly from behind the barricade of carts, assuring the Spaniards that he was only a captain. But when, after waiting for five hours, his army had no chief officers left, he placed himself at the head of the Spaniards, rallied the scattered musketeers, and put the Huguenots to flight, taking Condé prisoner.

De Coligny and Dandelot, however, retained their cool intrepidity. At the head of twelve hundred horsemen they threw themselves in a mad gallop on the victorious enemy, brought him to a standstill, and took prisoner Marshal Saint-André. The Marshal, who had dishonestly enriched himself, ended his life miserably. He quarrelled with one of his former servants; he begged for his life, but the servant shattered his head with a pistol-shot. So the tables were once again turned, but the balance, heavy with so much blood, stood still, and the battle of Dreux was a defeat for the Protestants, since it had not been a victory.

A victory would have opened the gates of Paris to them, without the Queen-Mother being able to turn back, and the war-hymn, chanted by the victorious Huguenots in the streets of Paris, would have sounded in mighty fanfares, and penetrated to the remotest cottages of France. It would have been a decisive victory for the Reformation; from the Pyrenees to the Meuse a Protestant nation would have been born, and two centuries afterward the Marseillaise of the Revolution would not have been raised, had not the Marseillaise of the Reformation been smothered in blood.

With sad surprise the Protestants heard that the Huguenot army had retreated, and that Condé had been taken prisoner. They had expected everything but defeat. They asked themselves why the Lord led them to this gloomy road; they were His friends, His children; and if there were a traitor in the army, an Achan, they fervently wished that He would reveal it to their stricken hearts.

Why had the Lord done this — why? This "why" was continually on the lips of Calvinists; it sounded wherever Protestant hearts beat; and in those sad days Calvin often preached on the words: "His ways are not our ways!" In the same spirit was Calvin's letter to Soubise, Governor of Lyons, once his pupil at Ferrara.

"When God takes the sword from our hands, we must quietly await the time when God will return it. The submission may be hard to bear, but that does not matter. God has sorely tried us . . . let us submit, until He raises us up again. And as it is God's will to afflict us, we should not rebel." Thus spoke Calvin; thus he taught — it was the Protestant Spartan who here spoke.

Guise shed no tears over the loss of Marshal Montmorency, who fell alive, and General Saint-André who fell dead into the hands of the Huguenots. He was satisfied; the day of Dreux had been a prosperous one to him; Condé, the head of the Huguenots, in his hands. Fortune smiled on him.

He treated Condé with effusive kindness; there was no end to it; Condé had to share his tent, and all that was done by Guise to shake the faith of the Protestants in their leaders.

The Germans soon gave loud voice to it. "Those French weathercocks," they said contemptuously, "one day they want to knock each other's brains out and the next they embrace each other." So Guise was at the height of his ambition. Not only was he the victor, but the sole victor. The Triumvirate no longer existed. Saint-André was dead, the Marshal a prisoner, and the Duke, who in the morning had modestly declared that he did not wish to command more than a company, was in the evening lieutenant-general of the kingdom.

He now determined to take short measures with Montargis, as officious individuals had informed him that the Protestant services were once again being held regularly in public, that the Duchess, as absolute mistress, had once again made her dominion a hotbed of rebellion and a place of refuge for Protestant preachers.

While his standard appeared before the gates of Orléans, he carried out his resolution to abduct his mother-in-law, willing or unwilling. And to enforce that resolution, he sent his captain, Malicoine, to Montargis at the head of a strong body of cavalry.

The Duchess's royal blood coursed more quickly through her veins when she heard of the misdeeds of those soldiers; with her own eyes she saw the blood of her fellow-believers staining the pavement; and powerless to protect the town, she was yet firmly determined to resist the whole of Roman Catholic France in her castle. Armed with her woman's cunning, she expressed her surprise at the town and castle being expected to surrender, and that the garrison of a town of which a royal officer had been appointed commander could be suspected. And raising her voice she asked Malicoine whether he remembered that the King was her nephew; she would not yield in obedience to anyone, but she could not but see some fearful misunderstanding at the bottom of it all, and she demanded a new enforcement of the royal mandate before she could consider herself at liberty to give in. So she appealed from her son-in-law to the King, whom she knew to be merely the tool of his subject.

By this appeal she gained time; and time gained meant much. For she knew enough of the political game of chess to be aware that a victorious Guise was as obnoxious to Catherine de Medici as a triumphant Huguenot army; she would hurry on the peace negotiations in order to frustrate Guise's conquest of Orléans, and the fact of Condé being a prisoner, could in Renata's eyes only promote peace.

But Guise had not sent a child to Montargis; Malicoine understood well enough that every moment was precious, and was not going to be imposed upon by an old woman. He informed the Duchess that it would be superfluous and merely loss of time to send for more definite instructions; she could follow him willingly, if she liked; otherwise he would find a way to break her obstinacy by razing her castle to the ground. He seemed to be fortunate; a company of artillery was just passing, which was to serve at the siege of Orléans. And he at once directed the guns against the walls of her castle.

But then the Duchess showed herself in all her greatness.

With the tenderness of a mother-hen spreading her wings over her little ones, she stretched out her arms over the poor wretches who would be left defenceless to the bitter animosity of the enemy if she withdrew her protection. Their cares had become her cares, their danger her danger.

A short space of scarcely a week had once been sufficient to bring her to a humiliating genuflexion at the feet of a Jesuit priest, but that time lay behind her. Suffering had refined her, as gold is refined in the furnace, and she wished to remain one with her fellow-believers to the bitter end.

With fearless mien she approached Montargis. "Shoot if you dare!" she said; "but I shall place myself in the breach! And we shall see whether you really have the courage to kill the daughter of King Louis XII!"

The captain of the Guise army was not easily daunted, yet now he hesitated. This woman would be capable of carrying out her desperate intention, and the responsibility of her death would fall upon him. That proved too much for him; without more definite

Gaspard de Coligny

orders he dared not carry out his plan, and before those orders arrived the fate of his master had been sealed for ever.

In the night following the battle of Dreux, De Coligny had rallied his decimated forces; his lion-like courage was unbroken, and he told his soldiers that nothing had yet been effected, that the work had to be done over again, and that it was their task to crush the enemy on the following morning. But the Germans showed him their wounds, their broken weapons; and two-thirds of the Huguenot army lay on the battle-field, dead or wounded.

The greatest difficulty for the Admiral was to keep the Germans, who had had blows instead of money, and who turned their faces toward the Rhine, within bounds. He told them that they could claim their money; they ought not, however, to look for it on the shores of the German Rhine, but at Hâvre, and on their way to conquer Normandy.

The question was now how to transform those warring nomads into a quiet and easily movable column. They carried with them their plunder and the possessions obtained in previous campaigns, in a long train of wagons, which prevented all rapid movement, and they would rather lose a battle than this baggage. De Coligny persuaded them to place this baggage in the nave of a large church at Orléans, and left his brother Dandelot, who was threatened by an attack of fever and by Guise, to defend the town.

In the middle of January De Coligny advanced. It was a severe winter; the plague depopulated the towns, while the forests were inhabited by fugitives, who succumbed to starvation and cold. The German horse-soldiers called the more loudly for their pay, and De Coligny conducted them to the shore to show them the storm-swept sea. "The money will be sure to come," he said consolingly, "but the sea is too tempestuous," they could see that for themselves.

The Germans drew their own conclusions; they began to pillage in order to compensate themselves, but they reckoned without their host, as De Coligny would not tolerate lawlessness. He had the first robber who was caught in the act hanged up by the legs, as a warning to the others, and by maintaining an iron discipline he made sure of the victory he was going to gain.

Guise besieged Orléans, while Dandelot, with the fever heating his blood, was its heroic defender. Every morning at six o'clock a service was held; then the Psalms sounded out of the depths, beseeching God for deliverance. And Guise, who never lacked patience, lost it before these stubborn walls.

"I could bite off my fingers," he wrote in a letter. And he assured the Queen-Mother that he would raze Orléans to the ground and kill every living thing, cats and dogs included.

But the man who wanted to murder everyone in the town was not to set his foot inside, but to fall himself by the hands of an assassin. That assassin was a young nobleman called Poltrot, who had fought at Saint-Quentin like a brave soldier, and had passed into Spanish captivity, and there in Spain had seen how Philip II illuminated his reign by flaming *Autos-da-fé*.

His heart full of vengeance and murderous thoughts, he returned to France. The terrible plan of assassinating Guise ripened in this Protestant heart; soon he spoke of nothing else; he stretched out his right arm, and said to his comrades: "This arm shall kill the Duke."

He told this to Soubise, by whom he had been educated, to De Coligny and many others, but no importance was attached to it.

He entered the service of the Admiral as a spy. He obtained money to buy a strong Spanish horse, rode into Guise's camp and offered the Duke his services.

He called himself a Spaniard. And Guise, usually very suspicious, believed it, as his accent, his face, his whole appearance confirmed his statement. The Duke expected great things from Poltrot's arrival; he grew enthusiastic and said: "Fifty thousand francs for you if you steal into the town and blow up the gunpowder-stores!" Thus the 18th of February arrived. Poltrot threw himself on his knees when alone, in order to ask the Lord to enlighten him, and he fancied he felt a divine incitement to this deed.

So all scruples had been overcome; a Protestant Balthasar Gerards[32] rose from his knees. Instead of listening to the voice of the Lord in the Scriptures, he followed the prompting of a misleading inward voice, and with a lie on his conscience, this fanatical man prepared to save Protestantism by means of assassination. He awaited the Duke on the outskirts of a forest, at dusk. He had calculated his chances; his hand did not shake; he had to let the Duke approach to a distance of six paces and then hit him in the vulnerable point above the arm-pits where there is an opening in the armour.

And so it happened. The shot was fired; the Duke fell backward, and six days after he died of the effects of this mortal wound.

Like a clap of thunder the tidings resounded throughout the Protestant and the Roman Catholic world; many Huguenots rejoiced, and more than one Protestant, mastered by his passion, exclaimed: "How fortunate that this murderer has been murdered! He has had his deserts, and this cruel persecutor of our brethren shall not escape eternal damnation!"

---

[32] The murderer of William of Orange.

Did the Duke of Guise really go to that terrible place where Judas Iscariot has his dwelling? Is it certain that he is eternally lost? How do we know? The Duchess Renata was his mother-in-law, and this purified Christian did not shrink from writing to Calvin: "If I knew that the King, my father, and the Queen, my mother, and my late husband, and all my children were rejected by God, I should hate them with a deadly hatred, and wish them to be in hell, and I should completely reconcile myself to God's will, if He would grant me grace for this." But the same pen from which these awful words flowed, then wrote: "I do not believe the Duke, my son-in-law, to be lost. I know he has been a cruel persecutor; but to speak candidly, I do not think and do not believe that God has cast him off, as he gave signs of the contrary before he died." Calvin replied in a remarkable letter, which exposed the stirrings of his heart like a flash of lightning.

"Concerning the Duke of Guise," he wrote, "it has been my constant prayer that God would show mercy to him, although I have also often wished that God would lay hands upon him and deliver the Church from the Duke, if He would not convert him. It was entirely due to me, that before the war, men refrained from ridding the world of him, for only my warning voice restrained them."

With these warnings he defied public opinion, which among both Roman Catholics and Protestants held that the slaying of a tyrant was a deed pleasing to God.

Calvin went even farther — he refused to doom Guise to eternal punishment. "If we damn the Duke," he wrote to Renata, "we go too far, if we have not a sure and unfailing sign of his reprobation. In such things we must refrain from suppositions and presumption. For there is only one Judge before whose judgment throne we must all appear."

When the Duke of Guise felt the end approaching he continually repeated words from the Scriptures; he begged his wife to forgive his shortcomings, as he forgave her, and thus he passed the threshold of Eternity. The murderer was taken prisoner and was put to the rack. He confessed all they wished, and mad with torture declared that De Coligny had incited him to the murder, while Beza had encouraged him in his plans. Once off the rack he recalled his words to once again confirm them when his limbs broke under the hellish torture. Poltrot's body was torn asunder by four horses, after the flesh had been wrenched off by hot pincers — according to the sentence. And the judges regretted that they could not pass the same sentence on De Coligny and Beza, although the latter declared himself most solemnly before God and the French nation to be altogether innocent of the murder.

That the Admiral was suspected of complicity was grist to the mill of Catherine de Medici, the Queen-Mother. It cast a stain on his character, which she eagerly applied to her own ends, and it weakened his influence, which was what she most earnestly desired.

He requested her to have Poltrot's case deferred till after the peace, that it might be thoroughly looked into. But she would not hear of it. This new investigation might have brought to light the innocence of both these distinguished Protestants, and that was just what she wished to prevent at any price.

She attained her purpose. In everything she attained her purpose. The proud dream of grandeur and glory dreamed by Francis Guise on the evening of the battle of Dreux, she now lived through. The reins of government were in her hands; she ruled; the seat on which she sat had actually become a throne.

She had Condé in her power. She kneaded this weak mind like clay. He did not hesitate to submit to the wishes of the Queen-Mother and to conclude a peace, which granted the Huguenots no greater privileges than the January edict, although the Queen promised to grant the Protestants more favourable conditions afterward and to raise him to the rank of lieutenant-general. These were vain promises; she never intended to keep them. It did not matter — Condé signed. And again we ask in sorrowful surprise: "Where was the iron Calvinist?"

An unnecessary question — Condé never was an iron Calvinist! The iron Calvinist in the Huguenot army bore another name. And this Calvinist, this hero, De Coligny, who in the middle of winter had conquered Normandy after a brilliant campaign, his was the right to wage war or make peace, for he had been chosen head of the Huguenots after the battle of Dreux. So the Protestants thought; so De Coligny thought; and he quickly pushed on to Amboise to say an earnest word at the peace conference.

But he was five days too late — the Peace of Amboise had been signed on March 12th.

For form's sake Condé had consulted the preachers, but notwithstanding their opposition he signed. And the indignation of the great Huguenot leader was so great, that at the meeting he flung the words in Condé's face, that he, Prince Condé, had, with one stroke of his pen, destroyed more churches than had been demolished in ten years.

But arguing was useless — the peace had been signed.

It had been stipulated that no Protestant services were to be held in Paris, and in a few other specially mentioned towns, including the place of residence of the Royal Court. But the Huguenots were permitted freedom of worship on the estates of all high vassals, in the houses of the nobles and in the towns where services had been held when the war broke out, while a general pardon was proclaimed.

So there was peace. And the Duchess Renata put her hand to the plough to heal the wounds the war had indicted. She opened wide the gates of her castle for the needy and suffering, while her generous character watched over the memory of her son-in-law. It cut her to the quick that his death meant life for the Huguenots; she braved the appearance of ambiguity by diminishing his crimes, and his tragic end washed out the stains of his character in her memory. She covered his glowing ambition with the mantle of charity, and at the flood of abuse which followed the dead Guise into his grave she burst into tears, while she unburdened her mind by writing to Calvin: "God is not the Father of lies, but a God of truth, and His word is sufficient to protect His children without their seizing the weapons of Satan!"

De Coligny was her faithful counsellor; the regular services were resumed, while Montargis became a second Geneva. Strict supervision on behaviour was held; the Church Council was quite independent of the Duchess; the Princess also tried to help De Morel in his work of evangelisation wherever possible.

Calvin corresponded with Renata to the last; he admonished, he warned and consoled — it was the voice of a father speaking to his daughter. She had to complain more than once of the masterful and hard tone assumed by De Morel in his sermons, while the latter was surprised that she did not take stronger measures to suppress Roman Catholic heresies. Calvin had to be mediator again and again, a difficult task, which required the greatest circumspection, as both parties were convinced of their being right. But De Morel's fanaticism he could not approve of, he was sorry that the zealous preacher was not always free from vanity and pride, and the gentle love shown by the Duchess brightened the evening of his life.

Generosity, wisdom, and tact Renata needed. When she opened the gates for the poor, the Huguenots poured into the town; and grown wild in the civil war, embittered by the ill-treatment they had undergone, they now thought they were at liberty to wreak their vengeance on the Roman Catholics.

But Renata thought otherwise. She would not tolerate that the oppressed of today should become the oppressors of tomorrow. She said without mincing matters that God had made her the protector not only of her Protestant subjects, but also of her Roman Catholic subjects, and that she would take short measures with regard to criminals who in the name of the purified faith lifted the tills of their Roman Catholic fellow-citizens. She did good to all alike; hungry monks, wandering along the roads, asked where Montargis lay, for there they should find bread and refreshment. In the midst of a sea of boiling passions which disturbed the land, the manor of Montargis lay like a peaceful and quiet island. The ticklish question of freedom of worship had been settled; Protestants and Roman Catholics passed each other on their way to church without gripping each other's throats or strangling each other. And this mutual respect for each other's convictions was so strange in those days that eminent men who were concerned for their country's welfare travelled to this singular spot.

The fatal knot tied at Amboise had been cut by the Duchess, as far as her estates were concerned; she acknowledged neither Guises nor Bourbons, and exacted obedience to royal authority. The world was full of suspicion, distrust, and bitterness, but the good faith of the Duchess remained untouched. Roman Catholics and Protestants trusted her; steeped in Calvin's doctrine, she walked on with a firm step, without swaying to the right or left.

By the gulfs of hatred which separated the children of the same country, her figure appears in a light all the more charming. She was a true daughter of Calvin, and loved all her subjects; bowed down by grief and cares, her eye lit up when she was able to lessen the cares of others or to assuage their grief. Duchess was her title, but she gained a more beautiful title, and the lady of Montargis has been called "a mother in Israel." So there was peace in the land.

Was it really peace, or merely a truce to recover breath, to restore exhausted strength and prepare for the mortal fray? The Roman Catholics infringed on the edict of Amboise wherever they could, and the Protestants did so wherever they felt strong enough to remove the barrier which obstructed their freedom of worship. It was a truce — nothing more. The Huguenots had pitched their camp on a volcano, but before a new eruption of this volcano took place, a long wail of sorrow ascended to heaven from Geneva.

Chapter XXXIV

BLESSED ARE THE DEAD THAT DIE IN THE LORD

"WE have this treasure in earthen vessels," says the apostle. And fragile and ruinous was the tent in which the Reformer lived. Matters did not improve as the years went by; it was said that he was ailing, and one Sunday he stopped in the middle of the sermon. A hot burning sensation came into his throat; he suddenly looked to the ground, and a stream of blood flowed from his mouth.

It made an anxious, uneasy impression on the congregation; it was now that they saw how strong the tie was which bound them to the remarkable preacher.

Calvin was carried home; Geneva was in mourning; "that will be the end," the people sighed.

It was rumoured abroad; there was a general rejoicing in the camp of the adversaries, and they flattered themselves that Calvin would take the Reformation with him to his grave.

Rumours of his death had been circulated before, and once it had been reported for a change that he had gone over to popery, bag and baggage. Calvin recovered, however, and resumed his work. He knew it would not be for long, and he redoubled his zeal to finish the great work his hand had begun. It was at that time that a special ambassador of France appeared at Geneva, and handed the Government a letter from his young master, Charles IX, with a stern, set face.

The contents of this letter were enough to frighten the Genevan authorities. It was full of the most bitter and threatening expressions. "The Privy Council and States of France," thus ran the letter, "were unanimously of opinion, that the fatal confusion which France was a prey to, was solely owing to the preachers sent out by Geneva. But the French Government no longer intended to look on patiently. They categorically demanded the recall of the ringleaders, who instigated the people, or otherwise France would take her measures." The menacing letter caused great consternation in the Council, and serious voices were raised to oppose going to extremes with regard to France. But Calvin, whose advice had been applied for, appeared at the town hall, and declared with the calmness of an ancient Roman that the safety of the town did not rest with France but with God. He told the councillors that it would be less dangerous to have the King of France for their enemy than the King of Kings, and warned them not to exchange the strong house built on a rock for the ruinous hut which was built on the quicksands of human favour. He explained to the councillors, as if expounding a mathematical problem, how they would do best to keep on the side of God, enforcing his explanation with the conviction of his unshakable faith. He proposed to modestly make the French King understand that the preachers educated at Geneva went forth on their own responsibility and could not be hindered in their movements by the Genevan Government. The preachers had besides always refrained from touching political questions, and if unrest and discord had notwithstanding been caused by their spreading the Gospel, then this was merely a confirmation of what the Great Sender had predicted.

It is highly improbable that such considerations would have made a deep impression in many council meetings, but these men had been formed in the school of Calvin; they were members of his Church, and through his words they had been initiated in the most holy faith.

They were no zealots, no fanatics. They knew very well that their small republic lay like a deserted post between three powerful Roman Catholic States, and that their town was only half an hour's distance from the French frontier. But the weak can do nothing against the strong, and the might of France could in no case be compared with the might of God, whom they would bitterly insult if they deserted him now.

Calvin was entrusted with the reply to this letter; the French Government was struck with surprise, but could not carry out its intentions, as the Lord prevented it.

At the same time a more threatening storm rose from the side of Savoy. Duke Philip Emanuel, who together with Egmond had beaten the French at Saint-Quentin, and had reconquered his hereditary duchy of Savoy, was now determined to increase his possessions by the desired annexation of the so eagerly desired town of Geneva. He was not only a soldier, but also a most dangerous diplomatist, and secretly called upon the exiled Libertines, who had connections in the town, to aid him. He understood that gold would be more powerful than steel, and in alliance with Bishop Allardet, he tried to attain his end by bribery.

The Bishop especially was full of courage; this man thought he knew for certain that they would find confederates among the councillors. But those confederates went straight to Cannon Street with the letters the Bishop had sent them, and when the secret was betrayed, the Bishop had enough of it.

Duke Emanuel laughed at the Bishop's pusillanimity, and Cardinal Borromeo, whose heroic philanthropy was only equalled by his fierce hatred of heresies, brought about an alliance between Philip II of Spain, Savoy, and the Pope, of whom the last-mentioned was willing to pay an amount of twenty thousand ducats to conquer the stronghold of heresy.

The Libertines, who had once boasted so of their patriotism, approved of it; they approved of everything, if only Calvinism was brought to ruin. But no blessing rested on this undertaking; two days before the scaling-ladders were to be placed against the walls, the secret of the conspiracy was divulged, and the Government took such vigorous measures that the enemy dared not attempt an assault. Geneva was saved; Calvin proposed holding a solemn day of thanksgiving, and the people streamed into the churches to thank the faithful Shepherd of Israel who neither sleeps nor slumbers.

Bishop Allardet, who would have liked to hold spiritual sway over Geneva, shrugged his shoulders contemptuously.

"It is useless," he said, "as long as the protector of Geneva is living; he employs demons, who frustrate all good plans."

Six months afterward they received news of Calvin's decease, and began to breathe more freely. This time it was positively true, there was no doubt of it; the arch-heretic, who was served by devils, because he had sold his soul to Beelzebub, the chief of devils, was dead, dead as a doornail. And Granvelle, that cunning statesman, wrote from the Royal Palace at Madrid to all friendly courts: "Now is the time to profit by this man's death. The Roman Catholic states must unite and set about it earnestly in order that an end may be put to the misery of the Church, and heresy be eradicated. His Majesty is fully prepared to employ all the resources of the realm for this purpose." All the resources of the realm — who ever doubted it! Did not Philip II make good his word in the Dutch Eighty Years' War?

But Calvin was still living; he was again seen in the streets; and to famous strangers, come to Geneva to see the Reformer, the citizens said: "Look, there goes our Master Calvin!"

Calvin's appearance in the decline of life must have made a deep and indelible impression on all who met him. He was emaciated and seemed to be nothing but skin and bone, yet his eye was not dim, but full of energy. It was quick and penetrating — a piercing falcon-like glance. His forehead was not high but arched, and denoted an iron will and invincible perseverance, while the strongly developed nose, together with the pale sunken cheeks, yet further enhanced the impression of firmness and keenness. He wore a long pointed beard, which flowed over his chest; he had black hair, and could not bear a speck of dust on his clothes — the Reformer was very particular with regard to his dress. And as he passed by in his long black gown, with his immovable serious face, more like a spirit than a man, he made an indelible impression of discipline, method, determination, and restrained force.

He was the man of logic, of conclusion, of iron consequence, who abhorred half-heartedness. The Reformer was unique; his words went forth like a river with a smooth bed, flowing along under a clouded sky. When the Lord guided him and made him understand His will and the essence of His word, Calvin bowed before the Divine will, the Bible became the lamp before his feet, and he grasped the salvation offered him, as the mighty who take the Kingdom of God by force.

To do God's will and to help to fulfil it everywhere in life, had become his life's task. That was the incitement to his iron strength, his never-resting activity, and the secret of the success which crowned his efforts.

As he himself testified, his character was naturally shy, sensitive, timorous, and he appealed to these qualities to make Farel understand that he was not fit to be a preacher in turbulent Geneva.

But when he saw his mistake, he sought no cowardly excuses, but without a moment's hesitation, like a brave soldier, mounted guard on the spot Farel had pointed out to him.

He was firmly convinced of being one of the elect, and praising God's almighty goodwill, he drew from this conviction the living water, which, above all, strengthened and refreshed him in his journey through desolate wildernesses. The mighty spiritual fights and temptations of Luther, the son of Noyon never knew, and whenever a believer fell into Satan's snares and sinned heavily, he declared that with such warnings before our eyes, we should walk our paths with the greater fear and trembling.

But this trembling is a thrill of awe for the impenetrable majesty of God and His judgments, and not fear for the uncertainty of his own election.

As the shades of evening fell, the Sun of righteousness brightened Calvin's inner being more and more. His life was rooted in God, this same God was the shield of his life; in this consciousness he approached the end of his existence, as if seeing the Invisible. "Before the face of God and His holy angels, who look down upon us," that is a standing expression in his letters and writings. God and His angels who are ever present, he calls upon as witnesses when his words are liable to meet with suspicion and mistrust. The angels he does not forget, and this is the more remarkable, as so many of those who regard themselves as true sons of Calvin, seldom mention the names of the angels. God and His angels — Calvin points them out to his friends, to warn, to console, to admonish them to be steadfast in their faith and to fulfil their promises. He shouts out to the martyrs mounting the stake that the eyes of the Lord and of His hosts of angels follow their steps and rejoice over them. He compares his own life, which is drawing to a close, to a campaign for God and His holy angels. The eye of the Judge of battles who dwells high in the heavens rests upon him; he feels it; and this consciousness heightens his courage. But not only that awe-inspiring eye, the hosts of angels are there too, to show their cordial sympathy, and to encourage him. And then that cloud of witnesses descending from heaven, whispering in his ear words of consolation and love!

Those are the judges whose opinion is all important to him. But the world's opinion — what is that opinion worth? What does it matter that the world spits in his face? What is human praise but night and darkness?

God, the Supreme Being, and His angels, serve him in the sixfold splendour of their wings — those are the friends in whose vicinity he lives. Before the Majesty of the eternal Being the tinsel of this world grows pale; the eternal lights burn, and in that light how insignificant does the toil and moil of human beings appear, whose only philosophy consists in the despairing cry: "Eat, drink, and be merry, for tomorrow we die!"

Calvin asked what task God had set him, and in his innermost soul was convinced that neither fire nor water, mountain nor precipice, human enmity nor satanic malignity would prevent him from carrying out that task. Boundaries were extended; roads were smoothed; impossibilities existed no longer, because God is omnipotent.

To carry out God's will — that was and became more and more Calvin's passion in life. That was the one thing necessary; the bells of eternity proclaimed it loudly with thunder peals through the air . . . God and His angels — it sounded through Calvin's words like a hymn. And on his death-bed he stammered in a broken voice: "Before God and His angels I confess and repent of my sins!" God stood between him and man, and while his outward form was decaying, his inward being was being strengthened and glorified day by day according to the image of that holy God. It was stamped on his face, his whole appearance; and when the councillors of Geneva stood in sorrowful silence around his death-bed, they were struck by the majesty on that marble face.

Calvin's death-bed, it would be death this time . . . He had preached on the preceding Wednesday — it was feared for the last time. But wrestling with death, which was sapping his strength, he once again appeared in the pulpit on the following Sunday to speak about the conformity of the Gospels.

That was his funeral-song, then everything was at an end; death was already busy demolishing the frail tabernacle. His pains increased, and when they overwhelmed him, the sufferer turned his eyes to heaven and sighed: "How long, oh Lord! how long!"

But stretched on his sick-bed by the grim hand of Death, this invincible hero still went on working by dictating his thoughts. And when begged to stop this work, he replied, looking up with his penetrating eyes: "What? Would you have the Lord find me idle when He comes?"

On March 10 the Council ordered a general hour of prayer to be held for the Reformer, and behold! there was a change for the better! Some friends, who had heard of this disquieting illness, came to visit him, and found him at his writing-desk fully dressed.

When they entered, Calvin rested his head in his hands for a time, as he was accustomed to do when deep in thought. Then he said in a weak, halting voice, but with a glad gleam in his eyes: "Beloved brethren! I thank you cordially for your tender care, and hope it will soon be unnecessary. In a fortnight's time I hope to see you gathered around me for the last time. Then the Lord will reveal to me, as I hope and believe, what He has decided concerning me, and He will take me into His eternal kingdom!"

The usual meeting of the court of censure[33] was indeed held at the Reformer's house on March 24. He said that the Lord had diminished his physical suffering, then took a French New Testament, and read over the remarks he had written in the margin. He then asked the opinion of his colleagues and said he wished to correct these notes. The brethren were surprised at his energy and clearness of mind — had the people's prayer really been heard? Would the angel of death really pass over that beloved head once again?

The attending of the meeting had greatly affected Calvin's health, he was very tired, and the following morning he did not feel so well. But he would not part from this world without having paid his grateful homage to the members of the Council. He was carried to the town hall, and, supported by two friends, mounted the steps slowly and with great difficulty.

Thus he reached the well-known council chamber with its four windows, and appeared before the gentlemen of the Council, who respectfully rose from their wooden chairs.

---

[33] This court of censure was basically the same as Article 73 of the Church Order of the Canadian Reformed Churches: The ministers, elders, and deacons shall mutually exercise Christian censure and shall exhort and kindly admonish one another with regard to the execution of their office.

First of all Calvin introduced a new rector for the University; then with his cap in his shaking hand, greatly moved, he thanked them for the many favours received. The councillors had but a short time before shown their good-will by offering him his salary, although, owing to his weakness, he had not been able to fulfil the duties of his post. And they had the sooner decided to do so, as Calvin was burdened with the support of his brother Antony, who, owing to adversity in business, had come down in the world. Calvin had refused the money, and when they had pressed him to accept his salary he had confessed the reason, which was that his conscience would not permit him to accept the money, now that he no longer performed his duties. And there the matter rested. But the Reformer no less appreciated the generosity of the Council, adding that he would now have the honour of addressing them for the last time in that place. So he bade a cordial farewell to all, but old recollections overpowered him; as in a vision he saw how these courageous men had braved the heat of the day and the cold of the night. The words stuck in his throat, and mournful tears glistened in those stern eyes.

Not one remained unmoved; the stern men of the Government wept, yes, now they knew how this iron heart had clung with a tender love to Geneva, his second country.

Easter fell on April 2. The sufferer had become very weak, but he longed to celebrate the Holy Supper with his flock. He was carried to church in a chair. Beza led the service; from his hands he took the bread and the cup. And at the end of this holy service the audience sang the Song of Simeon:

> *O Lord and Master, Thou*
> *Dost let Thy servant now*
> *Depart in exultation;*
> *Thy promise is fulfilled,*
> *For now have I beheld*
> *Thy wonderful salvation.*[34]

It was a touching scene. The angels were present at it. Softly, inaudibly their wings rustled through the lofty building. The

[34] Hymn 18:1 (*Book of Praise*).

audience wept; deeply moved they sang the hymn, their eyes turned on their departing shepherd. But he wept not; his soul was full of holy joy; he saw the golden gates of the eternal Home shining before him. It was his last walk. Once again he wished to address the Council to unburden his conscience, but the councillors would not suffer him to come, but went to him. The Council went in a solemn procession to Cannon Street; they grouped themselves around his bed to hear his last words.

"Your worships," said Calvin, "I cannot thank you enough for the honour and kindness you have shown me, and especially for the inexhaustible patience with which you have borne with my great shortcomings and faults. I have met with many discouragements and great opposition in my career, but that was not your fault, but was according to the decree of God who tries each of His servants. Wherever I have failed in my duty I earnestly beg you not to impute this to my will, but to my inability. For of a truth I may say, that I was devoted to your Republic heart and soul and, notwithstanding all omissions and faults, I have always laboured, as much as was in my power, for the public welfare. It would also be ungrateful hypocrisy, were I to deny that God had desired to use me as his instrument in performing certain things. Only this I repeat; excuse and forgive if my work in public and private life has been so insignificant in comparison to what it might have been. Above all, venerable sirs, am I indebted to you for so kindly and gently bearing with my too great vehemence. This and my other faults I am heartily sorry for, but I earnestly hope that God has pardoned these faults.

"Concerning the doctrine I preached to you, I confess before God and my Saviour that I had no other desire than to proclaim the Word of God which had been entrusted to me, in all its purity, while I feel assured that I have not gone my way in uncertainty. Had it been otherwise, I know well enough that God's wrath would now be threatening me, while, on the contrary, I am convinced that my labour and care in preaching His Word have not displeased Him."

He reminded them of the Lord's striking deliverances of the anxious year which lay behind them, assuring them that that faithful God who was then the Protector of the town would continue to be so in the future.

If you wish God to preserve your Republic in the happy condition it is in at present, guard well the holy place where He Himself lives in your midst, namely, His Holy Church, that it be not stained with sin! For He has said, that He will honour those who honour Him, and despise those who despise Him. He alone is the great God, the King of Kings, the Lord of all . . .

"The older ones among you I admonish not to envy the younger ones, should they surpass you. I wish to remind the younger ones that it behoves them, above all things, to be modest, humble, and moderate."

It was a father who before departing takes leave of his beloved children. They asked his blessing, and he prayed with them; then he gave them his hand and bade them a last farewell. The councillors went home full of sorrow; never had the town witnessed such a scene.

"When he had finished his speech," says Beza, "he called us to him one by one, and pressed our hands. And we went away, our eyes swimming with tears and our hearts full of unspeakable sorrow."

Those last farewell visits were a sweet consolation to Calvin in his great suffering. Farel, almost eighty, came from Neuchâtel.

The Reformer had written to him not to undertake the difficult journey, but he came notwithstanding, impelled by the mysterious force of love which counts all troubles as nothing.

Calvin was exceedingly rejoiced to see this faithful brother-in-arms once more on earth. They talked of days long past, of strife and victory, and they strengthened each other in the holy faith. Did Farel envy his brother's fate? Farel was twenty-five years older, and had to return to his post. And he would remain behind like a solitary tree in a forest, devastated by the storm. But the parting would not be for long, and so they doubtless consoled each other with the prospect of a speedy, eternal, and blessed reunion. On May 19, two days before Pentecost, another meeting of the preacher's court of censure took place, and it was decided to have dinner at Calvin's house. It was a sorrowful surprise when Calvin was carried into the room, and tears rose in the preacher's eyes when he said: "Brethren, I have come to meet you for the last time and to sit down at table with you." His strong will forced his body to obey it; he said grace, partook of some food, and talked as cheerfully as possible to comfort his sorrowing brethren.

But before the meal was at an end, the reaction set in; he had to be carried to his bed in the adjoining room. All those present were greatly dismayed, but he said with a gentle smile: "The partition-wall will not prevent me from being with you in the spirit."

The end was fast approaching now. And while the Reformer had finished with all earthly things, he was like a traveller, who having bidden farewell to all, waits for the signal to depart.

He was praying almost continually. His breath came and went in gasps; his voice was scarcely audible — his prayer was no more than a sigh. But those penetrating eyes, turned heavenward, shone with a wonderful light.

Sometimes when the pains made him writhe, he was heard repeating these words from the Psalms: "Lord, I have not opened my mouth because Thou hast done it."

The sympathy shown him was great and touching, but the Reformer regretted that the sight of his suffering should cause pain to others. In the midst of his greatest pains, this great heart remained full of tender solicitude for others, and while his soul thirsted for personal sympathy he would have refused it in order to cause no pain to others.

May 29 was his dying day. He seemed slightly better in the morning — it was the last flickering of the lamp before it went out for ever. In the afternoon death began to set in, but nobody was aware of it. For the Lord had made His faithful servant's death-bed as soft as possible.

Beza was called; he rushed to the bedchamber — the sufferer had already crossed the River of Jordan. It was eight o'clock; the May sun which had shone so brightly the whole day was setting and twilight was falling.

Calvin had retained consciousness, the power of thought, and his voice to the last. And he had fallen asleep; peacefully, like a child tired out by the long day.

It was Saturday — the end of the week of labour. And on this Saturday ended the life's labour of the great Reformer. When late at night the news of Calvin's death spread, there was much weeping in the town, as a nation weeps when it loses its benefactor.

Cannon Street was crowded with people; it became a pilgrimage to the Reformer's death-bed, and the Government had to take measures to prevent too great a pressure.

On the following morning the corpse, in its white graveclothes, was put into a wooden coffin, and at two o'clock in the afternoon the funeral took place — according to Calvin's express desire — with touching simplicity. The whole of the Council, all the professors, teachers, preachers, the Church Council, and nearly the whole town followed the body to the grave. A low cry of anguish arose from the crowd.

"My father! My father!" exclaimed Beza, "the chariot of Israel and the horsemen thereof!" The coffin descended into the gloomy pit; the May sun shone in all its glory, and its beams followed the Reformer into the bosom of the earth. The bells tolled solemnly; the echoes replied softly from afar; and the birds sang their songs.

The blue lake sparkled like a sapphire; unmovable, like a gigantic guard towered Mont Blanc; and the Jura Mountains stretched out their hands to one another, and the doves whispered to one another that it was the Lord's Day.

The noble grain is laid in the earth — hark! The sods fall on the coffin with a dull thud!

Church of Geneva, why do you lament? The grain is scattered into the furrow with tears, and soon the harvest will be gathered in amid shouts of joy and the song of the sickle.

Blessed are the dead that die in the Lord from this day forth! Yes, says the Spirit, that they may rest from their labour, and their works do follow them.

No monument marks the spot where Calvin was buried. It is not necessary; angels, whom the Reformer met on his toilsome journey, know the spot and guard it, until the day when the dead shall arise from their graves.

Israel's Hope and Expectation by **Rudolf Van Reest**

G. Nederveen in *Clarion*: This is one of the best novels I have read of late. I found it captivating and hard to put down. Here is a book that is not time-bound and therefore it will never be outdated.

The story takes place around the time of Jesus' birth. It is written by someone who has done his research about the times between the Old and New Testament period. The author informs you in an easy style about the period of the Maccabees. . . Van Reest is a good storyteller. His love for the Bible and biblical times is evident from the start. He shows a good knowledge of the customs and mannerisms in Israel. Many fine details add to the quality of the book. You will be enriched in your understanding of the ways in the Old Testament.

Time: Inter-Testament Period   **Age: 15-99**
ISBN 0-921100-22-1   **Can.$19.95 U.S.$17.90**

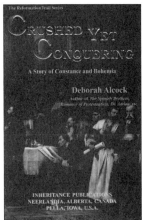

Crushed Yet Conquering by **Deborah Alcock**

A gripping story filled with accurate historical facts about John Huss and the Hussite wars. **Hardly any historical novel can be more captivating and edifying than this book.** Even if Deborah Alcock was not the greatest of nineteenth century authors, certainly she is our most favourite.
— Roelof & Theresa Janssen

Time: 1414-1436   **Age: 11-99**
ISBN 1-894666-01-1   **Can.$19.95 U.S.$16.90**

Quintus by **R. Weerstand**
A Story About the
Persecution of Christians
at the Time of Emperor Nero

The history of the Church in A.D. 64 is written with blood and tears. This book, based on historical facts, relates what happened in Rome in the summer of that year. It is a gripping chronicle. In the story we meet Quintus, the central character. He is a typical Roman boy, who through a number of ordeals experiences the grace of God.

Time: A.D. 64   **Age: 12-99**
ISBN 1-894666-70-4   **Can.$9.95 U.S.$8.90**

Against the World - The Odyssey of Athanasius
by **Henry W. Coray**

Muriel R. Lippencott in *The Christian Observer*: [it] . . . is a partially fictionalized profile of the life of Athanasius . . . who died in A.D. 373. Much of the historical content is from the writing of reliable historians. Some parts of the book, while the product of the author's imagination, set forth accurately the spirit and the temper of the times, including the proceedings and vigorous debates that took place in Alexandria and Nicea. . . This is the story that Rev. Coray so brilliantly tells.

Time: A.D. 331-373   **Age: 16-99**
ISBN 0-921100-35-3   **Can.$8.95 U.S.$7.90**

Hubert Ellerdale by W. Oak Rhind
A Tale of the Days of Wycliffe

Christine Farenhorst in *Christian Renewal*: Christians often tend to look on the Reformation as the pivotal turning point in history during which the Protestants took off the chains of Rome. This small work of fiction draws back the curtains of history a bit further than Luther's theses. Wycliffe was the morning star of the Reformation and his band of Lollards a band of faithful men who were persecuted because they spoke out against salvation by works. Hubert Ellerdale was such a man and his life (youth, marriage, and death), albeit fiction, is set parallel to Wycliffe's and Purvey's.

Rhind writes with pathos and the reader can readily identify with his lead characters. This novel deserves a well-dusted place in a home, school, or church library.

Time: 1380-1420	**Age: 13-99**
ISBN 0-921100-09-4	**Can.$12.95 U.S.$10.90**

With Wolfe in Canada:
or, The Winning of a Continent by G.A. Henty

Through misadventure the hero of the story, James Walsham, becomes involved in the historic struggle between Britain and France for supremacy on the North American continent. The issue of this war determined not only the destinies of North America, but to a large extent those of the mother countries themselves. *With Wolfe in Canada* will take the reader through many battles of this conflict. Meet a young George Washington and General Braddock as they fight the French and Indians, join up with Rogers' Rangers, and learn of the legendary generals Wolfe and Montcalm. *With Wolfe in Canada* is a model of what a children's book should be with its moving tale of military exploit and thrilling adventure. This classic provides a lesson in history instructively and graphically, whilst infusing into the dead facts of history new life. Mr. Henty's classic *With Wolfe in Canada* is a useful aid to study as well as amusement.

Time: 1755-1760	**Age: 14-99**
Cloth ISBN 0-921100-86-8	**Can.$28.95 U.S.$19.99**
Paperback ISBN 0-921100-87-6	**Can.$20.95 U.S.$13.99**

The Romance of Protestantism by Deborah Alcock

A wonderfully warm and loving book about the beauty of Protestantism. This topic, too often neglected and forgotten, has been revived by the author in a delightful way. Glimpses of our Protestant history are strewn in our path like jewels, whetting our appetite to read on and discover the depth of our history. Too often our role models tend to be found outside of our Christian heritage "to the neglect of the great cloud of witnesses, the magnificent roll of saints, heroes, and martyrs that belong to us as Protestants." This book is not only for adults. Young people and even older children will find riches in its depth which will encourage and build up to carry on the work of God in our own day and age.

— Theresa E. Janssen, home educating mother

Time: 1300-1700	**Age: 12-99**
ISBN 0-921100-88-4	**Can.$11.95 U.S.$9.90**

Under Calvin's Spell by Deborah Alcock
A Tale of theHeroic Times in Old Geneva

They had now reached the Forte Neuve, by which they entered the town, with many others who were returning from the Plain-palais. As they walked along the Corratorie they met Berthelier and Gabrielle, taking the air, as the afternoon was very fine for the season of the year. Both the lads saluted; De Marsac with a flush and a beaming smile.

"I did not know you knew them," said Norbert.

"Oh yes; did I not tell you I was going to see them? Master Berthelier's sister, Damoiselle Claudine, and I are fast friends. Some years ago when I came here first, a mere child, I was one day in the market, looking about me and buying cherries or the like, when I saw this poor damoiselle being frightened half out of her senses by a group of angry, scolding fish-women. That was before such good order was put in the market, and in all the town, thanks to Master Calvin. She had told them, quite truly, that they were trying to cheat her. I fought her battle with all my might, which in truth was not great, and at last brought her home in triumph. She was much more grateful than the occasion required, and has been my very good friend ever since. I — they — they are all good to me, though lately, being much occupied with my studies, I have seen them but seldom."

"Do you not think the young damoiselle very pretty?" asked Norbert. "I do."

"She is beautiful," Louis answered quietly; and the subject dropped.

Time: 1542-1564	**Age:14-99**
ISBN 1-894666-04-6	**Can.$14.95 U.S.$12.90**

The Spanish Brothers by Deborah Alcock
A Tale of the Sixteenth Century

"He could not die thus for his faith. On the contrary, it cost him but little to conceal it. What, then, had they which he had not? Something that enabled even poor, wild, passionate Gonsalvo to forgive and pray for the murderers of the woman he loved. What was it?"

Time: 1550-1565	**Age: 14-99**
ISBN 1-894666-02-x	**Can.$14.95 U.S.$12.90**

The Heroes of Castle Bretten
by Margaret S. Comrie

Eleonore, Lady of Castle Bretten, has been alienated from her friends and allies by false rumours spread by her nephew, General Lucas von Ruprecht, Count of Zamosc. When Guido, a young Protestant, comes to live at the castle, he wins the love and trust of Lady Eleonore and Felix, the General's son. With lots of excitement and action Guido and Felix uncover a plot to gain control of the castle.

Time: 1618-1648	**Age: 11-99**
ISBN 1-894666-65-8	**Can.$14.95 U.S.$12.90**

Doctor Adrian by Deborah Alcock
A Story of Old Holland

Doctor Adrian was a scholar living in quiet seclusion in Antwerp, the Netherlands, until a fugitive Protestant preacher and his daughter Rose sought sanctuary in his rooms. Before he knew it, he became involved with the Protestant cause, and eventually embraced it in theory. When the persecution of the Reformed was stepped up, Doctor Adrian made the dangerous journey to Leyden with his family. They survived the siege of Leyden, along with Adrian's sister Marie. When the siege was lifted by the fleets of William of Orange, they moved to Utrecht. Doctor Adrian's faith in the Reformed religion died when he experienced the loss of some of his loved ones, but a new faith in the Author of that religion took its place.

This is a tale of a doctor and his contact with William, Prince of Orange, and of his spiritual journey.

Time: 1560-1584	Age: 12-99
ISBN 1-894666-05-4	Can.$15.95 U.S.$13.90

Love in Times of Reformation
by William P. Balkenende

N.N. in *The Trumpet*: This historical novel plays in The Netherlands during the rise of the protestant Churches, under the persecution of Spain, in the latter half of the sixteenth century. Breaking with the Roman Catholic Church in favor of the new faith is for many an intense struggle. Anthony Tharret, the baker's apprentice, faces his choice before the R.C. Church's influenced Baker's Guild. His love for Jeanne la Solitude, the French Huguenot refugee, gives a fresh dimension to the story. Recommended! Especially for young people.

Time: 1560-1585	Age: 14-99
ISBN 0-921100-32-9	Can.$8.95 U.S.$7.90

The TowerClock Stopped by J. DeHaan
A story during the time of the Reformation

An amazingly true story about a surprise attack by the Spanish army on Sluis, a small city in a southern coastal province of The Low Countries, now known as The Netherlands. The Dutch fought for their freedom from Spain in an eighty-year war, from 1568 to 1648. The surprise attack on Sluis is part of that war.

"As soon as I finished reading this book, I had to check Motley's *United Netherlands* to see if these amazing facts really happened! Yes, the Towerclock truly stopped!"   — Roelof A. Janssen

Time: 1606	Age: 8-99
IP0000008516	Can.$9.95 U.S.$8.90

Coronation of Glory by Deborah Meroff

The true story of seventeen-year-old Lady Jane Grey, Queen of England for nine days.

"Miss Meroff . . . has fictionalized the story of Lady Jane Grey in a thoroughly absorbing manner . . . she has succeeded in making me believe this is what really happened. I kept wanting to read on — the book is full of action and interest."
— Elisabeth Elliot

Time: 1537-1554	Age: 14-99
ISBN 0-921100-78-7	Can.$14.95 U.S.$12.90

The Governor of England by Marjorie Bowen
A Novel on Oliver Cromwell

An historical novel in which the whole story of Cromwell's dealings with Parliament and the King is played out. It is written with dignity and conviction, and with the author's characteristic power of grasping the essential details needed to supply colour and atmosphere for the reader of the standard histories.

Time: 1645-1660   Age: 14-99
ISBN 0-921100-58-2   Can.$17.95 U.S.$15.90

The William & Mary Trilogy
by Marjorie Bowen

The life of William III, Prince of Orange, Stadtholder of the United Netherlands, and King of England (with Queen Mary II) is one of the most fascinating in all of history. Both the author and the publisher of these books have been interested in this subject for many years. Although the stories as told in these books are partly fictional, all the main events are faithful to history.

F. Pronk wrote in *The Messenger* about Volume 1: The author is well-known for her well-researched fiction based on the lives of famous historical characters. The religious convictions of the main characters are portrayed with authenticity and integrity. This book is sure to enrich one's understanding of Protestant Holland and will hold the reader spell-bound.

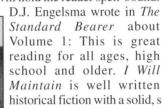

D.J. Engelsma wrote in *The Standard Bearer* about Volume 1: This is great reading for all ages, high school and older. *I Will Maintain* is well written historical fiction with a solid, significant, moving historical base . . . No small part of the appeal and worth of the book is the lively account of the important history of one of the world's greatest nations, the Dutch. This history was bound up with the Reformed faith and had implications for the exercise of Protestantism throughout Europe. Christian high schools could profitably assign the book, indeed, the whole trilogy, for history or literature classes.

C. Farenhorst wrote in *Christian Renewal* about Volume 1: An excellent tool for assimilating historical knowledge without being pained in the process, *I Will Maintain* is a very good read. Take it along on your holidays. Its sequel *Defender of the Faith*, is much looked forward to.

Time: 1670-1702   Age: 14-99

Volume 1 - *I Will Maintain*	ISBN 0-921100-42-6	Can.$17.95 U.S.$15.90
Volume 2 - *Defender of the Faith*	ISBN 0-921100-43-4	Can.$15.95 U.S.$13.90
Volume 3 - *For God and the King*	ISBN 0-921100-44-2	Can.$17.95 U.S.$15.90

The Lion of Modderspruit by Lawrence Penning
The Louis Wessels Commando #1

A wonderful historical novel in which Penning has interwoven love, pathos, and loyalty. The conflict the Boers endure with England involves not only a fight to maintain their independence (to which the British agreed in 1881) but also a deep religious significance. Louis Wessels, eldest son of a well-established Transvaal Boer family, is betrothed to Truida, a Boer maiden living in the British colony of Natal, and educated in British-governed schools. When England sends over thousands of troops to invade the independent Boer colony of the Orange Free State, causing the Boers of the Transvaal Colony to prepare to invade Natal, the two lovers are confronted by more than a political conflict — two loyal hearts separated by loyalty to conflicting causes. The horrors of the war drag both Louis and Truida through heights of joy and depths of despair. How can these two hearts, beating strongly for each other but also strongly for their separate causes, ever be reconciled? On which side is justice to be found?

Time: 1899   Age:11-99
ISBN 1-894666-91-7   Can.$10.95 U.S.$9.90

The Hero of Spionkop by Lawrence Penning
The Louis Wessels Commando #2

A company of twenty-five horsemen with an officer in command galloped into the yard. They jumped down, fastened their horses to the young fig trees which bordered the broad driveway, and in silence awaited orders from their commanding officer.

He carefully scrutinized the terrain and set out five soldiers as watchmen. Five others were ordered to make a thorough search of the barn. Ten were posted at the various exits from the house and with the remaining five the officer entered the livingroom . . .

"Do you have a Boer from the Transvaal hiding here?" asked the officer.

"If I should deny it, you wouldn't believe me in any case, Lieutenant."

Time: 1900   Age:11-99
ISBN 1-894666-92-5   Can.$10.95 U.S.$9.90

ALL FOUR IN ONE

Journey Through the Night by Anne De Vries

After the Second World War, Anne De Vries, one of the most popular novelists in The Netherlands, was commissioned to capture in literary form the spirit and agony of those five harrowing years of Nazi occupation. The result was *Journey Through the Night*, a four volume bestseller that has gone through more than thirty printings in The Netherlands.

"An Old Testament Professor of mine who bought the books could not put them down — nor could I."
— Dr. Edwin H. Palmer

"This is more than just a war-time adventure. The characters have vitality, depth and great humanity."
— *The Ottawa Citizen*

Time: 1940-1945   Age: 10-99
ISBN 0-921100-25-6   Can.$19.95 U.S.$16.90

In This Hour by **Rudolf Van Reest**
A Story of World War II and the Floods of 1953

"That's a rather rough expression, brother Melse — 'traitor.' How could you call someone a traitor if he's simply obeying the government? I would rather not hear such language from the mouth of an elder."

"I maintain that such work as building bunkers is treason against our land," repeated David Melse. "The bunkers have a definite purpose: when armies come to liberate us from the power of the Germans, the bunkers are supposed to hold them back. Each bunker could help sink one of the naval vessels approaching our coast. And on those vessels are our friends — perhaps even our own soldiers. Reverend, you should think carefully what those bunkers represent."

Rev. Verhulst shook his head. "You people have completely the wrong idea about those bunkers. Do you really believe that Germany will one day sink to its knees before England? If you do, you're completely mistaken, brother Melse. Germany will take control of all of Europe and will never let itself be overthrown. Germany is much too powerful to be defeated. Moreover, if you had listened carefully to last Sunday's sermon, you would know full well how I think about these matters. The apostate covenant people spent seventy years in the grip of Babylon, and I'm sure that our time under foreign domination will not be any less.

Time: 1942-1953   **Age: 15-99**
ISBN 0-894666-68-2   **Can.$15.95 U.S.$13.90**

He Gathers the Lambs by **Cornelius Lambregtse**

A moving book, written not only with deep insight into the ecclesiastical, religious, social, and historical situation in which the story takes place, but also with a warm, rich understanding of a child's soul. Every page of the book carries proof that it was eked out of the author's own experience. It is written from the inside out, and the people who appear in it are flesh-and-blood people as they walked the streets of southeastern Zeeland. Zeelanders with a mystical character . . . who had great difficulty appropriating in faith the redemptive deeds of the covenant God.

Also beautiful in this story are the descriptions of the natural beauty of the island on which it takes place. The author views nature with a loving but also with a knowledgeable eye. The landscape through all the seasons. . . But what is most striking is his knowledge of the soul of a child, a knowledge born out of love.   — Rudolf Van Reest

Subject: Fiction   **Age: 14-99**
ISBN 0-921100-77-9   **Can.$14.95 U.S.$12.90**

The Crown of Honour by **L. Erkelens**

Rachel Manesajian in *Chalcedon Report*: This book is about an illegitimate girl whose mother died when she was born, and no one knows who her father is. She grows up in an orphanage, and she goes through many hardships and is treated poorly because she is illegitimate. The few people she loves are taken away from her. Because of all her trials, she thinks God is against her, and so, in rebellion, she refuses to go to church or pray. However, the prayers of an old man who loves and prays for her are answered and she realizes . . . a wonderful story.

Fiction   **Age: 14-99**
ISBN 0-921100-14-0   **Can.$11.95 U.S.$10.90**

The Seventh Earl by Grace Irwin

A dramatized biography on Anthony Ashley Cooper, the Seventh Earl of Shaftesbury, who is most widely remembered as a 19th-century British philanthropist and factory reformer. "This is Grace Irwin's strongest and most poignant book . . . I have been moved and enriched by my hours with *The Seventh Earl*," wrote V.R. Mollenkott.

Time: 1801-1885	Age: 14-99
ISBN 0-8028-6059-1	Can.$11.95 U.S.$9.95

A Stranger in a Strange Land
by Leonora Scholte

John E. Marshall in *The Banner of Truth*: This is a delightful book. It tells the story of H.P. Scholte, a preacher in The Netherlands, who being persecuted for his faith in his own country, emigrated to the U.S.A., and there established a settlement in Pella, Iowa, in the midst of the vast undeveloped prairie. . . The greater part of the book is taken up in telling the stories of the immense hardships known after emigration. Interwoven with this story is an account of Scholte's marriage and family life. . . It is a most heartwarming and instructive story.

Time: 1825-1880	Age: 14-99
ISBN 0-921100-01-9	Can.$7.95 U.S.$6.90

Captain My Captain by Deborah Meroff
author of *Coronation of Glory*

Willy-Jane VanDyken in *The Trumpet*: This romantic novel is so filled with excitement and drama, it is difficult to put it down once one has begun it. Its pages reflect the struggle between choosing Satan's ways or God's ways. Mary's struggles with materialism, being a submissive wife, coping with the criticism of others, learning how to deal with sickness and death of loved ones, trusting in God and overcoming the fear of death forces the reader to reflect on his own struggles in life.

This story of Mary Ann Patten (remembered for being the first woman to take full command of a merchant sailing ship) is one that any teen or adult reader will enjoy. It will perhaps cause you to shed a few tears but it is bound to touch your heart and encourage you in your faith.

Time: 1837-1861	Age: 14-99
ISBN 0-921100-79-5	Can.$14.95 U.S.$12.90

By Far Euphrates by Deborah Alcock
A Tale on Armenia in the 19th century

Alcock has provided sufficient graphics describing the atrocities committed against the Armenian Christians to make the reader emotionally moved by the intense suffering these Christians endured at the hands of Muslim Turks and Kurds. At the same time, the author herself has confessed to not wanting to provide full detail, which would take away from the focus on how those facing death did so with peace, being confident they would go to see their LORD, and so enjoy eternal peace. **As such it is not only an enjoyable novel, but also encouraging reading.** These Christians were determined to remain faithful to their God, regardless of the consequences.

Time: 1887-1895	Age: 11-99
ISBN 1-894666-00-3	Can.$14.95 U.S.$12.90

The Soldier of Virginia - A Novel on George Washington by Marjorie Bowen

"Mr. Washington — and who is Mr. Washington?"
"It is the Governor of Virginia's envoy, Monsieur — bearing a letter from his Excellency."
St. Pierre gave his inferior officer a quick glance; two things occurred to him: the first was that Dinwiddie must be serious if he had sent a messenger in such weather; the second was that it would have been more courteous if the envoy had been a man of some rank; he remarked on neither of these things, but quietly requested that Mr. Washington should be brought into his presence.
The scene was St. Pierre's room in the newly erected Fort le Bœuf; December cold filled the apartment despite the huge fire of logs that roared on the hearth; and the view from the window was of a frozen lake, great trees against a drab sky, and the steady falling of snowflakes.

Originally published in 1912, this is a fictionalized biography on America's first President by one of the best authors of historical fiction.

Time: 1755-1775	**Age: 14-99**
ISBN 0-921100-99-X	**Can.$14.95 U.S.$12.90**

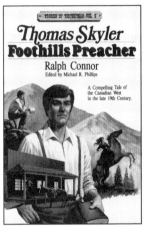

Thomas Skyler: Foothills Preacher by Ralph Connor
Another compelling tale of the Canadian West in the late 19th century by Ralph Connor. Meet Bronco Bill . . . Hi Kendal . . . the Duke . . . the Old Timer . . . and of course Gwen . . . and discover why the impact of "the Sky Pilot" was far different than any would have expected.

Subject: Fiction	**Age: 12-99**
ISBN 0-940652-07-2	**Can.$9.99 U.S.$7.90**

Winterflight A novel by Joseph Bayly
A disturbing, unsettling vision (some would call it nightmare) of the future. A chilling story that will rivet your interest, leave you with questions about moral and political trends in American life today.

Time: Future	**Age: 18-99**
ISBN 0-8499-0297-5	**Can.$8.95 U.S.$7.90**

Tales & Tellings by Paulina M. Rustenburg-Bootsma
J. Tangelder in *Christian Renewal*: This book begins with the story of Polle and Henderkien Eijsinga, great-grandparents of the author. The author also tells about her own experiences growing up in a new country, the people she came to know, as well as the tales and happenings she heard or read about. Each story is inspirational and Christ-centered and shows how God guides and sustains His people in times of joy, dangers, and sorrow. The poems which precede each chapter show the work of a God-fearing craftsman. A welcome addition to one's personal or church library.

Time: 1870 - 1997	**Age: 11-99**
IP0000005790	**Can.$12.95 U.S.$11.90**

The Dort Study Bible

*An English translation of the Annotations to the
Dutch Staten Bijbel of 1637 in accordance with a
decree of the Synod of Dort 1618-1619*

Rev. Jerome Julien in *The Outlook*: This is a wonderful addition to a home, church, school, or minister's library . . . Originally, these notes were commissioned by the Great Synod of Dort, 1618-1619, along with the Staten Bijbel, a completely new translation of Scripture. In a very real sense, this is probably the earliest study Bible ever produced. We might say of it that it is a short commentary on the Bible.

This volume, the first of what is planned, D.V., to be a republication of the whole set of annotations, contains an historical sketch — written most likely by Theodore Haak, and other documents from the 1637 Dutch edition. There is also an account of a gold coin produced by the States General of the United Netherlands commemorating the Synod. This coin is also stamped in gold on the front and back covers. (It *must* be added that the binding is beautiful!) Inside the front and back covers are reprinted the title pages of the Dutch Staten Bijbel and the English translation by Haak, dated 1657.

The notes are preceded by an introduction to each Bible book, and a summary at the head of each chapter. While the notes on Genesis are much more detailed due to the nature of the content, many insights are found on all the pages. These notes might not be what you would read in a commentary published today, but they give concise explanations of the verses. Regularly, they give cross references to other Biblical passages which shed further light on what God says in the text. Also, these notes give a historic-redemptive understanding of the Bible history. Ministers, as well as Bible students, will find helpful information here, as well as ideas to develop.

For those who might be interested, the position on creation days is "that night and day . . . made up one natural day together . . . comprehending twenty-four hours" (see Genesis 1:5). Further, the Book of Genesis lays open God's "everlasting covenant." The note on Genesis 17:7 states that it is "Everlasting for all believers in Christ . . ." This subject is discussed at great length in the appropriate places.

Of what value is this new, but very old set of notes? Some scholars might look with disdain on a republication of these notes. Yet, historically they have value because we can read in English what our fathers at Dort taught and believed concerning Biblical teachings other than those well explained in the Canons of Dort. It is foolhardy to cut ourselves off from our heritage, as so many wish to do today. Now, what has been readily available in the Dutch language for the last 350 years, is in a newly translated and typeset English edition for our reading and spiritual benefit.

Further, this volume has a practical value. For those who still attend church society meetings, or for those involved in Bible studies, here is a concise and helpful Reformed commentary. Its format allows it to be on the table with our Bibles, Psalters, and notes.

This is an ambitious project which Inheritance has undertaken. We must be grateful for their dedicated work. It is the hope of this reviewer that the day will come, beginning now, when this set will not only be displayed in many, many homes, but also well worn through use. In this day of seemingly shrinking interest in the Reformed Faith we and our children must be grounded in God's Truth!

Vol. 1 Genesis and Exodus	ISBN 1-894666-51-8	Can.$24.95 U.S.$21.90
Vol. 2 Leviticus - Deuteronomy	ISBN 1-894666-52-6	Can.$24.95 U.S.$21.90
Vol. 3 Joshua - 2 Samuel	ISBN 1-894666-53-4	Can.$24.95 U.S.$21.90

Sample Pages of *The Dort Study Bible*

In a time of much confusion and debate about reliable manuscripts of God's Word, as well as the proper place of God's Church, Covenant, and the Christ-centeredness of the whole Bible, there is an urgent need to reach back to one of the best and possibly only ecclesiastical translation of the Bible ever made. Even though the States General of the United Netherlands authorized this translation, it did so upon a decree of the famous Synod of Dort (1618-1619). The high value of this translation and its annotations — also written by the translators, who were among the best theologians of the early seventeenth century — is evident in the example below. The translators were not bothered by publishers who wanted to have as big a market as possible and so make compromises to avoid controversies — as is the case so much today — but seriously looked at what God revealed in His Word and stuck faithfully to the text. Their humbleness in often not being sure of what the text really means is evident throughout the annotations, nevertheless they have given a faithful translation of these texts. There is no better tool for the unity of God's church today then abiding by a reliable Bible translation and explanation. Since this English translation is not a direct translation of the original texts, it would not be suitable as a current ecclesiastical translation, but nevertheless it may be one of the best tools to come to a new ecclesiastical translation. In the meantime it is a number one tool for personal and group Bible study for those who cannot read the original languages.
— Roelof A. Janssen, editor and publisher.

2 Samuel 23

The last words of David, in which he testifies of his calling from God to the royal and prophetical office, v. 1. He prophesies of the Messiah Jesus Christ, and the blessed salvation under His reign, with the acknowledgment of the faults of his house, and a confession of his confidence in God's everlasting covenant of grace, v. 3. He announces everlasting destruction to the ungodly, v. 6. A history of David's heroes and their courage, v. 8.

1. Moreover, these are the last words[1] of David. David the son of Jesse says, and the man who was raised up on high, the anointed[2] of the God of Jacob, and pleasant *in* Psalms[3] of Israel, says:

[1] Before his death, according to the example of Jacob in Gen. 49, and of Moses in Deut. 32 & 33.

[2] Lifted up from low conditions and anointed as king over the people of God.

[3] Which he wrote for the church of God by the inspiration of the Holy Spirit.

2. "The Spirit of the LORD has spoken through me, and His word has been upon my tongue. 3. "The God of Israel has said, the Rock[4] of Israel has spoken to me:[5] *"There shall be* a Ruler over the people, a righteous *Person*,[6] a Ruler *in the* fear of God.[7]

[4] As also in 2 Sam. 22:2. Compare 1 Cor. 10:4.

[5] Or, *of me*; meaning that David here relates the prophecies which God had given him concerning himself, his kingdom, and his house, partly to David himself, partly to the prophets, Samuel, Nathan, etc.

[6] See Is. 53:11; Jer. 23:5, 6; 33:15, 16; Zech. 9:9 and its annotations.

[7] Compare Is. 11:2, 3. Understand by this Ruler our eternal spiritual King and Lord Jesus Christ, whose type David (as also Solomon) was, and of whom God had revealed to him that He should proceed from his seed, (according to the flesh). See Ps. 2:8; 72:8; Jer. 30:21; Micah 5:2. Others understand it as a description of the virtues and duties of rulers or governors, applying to it also the following comparison in 2 Sam. 23:4, as by this the graciousness and usefulness of such rulers as David and Solomon is meant, though lacking in much.

4. "And He shall be as the light of the morning, *when* the sun rises; of the morning without clouds, *when* from the glaring after the rain, the *tender* grasses *spring up* out of the earth.[8]

[8] That is, the coming of the Messiah and the carrying out of His soul-saving office will be so pleasant, acceptable, profitable, and fruitful for His church, as the things mentioned in this comparison are for the earth and its harvest. Compare with this verse Hosea 6:3; Ps. 110:3. Compare also Is. 60:1, 2; Mal. 4:2; Luke 1:78. And compare Is. 44:3, 4ff; 55:10, 11; etc.

5. "Although my house is not thus with God, yet He has made an everlasting covenant with me,[9] which is well-ordained and kept in all things.[10] Certain is *there in* all my salvation, and all desire, although He does not *yet* make it to spring forth.[11]

[9] David confesses here his sin and unworthiness and also those of his house (compare 2 Sam. 7:18, 19, etc. and see also 2 Sam. 11-13, & 15, etc.) and on the contrary praises God's undeserved bounty, shown to him in the everlasting and unchangeable covenant of grace, being founded in the Messiah, whose day David (as also Abraham) saw by faith, by which he was comforted, falling joyfully asleep in the LORD. Compare 2 Sam. 22:51; Ps. 72:20 and its annotations.

[10] That is, which in God's everlasting counsel, for His own glory and the salvation of His people, with all the means belonging to it, is wisely decided and previously ordained and shall be so firmly kept and preserved to the final fulfilling thereof, that the gates of hell shall not be able to prevail anything against it. Compare Matt. 16:18; Acts 13:23, 32, 33ff; Eph. 1:3, 4ff; 1 Peter 1:5, 10, 11ff.

[11] Although the promised shoot or stem of Jesse and David, the Mediator of the covenant, the Messiah, has not yet come. Compare Is. 4:2, 11:1; Jer. 23:5; 33:15; Zech. 3:8; 6:12. Some believe that in the verses 4 and 5 David places opposite one another the temporariness of things, related in verse 4, and the everlastingness of his kingdom and house in the Messiah, who would spring forth from his seed; they translate these two verses thus: 4. "And as a light of the morning, *when* the sun rises; the morning being without clouds, by the glaring, by the rain, the *tender* grasses *springing* out of the earth; 5. "That my house will not be thus with God, for He has made me an everlasting covenant, in all things well prepared and kept. Certainly all my salvation and delight is that He will not cause it to spring forth (as that which now already has sprouted forth, and shall in eternity not perish).

6. "But the *men* of Belial,[12] they shall be all as thorns that are cast away because they cannot be taken hold of with the hand.

[12] That is, reprobates, ungodly ones, wretches, despisers and enemies of the kingdom of Christ. Of this word, see the annotation to Deut. 13:13.

7. "But everyone who shall touch them, furnishes[13] himself with iron and the wood of a spear; and they shall be utterly burned[14] with fire in the same place."[15]

[13] Heb. *is filled with*, etc.; that is, he fills his hand, he furnishes himself first with some instruments with which he may handle the thorns without hurting himself.

[14] Heb. *burning will burn*.

[15] In the place where they grow or were cast, where they lie. Heb. actually *in the seating place* or *place of abode* or *chair*.

8. These are the names of the heroes[16] whom David has had:

[16] Thus David's chief officers are called here because of their outstanding courage, bravery, and fearlessness in the war. The order appointed by David among them according to their courage and deserving is very remarkable. See 1 Chron. 11:11ff.

Annotations to the Heidelberg Catechism
by J. Van Bruggen

John A. Hawthorne in *Reformed Theological Journal*: . . . The individual Christian would find it a constructive way to employ part of the Sabbath day by working through the lesson that is set for each Lord's Day. No one can study this volume without increasing his knowledge of truth and being made to worship and adore the God of all grace. This book will help every minister in the instruction of his people, both young and not so young, every parent in the task of catechizing and is commended to every Christian for personal study.

Subject: Catechism   Age: 13-99
ISBN 0-921100-33-7   Can.$15.95 U.S.$13.90

The Church Says Amen
by J. Van Bruggen
An Exposition of the Belgic Confession

We need to stand on the shoulders of those who have gone before us, to learn how they applied God's promises in the grit and grime of life's struggles . . .
— from the *Preface* by C. Bouwman

W.L. Bredenhof in *Clarion*: This would be an excellent book for the use of study societies, for individual refreshment on the doctrines of the church, or as a textbook for preconfession or adult education.

Subject: Belgic Confession   Age: 13-99
ISBN 0-921100-17-5   Can.$15.95 U.S.$13.90

The Belgic Confession and its Biblical Basis
by Lepusculus Vallensis

The Belgic Confession is a Reformed Confession, dating from the 16th Century, written by Guido de Brès, a preacher in the Reformed Churches of The Netherlands. The great synod of Dort in 1618-19 adopted this Confession as one of the doctrinal standards of the Reformed Churches, to which all office-bearers of the Churches were (and still are) to subscribe. This book provides and explains the Scriptural proof texts for the Belgic Confession by using the marginal notes of the Dutch *Staten Bijbel*. The *Staten Bijbel* is a Dutch translation of the Bible, by order of the States General of the United Netherlands, in accordance with a decree of the Synod of Dort. It was first published in 1637 and included 'new explanations of difficult passages and annotations to comparative texts.'

Subject: Creeds   Age: 15-99
ISBN 0-921100-41-8   Can.$17.95 U.S.$15.90

Christian Faith in Focus
by Gordon Spykman

This book is designed to serve the Christian Community as a study guide for personal enrichment and group discussions. Each of the thirty-two chapters is introduced by a pertinent Scripture passage, followed by brief explanations, leading up to questions which act as pump-primers for a free exchange of ideas.

Subject: Theology / Chr. Life   Age: 16-99
ISBN 0-88815-053-9   Can.$9.95 U.S.$8.90

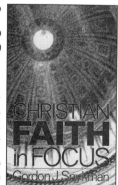

J. Geertsema in *Clarion* about Vol. 1: As the title says, this is the re-publication of the Dutch State translation with the added *Annotations* (in Dutch *Staten vertaling met Kanttekeningen*), in the English language. The Dutch States (government) gave the order for this State translation to the Synod of Dort. We read (p. 21f) that the States "found it fitting . . . to authorize, and require those at the National Synod held at Dort, in the years 1618 and 1619 that they would take in hand the aforesaid translation, and appoint some learned and experienced theologians . . . ." This Synod also gave order to add notes ('annotations'), as was the custom in those days. The article "Kanttekeningen" (in *Christelijke Encyclopaedie*, vol. 3, p 285) tells us that:

In its eighth session, the Synod of Dort has established the rules with which the Annotations had to comply. If a Hebrew or Greek expression had to be translated in a somewhat freer way because of the different Dutch idiom, then the more literal translation had to be taken up in the Annotations. Further, some short explanations could be given, but without presenting thereby the development of any point of doctrine. Finally, similar texts must be noted. . . . For the explanation the translators made use of the best available to them, in particular the commentaries of Calvin and Beza . . . [while the "learned and experienced theologians" also added their own, J.G.]. One can say that the annotations on the State translation present a precious piece of work and have been of great importance for our people.

These last words appear true, since even in 1980 and again in 1997 new editions of the Dutch State translation with their Annotations were published (see p. 7). Their importance is also evident in the fact that in 1648 the Westminster Assembly in England decided that it was good to have these Annotations translated into the English language for the English people. When the publisher of Inheritance publications, br. Roelof Janssen, planned to publish these "Annotations" in the English language, he was told about this existing English translation of about 1650. He found it and used it for this revised 2003 English edition (p.7-8).

Now it is true that today there are many, more or less extensive, commentaries on the market. Yet, these "Annotations" hold their value. For they present a Reformed interpretation of the Scriptures, going back to Calvin, Beza, and other Reformed Scholars from 1619 till 1637. One of the strengths of these Annotations is their reading of Old and New Testament as a unity: as the one Word of God that in both Testaments gives us testimony about Christ Jesus. At Gen. 3:15 the following note is added at the word "Seed" (with a capital letter): "This Seed is actually the Lord Jesus Christ, the only begotten Son of God, who was to be born in the fulness of time, of a woman, a virgin, by the working of God's Spirit, in order to dispossess the devil of all his brute force, through the merit of His death and the power of His Spirit, and to tread him under His and His Church's feet. See Ps. 110:1; John 12:31; Rom. 16:20; Hebrews 2:14;1 John 3:8. This is the first Gospel promise of life, put in opposition to the first denunciation of death. See also Col. 2:15." And the note with the words that Satan will "crush His heel" reads, "That is, the devil and his seed shall persecute Christ and His Church, but never be able to eliminate or destroy them." These Annotations belong to the books I personally consult; and I know colleagues who do the same.

I thank the publisher, and congratulate ourselves and our global English speaking brotherhood with this second, revised, publication of the Annotations in the English language, now in a modern format. I sure wish and hope that this book too will find many buyers, and that this first volume with Genesis and Exodus will be followed by all the other books of the Bible.

Music Books, Compact Discs & Cassettes on the Genevan Psalms

The Genevan Psalms in Harmony
by Claude Goudimel

This book is ideal for churches, organists, choirs, and Christian families. Approximately 450 4-part settings of the Psalms. The melody is both in a Soprano and a Tenor setting, and all the stanzas of the Psalms from the *Book of Praise* are included.
ISBN 1-894666-66-6   Can.$ 59.95 U.S.$ 49.90
(15% discount for 6 or more copies!)

Theresa Janssen Plays the Genevan Psalms of Claude Goudimel
for you to sing along
(or play along on your favourite solo instrument)

An ideal set of 4 Compact Discs for those who want to learn to sing the Genevan Psalms by heart. Each of the 150 Psalms is played twice, once with the melody in the Soprano and once with the melody in the Tenor. The organ registrations (of the organs at West End Christian Reformed Church, Robertson-Wesley United Church, and Grace Lutheran Church in Edmonton, Alberta) used for each of the Psalms are available at **http://www.telusplanet.net/public/inhpubl/Goudimel.htm** which can be of great help for (young) organists.

4 Compact Discs CMR 109-112   **Can.$ 40.00 U.S.$34.00**

Great is the Lord! Him Greatly Laud
The Odé Ensemble Sings Anglo-Genevan Psalms of Claude Goudimel
Annelize Viljoen, soprano;
Helga Schabort & Philna Badenhorst, altos;
Antonie Fourie, tenor; Eric Kayayan, bass.
(The sheet music of this C.D, is published in *The Genevan Psalms in Harmony* by Claude Goudimel.)

Psalm 65:1 & 6; Psalm 38:1 & 10; Psalm 9:1 & 6; Psalm 28:1 & 5; Psalm 13:1 & 3; Psalm 43:1 & 5; Psalm 45:1 & 6; Psalm 37:1 & 5; Psalm 54:1 & 3; Psalm 32:1 & 5; Psalm 2:1 & 4; Psalm 40:1 & 7; Psalm 46:1 & 5; Psalm 62:1 & 6; Psalm 53:1 & 5; Psalm 17:1 & 5; Psalm 50:1 & 11; Psalm 34:1 & 7; Psalm 11:1 & 2; Psalm 41:1 & 4; Psalm 57:1 & 5; Psalm 59:1 & 8; Psalm 10:1 & 7; Psalm 26:1 & 7; Psalm 33:1 & 6; Psalm 48:1 & 4.

Compact Disc CMR 108-2   **Can. $21.99 U.S.$ 18.99**

The Church: Its Unity in Confession and History
by G. Van Rongen

"The planet on which we live is becoming smaller and smaller. It seems as if it is no longer true that the East is far from the West. Distances are shrinking. At the same time, our world of interest is becoming larger and larger. What is happening on the other side of the globe can be watched as it happens.

"In the field of church life, too, this process of shrinkage and expansion is going on. These modern times have brought us into contact with other churches which we had hardly ever heard of a few decades ago. After the war, our immigrant churches went through a period in which we settled into a new country and had to build up our church life from scratch. Now, however, we are able to have closer contact with our ecclesiastical environment and have discovered some of these churches.

"This has raised the question: How are these other churches to be regarded? Must we, with a good conscience, leave them alone? Or, knowing that Christ wants His Church to be one, ought we to initiate dialogue with them? This is why our immigrant churches in various countries have been involved, sometimes for many years, in discussions with other churches."

"The best we can do in such a situation is to read and study our confessional standards and try to learn some lessons from history. That is the aim of this book. For that reason, we shall pay particular attention, first of all, to what the Belgic Confession says about this important subject, focusing on Articles 27, 28, and 29, since they contain the Scriptural fundamentals. Then we shall listen to what Church history teaches us about unity of faith as something basic to Church unity. Finally, we shall see how Church unity was endangered but, by God's grace, also preserved in the events connected with the Liberation in the Dutch churches during the 1940s."

This is what eighty-year-old Rev. G. Van Rongen writes in the Prologue of his book, which deals with what we believe concerning the Church of our Lord Jesus Christ. Rev. Van Rongen has spent the major part of his life pastoring and shepherding God's people in Reformed Churches in The Netherlands, the U.S.A., and Australia. Throughout this book and many of his other writings, it is clear that it is a great joy for him to serve his God and Saviour, as well as God's covenant community, the Church, by following in the footsteps of one of his earthly mentors, Dr. Klaas Schilder. Like Dr. Schilder, he has laboured in obedience to the prayer of the Lord Jesus Christ in John 17: "That they all may be one!"

It is no surprise to find the following paragraphs at the end of this book: "In our church life, we try to avoid synodocracy, ministeriocracy, and even consistoriocracy. All of our church members are involved in the issues that require our attention, and that is why I express the hope that all who have reached the years of responsibility would join me in contemplating what we actually believe regarding the Church.

"Let us not forget that it is the Church of our beloved Saviour!"

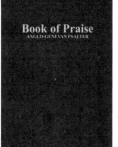

Subject: History / Doctrine   **Age: 13-99**
ISBN 0-921100-90-6   **Can.$14.95 U.S.$12.90**

Book of Praise, Anglo-Genevan Psalter
of the Canadian Reformed Churches.

This book contains the 150 Psalms, 65 Hymns, the Ecumenical Creeds, the Three Forms of Unity, Liturgical Forms, Prayers, and Church Order.
Subject: Genevan Psalms   **Age: 3-99**
ISBN 0-88756-029-6 (in Black & Maroon)   Can.$21.00 U.S.$18.00